NEPTUNUS REX

VOICES OF THE NAVY MEMORIAL

NEPTUNUS REX: Naval Stories of the Normandy Invasion, June 6, 1944

Edited by Edward F. Prados

U.S. Navy Memorial Foundation

STACEY ALLEN JACKSON
U.S. NAVY 20 OCT 1943 - 16 DEC 1945
U.S.S. LST. 55. 6 JUNE 1944 NORMANDY
INVASION. 8 JUNE 1944 UNLOADED ON
EASY RED BEACH (OMAHA).

To Mr. James Fucks
From. Stacey a. Jackson
25 Dec 1998.

★

PRESIDIO

Published by Presidio Press
505 B San Marin Drive, Suite 300
Novato, CA 94945-1340

Library of Congress Cataloging-in-Publication Data

Neptunus Rex : naval stories of the Normandy Invasion. June 6, 1944
  / edited by Edward F. Prados.
      p.   cm.
   ISBN: 0-89141-648-X (hardcover)
   Includes bibliographical references and index.
  1. World War, 1939–1945—Naval operations, American. 2.
Operation Neptune. 3. World War, 1939–1945—Campaigns—
France—Normandy. 4. World War, 1939–1945—Personal narratives, American. 5. Normandy (France)—History, Military. I.
  Prados, Edward F.
  D773.N47   1998
  940.54'5973—dc21   98-6151
                               CIP

Printed in the United States of America

For CYN Warren Prados, USN

*And all other sailors and soldiers
who fought in the Normandy invasion.
Although we may never know their stories,
we cannot forget their sacrifice.*

CONTENTS

CONTENTS

CONTENTS

ACKNOWLEDGMENTS

First and foremost, I wish to thank all of the individual authors whose stories are preserved in these pages. Without their willingness to share their experiences, both orally and in writing, this book would never have been written and their stories would remain untold. I have greatly enjoyed my conversations and correspondence with these veterans; their wisdom and experience have taught me much. I wish to thank Tracy Sugarman in particular for his assistance and effort in integrating his fine works into this book.

I also wish to acknowledge the staff and volunteers at the U.S. Navy Memorial Foundation who helped support this project. Special mention goes to Mrs. Anna Miller, wife of former President and CEO Admiral James E. Miller, USN (Ret.), who transcribed many of the oral histories contained in these pages. Captain Tom Coldwell, USN (Ret.), Commander John Hoshko, USN (Ret.), Bob Stevenson, John Small, Robert Smith, Catherine Kaplan, Stephen Langevin, and David Abruzzino all assisted with various phases of the project, especially editing. The U.S. Navy Memorial's Victory Club provided financial backing for the book.

The staff at the Still Pictures Branch of the National Archives were most helpful in furthering my research. Their suggestions, friendliness, and professionalism made research enjoyable and stimulating. I also owe a debt of gratitude to Paul Stillwell of the U.S. Naval Institute, who graciously permitted publication of Captain Quentin Walsh's account of the capture of Cherbourg. Dr. Ed Marolda, Senior Historian of the Naval Historical Center, lent his expertise to the book's introduction.

Finally, the support of my family was instrumental in helping me to complete this effort. My father, Colonel Alfred B. Prados, USA (Ret.), helped in clarifying the "lubberly" aspects of the invasion. The multi-faceted assistance of my wife, Sabrina, made it all possible.

VICTORY CLUB EDITION

RADM Philip F. Ashler, USN (Ret.)
Mrs. Richard W. Buxton
SKCS Eugene V. Buzelli, USNR (Ret.)
RDCS Bradford H. Carr, USN (Ret.)
Mr. Howard Chastain
LT Philip D. Christopher, USNR (Ret.)
Mr. John P. Cosgrove
ADM William J. Crowe, Jr., USN (Ret.)
LCDR Arnold R. Cutler, USCG
CDR Roy M. Dunham, USNR (Ret.)
Mr. Frank M. Ellis
RADM Robert B. Erly, USN (Ret.)
CAPT J.W. Evans, USNR (Ret.)
CAPT William Fedarko, USNR
CDR John C. Glenn, Jr., USNR (Ret.)
Ms. Anna L. Godsho
LCDR Charles L. Grannon
Mr. William J. Halligan, Jr.
RADM Roberta L. Hazard, USN (Ret.)
ALC Richard W. Johnson, USN
CAPT Kenneth K. Kaneshiro, USN (Ret.)
LCDR Anna Knoll, USNR (Ret.)
Mr. Max Koontz
LCDR Jack Lancaster, USN (Ret.)
MAJ G.R. Lanham
Mr. John A. Lednicky
CDR Stephen E. Mandia, MC, USN
Mr. John W. McIntyre
AKCS John Nici, USN (Ret.)
LCDR Russell K. Ningen, Jr.
CAPT George A. Oberle, USNR (Ret.)
LTC James N. Pritzker
HMCS Donald W. Ritchie, USN (Ret.)
CWO W4 Warren L. Shelton, USN (Ret.)

PREFACE

Innumerable works have been written about June 6, 1944. What then justifies the addition of yet another volume to this already over-crowded corner of history? First, many previous works are secondary accounts. While they are invaluable historical records of the invasion, they leave untold the eyewitness stories of soldiers and sailors involved in this Herculean operation. Second, those narratives that do contain first-person accounts focus on the land aspects of the invasion . . . withering fire at Omaha Beach, ambushes in the hedgerows, and drops behind enemy lines in the pre-dawn blackness of D-Day. Relatively little has been written about the contributions and experiences of the tens of thousands of sea service veterans who also were witnesses to, and participants in, one of the most epic events in modern history.

Yet that great, gray fleet massed off the shores of Normandy was essential to the success of the invasion, and the sailors who manned the five thousand ships and craft present were inextricably bound up in all aspects of the assault. Only recently has Paul Stillwell's *Assault on Normandy* appended to the D-Day record personal histories of Operation Neptune, the naval phase of the invasion. Named after King Neptune or *Neptunus Rex*, the Roman god of the sea, this book adds more than fifty eyewitness accounts to the historical record. Many of these accounts come from men who were young bluejackets—enlisted sailors—and who were experiencing their first taste of war. It is now more critical than ever to preserve and disseminate such first-hand reports, for within a generation, few veterans of the Normandy invasion will remain to tell their stories.

The sea service veterans included in this book witnessed Operation Neptune from all perspectives—from battleships, cruisers, destroyers and landing craft, on the beach, and even inland. Several narrators describe their experiences with the almost unknown—but essential—Naval Beach Battalions, which accomplished everything from patching up the wounded to directing offshore naval gunnery.

The sailors' narratives in *Neptunus Rex* were recorded over a fifty-year period. Many of the following accounts are oral histories culled from a D-Day fiftieth-anniversary reunion trip to Normandy sponsored by the U.S. Navy Memorial Foundation. Others were written soon after D-Day in letters home or in diaries. Still others are verse tributes or carefully worded reflections on the day's events and their significance. All of these histories, unless otherwise indicated, are housed at the U.S. Navy Memorial Foundation and are available for study by researchers. All ensure that the bravery, fear, joy, and despair that accompanied this epochal invasion will not be forgotten.

This book is graced by the drawings and watercolors of Lieutenant (j.g.) Tracy Sugarman, USNR. The young artist served as an amphibious officer during the invasion and was at Utah Beach from D-Day until the beach was secured in November 1944. These drawings and excerpts from correspondence to his wife, June, reflect the emotions that he experienced as the invasion unfolded around him.

Regardless of how these sailors present their views of the Normandy invasion—in pictures, text, oral accounts, or poetry—they relate history as they experienced it. Some readers may doubt the accuracy of their recollections. Yet, strikingly, there are many subtle links between the stories, ranging from shared ships or units to shared battle experiences. Further, official photographs and histories confirm much of what the authors witnessed. Finally, accounts can and should differ from one another and from official accounts. As one destroyer sailor notes, "Many times when we compared notes after General Quarters was secured, we found out that we had been observing two different actions. What was happening on the port side was not necessarily happening on the starboard side." In war, perspective is everything; these accounts lend fresh insights to a moment that can never be fully described, whether in prose, verse, or pictures.

Dear June,

This Spring of '44 will be engraved on my mind. What a strange and terrible time this is. Someday our kids will read in school about the Spring of '44 and it will be dusty and meaningless to them. Yet how very vivid and momentous to live through it. To see the weight, to sense the power, to speculate on where, when, how—to be a tiny, insignificant part of it all . . . and yet to have so much at stake in the game. You've placed your bet and somebody else is rolling the dice . . .

I
THE INVASION STORY

A landing against organized and highly trained opposition is probably the most difficult undertaking which military forces are called upon to face.

—General George C. Marshall, U.S. Army

In landing operations, retreat is impossible. To surrender is as ignoble as it is foolish. . . . Above all else remember that we as the attackers have the initiative. We know exactly what we are going to do, while the enemy is ignorant of our intentions and can only parry our blows. We must retain this tremendous advantage by always attacking rapidly, ruthlessly, viciously, and without rest.

—General George S. Patton, Jr., U.S. Army

EARLY PLANNING

The British Joint Planning staff, recognizing the complexity of mounting a large amphibious operation, had drawn up long-range plans for a cross-channel invasion of France as early as September 1941, under the code name "Roundup." Serious consideration of a continental invasion, however, only began with the United States' entry into World War II following the Japanese surprise attack on Pearl Harbor on December 7, 1941. Formal planning for the invasion, designated Operation Overlord, commenced in earnest in March 1943 with the establishment of the combined Anglo-American headquarters. British General Frederick Morgan commanded this team, known formally as Chief of Staff, Supreme Allied Command (COSSAC).

COSSAC was responsible for coordinating all invasion planning, including the deception plans designed to lure German forces away from the invasion site. The entire deception phase of the operation relied on information obtained from a German Enigma decoding machine, which had been captured by the British early in the war. So secret was the "Ultra" program that decrypted the Enigma machine that its existence was not publicly revealed until 1974.

COSSAC included officers from every branch of the American and British military forces, with Captains Lyman Thackery and Gordon Hutchins representing the U.S. Navy on the planning committee. The experience of U.S. Navy and Marine Corps planners in conducting amphibious warfare was essential in preparing the U.S. Army for its role in the Normandy invasion.

At the Trident and Tehran Conferences during 1943, Stalin and Roosevelt pressured Churchill—who wanted to continue the Allied push from Italy northward—to accept the French invasion plans by the end of that year. The target date for the invasion was set for May 1944. At this stage the planning for Overlord was handed to General Dwight D. Eisenhower, the newly-appointed Supreme Allied Commander, at his headquarters in London. His terse orders belied the complexity of the task ahead: "You will enter the continent of Europe, and in conjunction with the other United Nations, undertake offensive operations aimed at the heart of Germany and the destruction of her armed forces." British Field Marshal Sir Bernard Montgomery, who was to be in operational control of the invasion, insisted that the plan be changed to accommodate more ground and airborne divisions for the landings. Montgomery also had the invasion postponed for one month so that the Allies could continue to pound the beleaguered Nazi air force, the Luftwaffe.

Many factors determined the location at which the invasion was to be staged. The planners considered elements such as the need for short-range fighter support, favorable beach gradients, water approaches and tides, and they pinpointed weaknesses in the German coastal defenses. Calais, the nearest French port to Britain, was rejected as the site of the invasion because of the heavy concentration of German forces and defensive works. Eventually, the Normandy beaches were chosen as the most suitable landing site. Although the designated locale was without adequate port facilities, the Allies hoped to capture the nearby ports of Cherbourg and Le Havre early in the offensive so that they could off-load men and matériel needed for the advance into Germany.

Accordingly, planners developed a plan that projected assaults on five beaches stretching along a sixty-mile section of the Bay of the Seine from the mouth of the Dives River to the base of the Cotentin Peninsula. Five Army divisions were to be landed between Cherbourg and Le Havre on these beaches, code-named Sword, Juno, Gold, Omaha, and Utah. The primary assaults were to be undertaken by the U.S. 1st Army under Lieutenant General Bradley and the British 2d Army under Lieutenant General Sir Miles Dempsey, which together constituted the 21st Army Group, commanded by Montgomery. Back-up forces included the American 3d Army under Lieutenant General George Patton and the Canadian 1st Army under Lieutenant General Henry Crerar. British Air Marshal Sir Arthur Tedder and his Vice Marshal, Trafford Leigh-Mallory, coordinated the strategic and tactical air aspects of the invasion, which involved over thirteen thousand American aircraft. Admiral Sir Bertram Ramsay, RN, commanded the Allied naval force of five thousand ships in the amphibious phase of Overlord, known as Operation Neptune. In addition to the American and British ships that constituted the majority of the fleet, several nations contributed ships to the invasion armada.

Among the contributors were Greece, the Netherlands, Norway, Poland, and France.

Rear Admiral Alan G. Kirk, USN, an officer well-versed in naval gunnery, in dealings with the British, and in amphibious operations, commanded the American naval forces. Kirk's forces were responsible for offshore fire support and for landing the U.S. 1st Army, under General Omar N. Bradley. Directly under Admiral Kirk were Rear Admiral Don P. Moon, leading Naval Task Force U (in charge of the Utah Beach landings) and Rear Admiral John Hall, commanding Naval Task Force O (in charge of the Omaha Beach landings).

Despite the vast number of naval ships and landing craft, the Allies did not have enough. Planners at the highest levels debated solutions to this problem. Although more than one thousand LSTs had been produced during the war, many were in the Pacific theater assisting the U.S. Marines in the "island-hopping" strategy on their steady journey toward Japan.

Once the Allies had isolated the battle zone and established beachheads in France, their armies were to be supplied by two artificial harbors known as "mulberries" until the ports of Le Havre and Cherbourg were captured. With the capture of the ports, the amphibious assault phase of the European invasion—known as the "lodgement"—would be over. The Allies would then begin their push through France toward Germany.

Fifty German divisions (including ten armored divisions) stationed across the English Channel in France stood ready to thwart an Allied invasion. Despite Germany's losses in North Africa and Russia, Hitler's forces in France, commanded by Field Marshal Karl Von Rundstedt, presented a formidable invasion obstacle. Field Marshal Erwin Rommel, commander of Army Group B, was tasked with defending the French coast against an Allied invasion. Rommel constructed an "Atlantic Wall" of fortifications—undersea obstacles, mines, barbed wire, pillboxes, and blockhouses—designed to frustrate Allied landings. So much effort was put into constructing these fortifications and improving the Germans' defensive posture that troops suspended training in an all-out effort to build as many defenses as possible before the anticipated invasion.

THE BUILDUP

As the planning progressed, all the war-fighting equipment and men needed for the invasion and the ensuing continental warfare began to arrive in Great Britain, the base of operations for Overlord. To accommodate the equipment and soldiers, three U.S. Naval Construction Units built bases, training camps, and repair facilities. Training was essential for the combined air-sea-land operation to be successful. Allied soldiers and sailors participated in rigorous training and engaged in amphibious invasion exercises off England's beaches.

As the buildup and training continued, German U-boat submarines and high-speed motor torpedo E-boats represented an ongoing concern. The Allies tirelessly patrolled the channel with boats, ships, and planes, assuring that German operations would not endanger the buildup or the invasion operation.

Nevertheless, E-boats could and did operate in foggy weather and on moonless nights. And they did manage to find prey. In one now infamous incident, E-boats attacked and sank two troop-laden LSTs and heavily damaged a third while the ships were engaged in exercises off Slapton Sands, England on April 27, 1944. More than seven hundred men perished in the pre-dawn attack. The casualties of this exercise, known as Exercise Tiger, exceeded Utah Beach's casualties by a factor of four. Admiral Moon, who led the Allied assault on Utah Beach and who was in charge of Exercise Tiger, took his own life several months after the incident, distraught over the loss of life. This disaster remained classified until the 1970s, and was only publicly acknowledged in the 1980s.

TO NORMANDY

On June 3, minesweepers left England for France. Their task was to prepare five four-hundred-foot-wide buoyed lanes for the Allied fleet, set to steam the following day. The weather, however, deteriorated rapidly. The next day, Eisenhower decided to call back the fleet, knowing all the while that significant delays threatened to reveal Allied plans as well as result in further postponement until the tides were again suitable for landings.

Although the weather forecast remained uncertain, the seas began to calm; Eisenhower decided at 0415 on June 5 to launch Overlord. As 2,727 ships (carrying 2,606 landing craft) prepared to leave the British ports of Milford Haven, Plymouth, Portsmouth, and Southampton for Normandy, Admiral Sir Bertram Ramsay, commander of the Allied naval forces, sent the following message:

> *It is our privilege to take part in the greatest amphibious operation in history. The hopes and prayers of the free world and of the enslaved people of Europe will be with us, and we cannot fail them. I count on every man to do his utmost to ensure the success of this great enterprise, which is the climax of the European War. Good luck to you and god speed.*

Nearly 200,000 men were crowded into the ships and craft that filled the English Channel on their voyage to France. Meanwhile, airborne troops (the British 6th Division and the U.S. 82nd and 101st Divisions) had been the first to land in France shortly after midnight under cover of darkness. The drops went awry, but the airborne troops succeeded in wreaking havoc behind enemy lines and in capturing strategic points.

Between midnight and dawn, Allied bombers saturated the entire northwestern coast of France. These attacks, however, were largely ineffective because most of the ordnance was dropped too far inland to damage coastal defenses. Then, shortly before dawn (0558), naval guns from the offshore armada opened up and continued firing until 0625. The eight hundred warships that pounded the beaches played a critical role in breaching Rommel's "Atlantic Wall" during this phase of the invasion. At 0625 the mighty guns of these ships went silent as droves of landing craft streamed toward the Normandy beaches. Small fire support craft such as LCM(R)s (landing craft, mechanized (rocket)), advanced toward shore firing barrages of one thousand rockets at a time. At 0630 (H-Hour), the first ground troops hit the beaches.

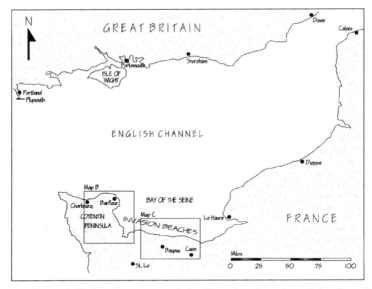

Map A: Great Britain, France, and the invasion beaches. Map by editor.

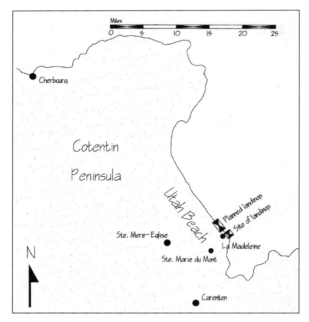

Map B: Utah Beach and vicinity. Map by editor.

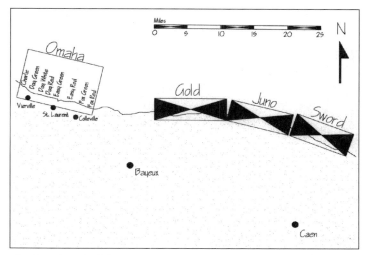

Map C: Omaha, Gold, Juno and Sword Beaches and vicinity. Map by editor.

Aboard an LCI, (left to right) LTG Omar N. Bradley, USA; RADM John L. Hall, USN; MG Leonard T. Gerow, USA; and MG Clarence L. Huedner, USA, observe an invasion rehearsal off the coast of England. *(U.S. Navy; National Archives)*

11

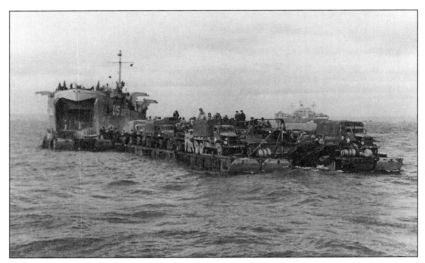

"Rhino" ferry RHF-7 off-loads from USS *LST-332* during a practice landing off Slapton Sands, England. *(U.S. Navy; National Archives)*

View of practice landing operations at Slapton Sands, England on March 17, 1944. Amphibious M-4 "Sherman" tanks are on the beach. *(U.S. Navy; National Archives)*

A U.S. Army field kitchen rolls aboard an LST during pre-invasion loading in England in early June 1944. *(U.S. Navy; National Archives)*

A convoy of attack transports and LSTs prepares for the June 6 invasion. *(U.S. Navy; National Archives)*

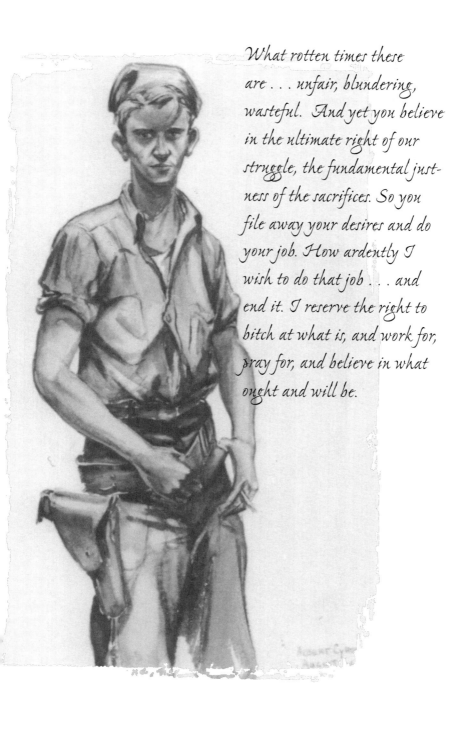

What rotten times these are . . . unfair, blundering, wasteful. And yet you believe in the ultimate right of our struggle, the fundamental justness of the sacrifices. So you file away your desires and do your job. How ardently I wish to do that job . . . and end it. I reserve the right to bitch at what is, and work for, pray for, and believe in what ought and will be.

II

Big Guns

The floating fortresses known as battleships and cruisers were among the most powerful weapons present at the Normandy invasion. These ships poured a steady stream of explosive shells into the coastal defenses of Normandy. While providing fire support for Allied ground forces, they were instrumental in helping dismantle Rommel's Atlantic Wall.

At Omaha Beach, the battleships USS *Texas* and USS *Arkansas* pounded the Atlantic Wall from five miles offshore. They were joined by three cruisers and eight destroyers. At Utah Beach, the heavy cruiser USS *Quincy* commenced the naval bombardment of Normandy; she was soon joined by the cruiser USS *Tuscaloosa* and by the 14-inch guns of the battleship USS *Nevada*, a battle-scarred Pearl Harbor veteran. In the pages to follow, sailors from USS *Quincy* and USS *Nevada* remember those opening shots and the trials of shipboard life during the invasion.

Boatswain's Mate Second
Class Joel E. Garner, U.S.
Naval Reserve.

OPENING SALVOS

By Boatswain's Mate Second Class Joel E. Garner, U.S. Naval Reserve.
Adapted from oral history transcript.

I was a coxswain serving on the heavy cruiser USS *Quincy* (CA-71)
in 1944. Our ship crossed the Atlantic with a convoy originating in
Boston, New York, and Halifax and we arrived in Belfast, Ireland on
May 14, 1944. We were stationed in the Irish Sea, where most of the
warships had assembled. We practiced maneuvers with the British
fleet off the coast of Scotland so we could be prepared to operate at
Normandy later. On May 19, 1944, General Eisenhower and several
British military figures came aboard to inspect us. The General said
this was the first time that he had been aboard a large American war-
ship, and we were proud because she was the newest ship there.

We returned to Belfast Lough on May 24, and waited there until
June 3. While anchored there, a British marine came aboard to present a shillelagh to the captain from the townspeople. We sailed on

June 3 and made it to the area of Land's End, England, but were forced by bad weather to return to the Irish Sea.

We sailed again on June 5. We were then issued three candy bars apiece and told to conserve them, as we might not have a meal again in a long time. We were all to take showers and put on clean clothes, so as to cut down on infections if wounded. Each gun position had water and a bucket for a toilet as all hatches would be closed. As we were manning the 20-millimeter anti-aircraft guns, we would be topside throughout the action. Captain Senn praised the crew and briefed us on what we were supposed to do. The chaplain then gave a prayer for our success. It was surprising how quiet it was. Everyone seemed to sense that we were all players in something much larger than ourselves.

We threaded our way through tiny strings of lights in the water leading us to our berth, which the minesweepers had cleared, although the Germans had magnetic mines that the sweepers could not detect. We had been degaussed; an electrical charge had been used to neutralize the ship's magnetism. The coast was aflame as the bombers attacked. Somewhere in the darkness, the paratroopers were preparing to land behind enemy lines.

As dawn broke, the enemy batteries opened up and a shell hit the water just in front of our bow, sending up a huge splash. These were the first shots fired by shore batteries on D-Day, and the *Quincy's* return salvos were the first to be returned. [Ed.: According to the USS *Quincy's* log, *Quincy* came under fire from shore batteries at 0520 and returned fire at 0537, initiating the planned 0550 shore bombardment thirteen minutes early.]

Once the firing started, it was non-stop until dusk. Shells were splashing all around us and shrapnel skittered across the deck. Our bow was holed by a near miss, and one compartment (containing ship's stores) was flooded. Somewhat later, the O'Henry candy bars that were in that compartment were removed. I never knew that candy could smell so bad after being wet. Shrapnel also pierced the sea rations tied to the life rafts, destroyed the antenna between the stacks, and put holes in our battle flag. Some of the men jumped out of the gun tubs to pick up shrapnel for souvenirs, all the while under fire. They had to be ordered to take cover.

Our 5-inch batteries were pumping out shell casings so quickly that there was no time to collect them. They formed huge piles that rolled around the deck and, eventually, over the side. During most of this time, the 20-millimeter crews looked for [shore] guns firing at us, as the Royal Air Force kept the German planes away.

Our gun tub was marked in degrees so that we could report shore fire to fire control. The Germans made it difficult, however, because they used smokeless powder to hide their positions from us. They also had guns mounted on a track that would disappear quickly after firing. Some of the 135-millimeter guns ashore could cover both Utah and Omaha beaches.

The water soon became filled with debris, including bodies that seemed to float just beneath the surface. We picked up some of the bodies with hooks and stored them temporarily aboard ship. A downed barrage balloon became lodged in our water intake, but fortunately a diver got it out in time.

Being topside in the superstructure, I had as good a view as could be had. One thing that amazed me were the planes (they looked like Piper Cubs), that floated lazily above the Germans, giving us firing ranges. Also, there were Frenchmen who were beach-combing under the cliffs that we were firing over. I'll also never forget the awesome sight as the B-25s pulling gliders came over our ship. The sky was full of gliders that looked similar to the planes pulling them. The B-25s came back at a lower altitude, many spurting flames or oil. The crews of some of the planes that ended up in the ocean were picked up by PT boats.

One hilarious moment was when our secondary batteries were firing at a locomotive pulling a rail gun. The scene looked like the Toonerville Trolley. It sure was putting out black smoke as the shells hit all around it. When the locomotive came around a hill, the 5-inch guns peppered it, but we were moving and we never saw what happened to the locomotive.

After dusk, we pulled out from shore and anchored for the night. That first night we shot down one Spitfire by mistake. The pilot survived, but the British said that if that happened one more time that we would get no more air cover. They didn't need to explain what would happen to us without air cover. Somewhat later, we had a

German plane almost take our mast off after dusk. Not a shot was fired!

On June 7 we made a mad rush across the Channel for more ammunition. As we were crossing, we passed between two columns of huge troop transports. We were traveling at flank speed, and I wondered what the soldiers thought about us leaving the fight so quickly.

Our destroyer escort could not keep up with us. Destroyers can do 45 knots [Ed.: actually, around 35 knots], so we finally found out what the *Quincy* could do, as our top speed was always kept secret [Ed.: *Quincy*'s maximum speed is listed as 33 knots]. The escort sent us a message of congratulations on our speed, saying that it would meet us in England.

After loading ammunition, the captain told the barge to cast off. The barge crew said that they couldn't, as they'd be left adrift. The captain said, "Cast off now or go to sea with us." They cast off hastily as the *Quincy's* screws began to turn.

We made it back to the firing line. The battleships remained some distance offshore, but we moved in closer and joined HMS *Enterprise* and HMS *Glasgow*. *Glasgow* took a hit amidships, and we soon arrived (mistakenly) in the spot where she had been hit. We braced ourselves for a hit too, as the Germans had the exact range. Luckily for us, we made it. We traveled up and down the coastline of Omaha and Utah beaches. At that time, we didn't know that the beaches had those names.

Later, we went to Cherbourg on June 24 to take on the German forts there. They had larger guns than at Normandy and there was less room to maneuver. We didn't get hit, but the *Texas* got it. We were just plain lucky. On July 4, we set sail for the Mediterranean and the invasion of Southern France.

At times, we all feared that we wouldn't make it through the battle, but there was never any panic. It all feels unreal, as though it isn't really happening. You feel sort of numb . . . devoid of emotion.

Lieutenant (Junior Grade) Stanley M. Mather, U.S. Navy.

SMASHING THE ATLANTIC WALL

By Lieutenant (Junior Grade) Stanley M. Mather, U.S. Navy. Adapted from "Neptune: 6 June 1944," unpublished manuscript.

H-hour was set at 0630. My ship [USS *Nevada* (BB-36)] pulled into the Bay of the Seine next to the Cotentin Peninsula around 0200. At about 0140, paratroop planes had flown low over our ship, homeward bound after dropping their troops. At 0230, heavy bombers of the Army Air Force began bombardment of Omaha Beach. It was a brilliant display of fireworks, accompanied by many large chandelier flares. The bombardment was very heavy, and we could see large bomb bursts visible on the distant shore about ten thousand yards away. All the while, tracers from the German anti-aircraft batteries were systematically sweeping the sky.

Prior to our moving in, minesweepers swept across the channel and into the fire support area where we were to anchor. Our ships—USS *Nevada*, USS *Quincy*, USS *Tuscaloosa*, HMS *Hacking*, HMS *Black Prince*, and HMS *Erebus*, in addition to about ten destroyers—moved

23

in. We were not bothered by any fire from shore or from German naval units.

The English Channel was marked all the way with lighted buoys to keep us in safe areas. Our ships were not scheduled to open bombardment until H—40 minutes (0550). Sun up was 0558. All during the early hours we were anchored some distance off shore, just inside the peninsula. Then at 0500, we took up our fire support position and anchored again. As yet, no shore batteries had opened up.

Our position was about eleven thousand yards from the beach. Beyond us, a picket line of destroyers, Coast Guard cutters, and PT boats roamed up and down to keep German boats out of the area. The transports for unloading the troops were about five thousand yards seaward of our area.

Between 0230 and 0500, two battalions of paratroopers were landed from DC-3s and C-47s. German ack-ack [anti-aircraft fire] brought down several planes. It was quite a sight; the planes dropped from the sky like giant flares or flaming torches. Upon hitting the deck, they exploded violently, lighting up the sky intensely. All in all, however, few were lost (less than two percent).

The illumination by the pathfinder planes was an amazing spectacle. The whole of the Bay of the Seine was lit up brilliantly enough to illuminate our ships. Why the shore batteries did not open up was beyond us. No German fighter or bomber resistance was observed; evidently they were surprised by the attack. Later, reports indicated that the Germans were expecting the attack at the Pas de Calais area.

The weather was fine; the full moon was, fortunately for us, obscured by a high layer of clouds. The pasting the bomber gave the beach area was terrific and thorough. Up to H—40 minutes, 110,000 tons of bombs were dropped on the Cotentin Peninsula, around through the Omaha area, and on the British section known as the Eastern Assault Group (Gold, Juneau, and Sword beaches). Ours was the Western Task Force in the Omaha and Utah area. The latter location was on the northern side of the Cotentin Peninsula. The Eastern Task Force was situated farther down to the east.

At daybreak (about one hour before the astronomical sunrise), the Germans began to open fire. This hour was to go by without our ships returning the fire. It was quite a feeling resting there like a "big sitting duck," being shot at and not retaliating. Gun flashes were visible up and down the beach areas. The guns consisted of, to the best of my knowledge, 6.1-inch, 150-millimeter, 75-millimeter, 4.14-inch, and probably some 200-millimeter guns. Also known to exist were a few batteries of 11-inch guns. Undoubtedly, some of these were knocked out by the bombardment, but many were still left. The main object of the bombing was to remove beach opposition as much as possible for our troops. It worked, too!

By daybreak the first assault wave was heading for the beach. They were to reach it at 0630 or "H-Hour," at which time our bombardment where they were to land was to stop. Shortly after the shore batteries opened up, several splashes were seen about one or two hundred yards off our port bow. The next salvo from the shore battery landed about five hundred yards off our starboard bow. They were getting the range. This was about 0530, and none of us had opened up yet. One landing craft (we think it was an LCVP), received a direct hit which set it tumbling end over end, up into the air about two or three hundred feet. We saw men hurtling through the air. At this time the Quincy opened up prior to the hour we were supposed to—thank God—and knocked out the battery that was firing at us. Good old Quincy.

Our fighter coverage, consisting of P-47s, P-38s, Spitfires, and a few Typhoons, was now overhead. A German ME-109 somehow got mixed up with about six Spitfires. The machine gun fire from the Spitfires was beautiful but rather wicked. The tracers licked out and seemed just to touch the fighter—black puffs of smoke were seen as it was hit and started off in a steep dive. Quite a show. That was the last Heinie seen that day.

At 0550, our scheduled 5-inch battery opened up with its planned "beach drenching" of Red Beach. The firing was to keep up until H-Hour (0630). We concentrated forty minutes of continuous fire in an area 875 yards along the beach and 250 yards deep. Close to two thousand rounds were fired from the same eight, port-side guns during this period. The shots were continually spotted up and down—four, fifty-four-pound projectiles spinning over into the area every five or six seconds. LCM(R) rocket boats launched rockets at the beach in waves of about two thousand at a time. Approximately 100,000 rockets, carrying seven pounds of TNT each, were fired.

A large group of B-17s was over the same beach flying due north. One plane in the last group received a direct hit, either from our guns or from the Germans. It exploded violently and went down in a shower of burning embers scattered over a wide area.

The troops reached the beach at 0635 and our signal to cease fire, a black rocket, was seen. We ceased fire accordingly and shifted to another target on Green Beach about twelve hundred yards up the beach. A great many obstacles were on the beach and underwater to stop the troops. Our invasion wave came in on a low tide so that the engineers plus our bombardment could clear this particular strip. About one thousand yards of beach were exposed, so we were successful.

A sea wall of concrete lay all around this area. One of our jobs was to breach this wall. To do this, our 14-inch main battery spotted through all the smoke and dust and fired ten full salvos (five salvos of anti-personnel bombs and five of high explosives) from our ten guns. Each 14-inch projectile weighed about 1,250 pounds, so the total amount fired was 125,000 pounds of high explosives within twenty minutes. We breached the wall okay.

The troops landed all right and men began to pour ashore. In the transport area there were hundreds of ships—LSTs, LCVPs, attack transports, Liberty ships, minesweepers, etc. At least a thousand if not more. It looked like this H-Hour was won . . . and it was.

The remainder of the day we spent firing at the targets our intelligence had gathered. By noon all the coastal batteries were silenced. Now and then some gun would take a whack at a destroyer. One destroyer was hit in the engine room and sank shortly afterwards. This was our first loss of any size. Several of the LCVPs were sunk. Through our glasses, we could see tanks on the beach and men walking around and standing on top of the wall. They were still under fire. Bursts could be seen in their vicinity. About one thousand yards back from the beach in a forest, gun flashes could be seen. A shell hit right in the center of the group of our men pinned down on the beach, but did not seem to affect them much.

Our main battery, using air spotting, broke up numerous tank and troop concentrations. Our own spotters could see targets of opportunity and we took them under fire too. We had very good success and did a lot of damage. None of our capital ships was touched and we faced no enemy aircraft opposition at all. We had complete control of the air and the sea, and were gaining control of the beachhead rapidly. Later in the day, one of the boat officers came alongside and said that little opposition was met in the immediate vicinity of Red Beach.

That evening, we retired to our anchorage nearer to the transport area and dropped the hook. Tracer fire and ack-ack lit up the skies the remainder of the night. Falling planes, rockets, and flares were rather frequent.

Just at daybreak, stream after stream of DC-3s and C-47s came in low over the ship and began to cut loose their gliders. Each plane towed three gliders almost as big as it was. The gliders could be seen landing beyond the trees not too far away. No casualties were noted with the exception of one which seemed to stall and nose down sharply, disappearing behind the trees. [Ed.: Approximately 850 British and American gliders landed in conjunction with the paratroopers, delivering additional troops and supplies to those in the vanguard.]

June 7 was a quiet night. At dawn droves of gliders (close to four hundred) came over and were let go in the same area. During the day we fired at various targets. A destroyer got hit by a mine at the stern, and its end was blown off. It settled down by the stern but was later saved. Three destroyer escorts went in to rescue the crew and one passed over a mine that exploded amidships. The ship was covered with white smoke and steam. When the haze cleared, only its stern was visible out of the water. During the day many mines were detonated by the minesweepers.

Bombers flew around all night on June 8. We saw lots of tracers and ack-ack from German and American positions. Later, there was a large splash and explosion about three thousand yards off the stern. About an hour later, there was a large splash and explosion one thousand yards off our starboard bow. We found out that these explosions were probably caused by rocket glide bombs. We did see one HE-111K over the ship, silhouetted against the moon. Out in the channel, flares and firing were seen on the surface. E-boat and destroyer attacks were countered by our screen.

At dawn, we took up our firing position. We shot the rest of our ammunition and headed for Plymouth, England at about 1600. We picked up a carrier pigeon en route and arrived at Plymouth at 0430 on June 9.

After reloading our ammo, we got underway on June 10 at about 0900. We arrived back in the Cherbourg area about 2130. We saw several sections of the mulberry being towed across the channel. The mulberry was a portable cement harbor that was being moved across the channel to assist in off-loading troops and supplies. Towing the mulberry was a gargantuan task, requiring over 150 tugs to tow its sections across the channel.

We spent another anxious night looking at ack-ack, tracer, and surface fire, and listening to the chug of German motors above us. Several planes came down in flames. They were probably ours, but we were not able to determine their true identity. Our ships never opened up that night.

The next day, June 11, we sat out in our fire support area and fired about forty-six rounds from our main battery. The weather was very hazy, overcast, and foggy. A shore battery was firing at the Quincy. One salvo landed about one thousand yards from our position. We spotted the gun firing and, with two of our own salvos, knocked it off with two direct hits. We struck a few more targets in the evening (about 2100–2200) in cooperation with a shore fire control party. The targets consisted of batteries, personnel, and tanks. We must have knocked the hell out of a bunch of them.

That night it was rather quiet, and there were only a couple of planes around. They didn't bother us. It was overcast and foggy until 0330, then the skies cleared. We sat there looking like a carnival concession—that moon can sure be bright! We saw lots of activity from E-boats again out in the channel at about twenty-five thousand yards, but our screen took care of them. Carentan could be seen burning fiercely in the distance. Our forces had bombarded it in preparation for moving our troops in. They had done a thorough job, and the whole area (about one thousand yards square) was on fire. Off the port bow, fighting among the troops could be seen. There were lots of flashes and explosions from tracer fire and star shells.

Dawn came and with it our much-awaited fighter protection. These nights had not been very much fun, although they were interesting. No one had any rest.

Lieutenant O. Alfred Granum, U.S. Naval Reserve.

STRADDLING A BATTLE WAGON
By Lieutenant O. Alfred Granum, U.S. Naval Reserve. Adapted from oral history transcript.

As an ensign on the battleship *Nevada* (BB-36), my first experiences involved convoy runs out of either Boston, Massachusetts or Bangor, Maine to Bangor, Northern Ireland, which was the port for Belfast. I was temporarily detached from the ship about three weeks prior to the invasion, on the beach with Lieutenant Jack Ward from the *Tuscaloosa*, who was a communications officer. I was a line officer and the two of us had the duty of attempting to obtain anything that any ship commander going into the Normandy invasion realized that he needed at the last minute.

One of the most interesting things we were able to do was to locate experts (from MIT in the states) in jamming the Germans' radio-controlled, rocket-accelerated bombs. The way in which they jammed the bombs was not to listen for the radio signal, but to use some sort of an oscilloscope, like a TV screen, which would visually give an indication of the frequency of the signal so they could immediately tune in to jam it.

We went into Normandy and bombarded Utah Beach the first morning. We were at General Quarters for three or four days and nights. It was miserably cold because of the damp and the breeze, although the temperature wasn't all that low. Then we headed to Plymouth, to get another load of ammunition, and went back to the beaches again. We made a number of trips like this to re-load our ammunition. Next we went to Cherbourg, ten days after the invasion because we were told that some of the big guns were being trained inland and were holding the Army back. The Air Corps couldn't hit them with high-level bombing and when they used low-level bombing, they were sitting ducks for machine-gun platforms on towers, so the idea was to send in the big ships to knock 'em out.

We were there for about three-and-a-half or four hours and were actually straddled twenty-seven times! I had nothing to do because we were not under air attack and I was on a machine gun director. So I had to just sit there and watch the flashes of gunfire on the beach, count about thirty-seven seconds, and whomp . . . their shells would come down around us. Many of the other ships were hit, but we were not; we got away scot-free.

After Cherbourg, we went through the Straits of Gibraltar to the Mediterranean where we participated in the invasion of Southern France.

Radarman Second Class Millard Cloutman, U.S. Navy.

SMOKING GUNS

By Radarman Second Class Millard Cloutman, U.S. Navy. Adapted from oral history transcript.

I served aboard the USS *Nevada* (BB-36) at Utah Beach. I can't tell you too much about it because my job was inside. I was a radar technician and my job was to see that the port and starboard transmitter for the 5-inch/38-caliber gun directors was operational and stayed operational during the invasion.

One of the things that stays with me more than anything else is that when we were on the way to the invasion, we got ahead of time and we had to make a 180-degree turn and go back for a certain length of time and then another 180-degree turn and head back for Utah Beach. And it really gets to you when you remember things like the planes flying over, the bombers and the paratrooper planes, and after a little while you see a ball of fire fall out of the sky ahead of you. It really touches you; it gets you where it hurts, because you know you're losing a lot of good men that way. And I want to tell you one thing: I am happy to have been able to be a part of trying to start a new democracy for the world.

Aboard the *Nevada* we stayed on our battle stations for seventy-two hours without getting off of them and then, after we got through with Utah Beach, we went in and helped them capture the harbor of Cherbourg. We were straddled approximately twenty-eight times at Cherbourg and about twenty-two times at Utah Beach. And we had shrapnel all over the fantail of the ship—that's how close they came to hitting us. I think we were fortunate and we were lucky. We fired approximately five thousand rounds of 5-inch/38-caliber ammunition at Utah and around twenty-five hundred rounds of 14-inch [ammunition]. At times we were firing six hundred yards ahead of our advancing troops. I give credit to the spotter and the fire-control crew on the *Nevada* for the accuracy of their fire.

I tell you one thing, if you are ever on a battleship that's firing all ten guns at once—a broadside—you are in for an experience. The broadside shoves a battle wagon sideways.

Boatswain's Mate Second Class Albert Buckholz, U.S. Navy.

"Grinding Up Spam"

By Boatswain's Mate Second Class Albert Buckholz, U.S. Navy. Adapted from oral history transcript.

I went into the Navy right out of high school in 1940. I went in on a "kiddie cruise" which would let me out on my twenty-first birthday, but that never happened because we were still at war.

I was sent to the USS *Nevada* out in Bremerton, Washington. My first tour of duty was to Pearl Harbor and during this time I was a lookout on the foretop of the USS *Nevada*. That was the job that I held for nearly four-and-a-half years, all the time I was in the service. The ship was damaged and grounded in Pearl Harbor, but later rebuilt at Bremerton Navy Yard. There have been a lot of stories about that, so I won't dwell on it.

Our job as lookouts consisted of reporting all of the things that we saw from the ship, so we spent a good deal of our time learning to identify foreign ships as well as U.S. ships. When we came down on our last trip before the D-Day invasion, we had to study the Normandy shoreline on relief maps that we had aboard the *Nevada*. These maps included the landmarks and showed us where all of the defenses were installed along the Normandy coast.

There were so many ships out in the English Channel that we could not begin to know all of them, but we knew a good share of them. There were many ships that we had never seen before and all we had for studying were the books we read and flash cards for quick identification of them. The big topographical map that we had on the ship gave us a chance to study all the defenses along the Normandy coast and become familiar with their names for communicating with the bridge. When the bombardment began, we were able to report to our navigation department all of the things that we could see that were happening, such as where our gunfire was effective and where it was ineffective. We were able to help correct our firing considerably by these reported observations.

The Normandy invasion was something that I never could begin to talk about and be able to do a good job of it, without some training as a public speaker. There were many things that I witnessed along the Normandy coast that were almost past comprehension, such as the number of ships, the number of planes, the number of gliders and the number of landing craft that were going in. We were able to see them extremely well from the foretop because of our height, as well as the good binoculars that we were using. We could watch every phase of what was going on. The *Nevada* fired many, many rounds on the beaches and was very, very effective in knocking out those things along the coast that were giving the troops the most trouble.

Some of the things that I always will remember about the Normandy invasion had to do with the way we lived for five days straight. We stayed in the foretop for five days, ate hardtack, had C rations [military food rations], had no showers or shaves during that time, had no change of clothing, and had very little rest. The food was indifferent, you were dirty, your eyes were tired from watching carefully for many hours at a time, and you rested by leaning against a wall. This was not our normal existence on the ship.

One of the amazing things that I always remembered was a quotation from Winston Churchill, after about the third or fourth day of the invasion. He got on the radio stations of all the ships and all the stations all over the area and said, "The Germans have developed a new type of weapon, a secret weapon, that they are using." He said, "They are grinding up Spam and throwing it all over England." That was one of the finest tension-breakers that could have happened. It was well received as a bit of humor, in an otherwise real grave situation.

One of the hard things to live with, as far as I was concerned, was the constant fear of buzz bombs that the Germans were throwing out in our area. Even though we had found ways to jam them, they were still a never-ending source of discomfort. We lived through it all and never did get hit on the initial first week or so of firing.

The next time we went into Cherbourg, we went in to bombard a big gun that looked as though it was in place on a railroad track. It seemed to go back into a hole in the mountain, there in the cliff, after firing. We spent quite a little time trying to knock that gun out. I have complete lists of the number of shells they fired at us. We were trying to operate under cover of smoke screens because the German gun had a longer range than we did; still they were putting straddles on us in quite big numbers. That probably was the scariest thing, with the exception of the Pearl Harbor attack, that ever happened to me in all the time that I was in the Navy. Not too long after that time, we headed back over to England, then down to Africa, Italy, and the bombardment of Southern France.

USS *Arkansas* (BB-33) fires on German installations during the invasion. (*U.S. Navy; National Archives*)

Heavy cruiser USS *Quincy* (CA-71) passes a convoy of LCTs off the English coast the evening before D-Day. (*U.S. Navy; National Archives*)

Battleship USS *Nevada* (BB-36) fires her 14-inch guns at enemy shore batteries north of Utah Beach on D-Day. *(U.S. Navy; National Archives)*

Just got back from a real funny
USO Camp Show and had a wonderful time! Three gals . . . strictly
Coney Island and Brooklyn . . .
some solid trumpeting and stompin!
It's things like tonite that snap a
guy out of himself.

Hope this gets out to you. It
will be the last word from me for a
long time. Don't worry. I'm feeling
wonderfully well and absolutely
squared away for anything that
may come my way. For this peace of
mind, I have you to thank.

III

TIN CANS: THE NAVY'S FIELD ARTILLERY

Destroyers played an integral role in assisting American foot soldiers during the early phases of the invasion. These "greyhounds of the sea" or "tin cans"—so called because of their thin armor-plating—brought their powerful 5-inch guns to bear against the German defenses. Venturing so close to the shore that they often risked running their ships aground, destroyer crews were able to spot targets from aboard ship rather than relying on shore fire control parties. On Omaha Beach, where the soldiers were bogged down by withering German fire and hampered by the loss of much of their field artillery to the unsettled seas, destroyers were particularly essential for they helped the Army maintain its initially tenuous hold.

To be aboard ship was not to be out of danger, and destroyer crews risked their lives and ships to assist the Allied ground troops. Performing admirably under hostile fire conditions, destroyers faced the ever-present dangers of air attacks, floating and submerged mines, and radio-controlled bombs. Destroyers were sunk and lives were lost. In the following stories, sailors recount their experiences in destroyer warfare off the Normandy coast.

Radioman Third Class
Angus S. Schmelz, U.S.
Navy.

LUCKY *HERNDON*

By Radioman Third Class Angus S. Schmelz, U.S. Navy. Excerpted from: Jane Moore Roberts, The Lucky *Herndon*: The Invasion of Normandy (*Privately printed, 1993*).

At the time of the invasion, I was twenty years old and had already served for three-and-a-half years in the U.S. Navy. My battle station was a 20-millimeter gun on the starboard side of the bridge of the destroyer USS *Herndon* (DD-638). Because of my vantage point, I also served as a lookout and observer. Throughout the invasion, I kept a log of the events. My memoirs are based on this log.

In early May 1944, *Herndon* crossed the Atlantic with Destroyer Squadron 17 and arrived in Bangor, Ireland. We continued on to Plymouth for some training, before returning to Belfast Lough, Ireland. On May 28, Lieutenant D.F. Chamberlain mustered us on the fantail. He told us the news we had been waiting for—what our job would be, what we were up against, and what the odds of our coming out of the invasion were. We were told that our position would be within range of two German batteries of 11-inch guns, five batteries of 155-millimeter guns, and four batteries of 75–150-millimeter guns. He also told us that we were scheduled to lead the assault.

The men of the *Herndon* seemed to love the news. Morale was high and there was no sign of fear. We had all known the invasion was coming soon, but we hadn't known when. And it was certainly news to us that we would lead it! I was not afraid of what was ahead, for I knew that I was on a good ship, with good officers and a good crew that had been well-trained for this action.

On June 2, all hands were issued gas masks. A whaleboat from the USS *Corry* (DD-462) came alongside and offered us bets at ten to one that we wouldn't make it back. By this time, as we rested at anchor, many sailors began to get restless. The next day, however, we left Ireland for France, testing our anti-aircraft guns as we were underway. On June 4, we were served steak and eggs—the usual invasion meal—for breakfast. However, the word came out that the invasion had been delayed for twenty-four hours because of the weather. We returned towards England on the fifth before heading across the Channel once again toward France.

Early on the morning of June 6, we entered the Bay of the Seine. At 0203 we were called to General Quarters, and we saw C-47s flying low over our ship, returning from their parachute drops. At 0510 we arrived at our assigned station. We were the first one in. At our masthead was the largest U.S. flag that I'd ever seen. How could the Germans miss that? Painted on our number 1 stack was a Confederate battle flag. The *Herndon* was built in Virginia, and we had many southern officers aboard; that is why we had painted the flag on the stack. Nevertheless, later that morning we received orders to remove the Confederate flag so that the Germans wouldn't be confused about who they were fighting!

When light dawned on the cool, cloudy, and choppy morning of D-Day, we could see the distant outlines of the battleship *Nevada* on our starboard side off Utah Beach, and the battleship *Texas* and destroyer *Satterlee* on our port side off Omaha Beach. When those battleships opened fire with their 14-inch guns, you could see the smoke, and then you heard a very loud and startling "whooshing" sound, like a freight train going overhead.

At 0547 we commenced firing with our main batteries on assigned enemy shore targets. At 0605 Allied bombers commenced heavy bombardment of the beach. A bomber was hit and it exploded into a million pieces. The planes alongside it were blown out of formation. But, as if nothing had happened, they closed into formation again and went on with their mission. It was an unbelievable sight. At 0610, rocket-loaded landing craft commenced moving towards the beach and released salvos of rockets. One ship, that must have hit a mine, blew up.

For several hours as we fired at targets, smoke and fire billowed from the beach area. As we were firing, at 0620, we learned that the *Corry* was being shelled. At 0730, we heard that the *Corry* had gone down. Two hours later, we recovered the body of a seaman first class in the water. Doc [John] Peck, our medical officer, stated that the death was due to drowning, as there were no visible wounds.

At 0954 an LCVP came alongside for assistance in pumping out water that was causing her to list badly. Our repair party got the "handy billy" pump and pumped her dry. The men in the boat looked seasick from the bouncing around they were receiving.

We were relieved by the *Barton* at 1300 and joined the *Walke* on patrol duty in the transport area.

Gus Schmelz's buddy, Radioman Second Class Bob Holloway, comments on his perspectives of the invasion:

"During General Quarters, Gus and I were no more than thirty feet apart. But many times when we compared notes after GQ was secured, we found out that we had been observing two different actions. What was happening on the port side was not necessarily happening on the starboard side. For instance, that morning, I was able to see the Rangers scaling the cliffs at Pointe du Hoc. Those guys were climbing right into a well-fortified German position! When I related the Ranger action to Gus, he said: 'What Rangers?' From the starboard side of the ship, he hadn't seen them climbing the cliffs.

Many times since, I have heard people stating very strongly: 'This is what happened!' That prompts me to ask: 'Were you on the port side or the starboard side?'"

On June 8, *Herndon* was patrolling the inner screen when at 0140 an HE-177 passed over us and released a glider bomb. We had our jamming equipment on, and counting that bomb, had jammed twelve that night. At 0148 we opened fire with our 5-inch guns on another HE-177 that crossed over our ship.

At 0158 the USS *Meredith* (DD-726) was rocked by an explosion caused by a glider bomb or a mine. We commenced laying a smoke screen. But then, something happened in our engine room. A sheet of flame about twenty to thirty feet high shot out of the number 1 stack with a loud roar. It sounded like the engines were exploding [engine room personnel had not removed the burner tips from the boilers, so instead of producing smoke, *Herndon* produced fire from her stacks]. It scared the heck out of us on the bridge. I was at my 20-millimeter gun, very close to the stack. I had to back off from the flames. We thought that we'd been hit. The Germans above us must have thought so too, because they soon departed.

At 0216 we sent our motor whaleboat to pick up the wounded from the *Meredith*. They returned with thirteen men at 0235. We understood our luck as we brought those survivors aboard our ship. Some of the poor guys had been scalded. And one of them came aboard with a missing arm. It was awful. Doc Peck treated the injured men until they were transferred to a temporary hospital ship [USS *LST-284*; see Earl Blair's account in Chapter IV] at 0549. He cleaned their wounds and gave them morphine for the pain. On my way to duty in the radio shack, I stopped by the wardroom to help. Doc Peck was so overworked that he even had me giving morphine shots.

Soon after, at 0815, USS *Glennon* (DD-620) struck a mine. The disabled ship was sunk by enemy gunfire two days later with my good friend Harley Alexander aboard. Harley and I had become good friends when I was in the Brooklyn Navy Yard hospital for a spinal operation. Later, when the *Herndon* was in Plymouth just before the invasion, I went aboard the *Glennon*, which was tied up alongside us, to visit Harley.

46

The first thing that he said on seeing me was: "Come down below. I have something for you." He went to his locker and reached for his wallet.

I had loaned him money, but I said, "What's the rush? I can get it later."

But he replied, "No, I have to give it to you now. I won't be able to later."

I didn't think anything more about it, but I realized later that he must have had a premonition. I sent him a V-mail letter in August that was later returned, marked "Unclaimed." Some time later, I met one of the *Glennon* survivors at the Brooklyn Navy Yard. He was the last one out of Harley's compartment and had called down to see if anyone else was still alive. When he received no answer, he closed and "dogged down" the hatch to keep the water from rising.

At 1305 we commenced firing on shore targets under the direction of an Army fire control party. We could see several ammunition dumps go up that we had targeted. We fired so much that we began to run out of ammunition, so we used star shells, just to keep the enemy on the run. We were firing so quickly that we had to hose down our guns as they were cherry-red from the heat. As we left the fire support area, USS *Jeffers* (DD-621) and USS *Rodman* (DD-456) arrived to relieve us. It made us feel good that it took two ships to replace the *Herndon*.

On June 9 we left Normandy and went to England for fuel and ammunition. While we were in Plymouth, we took on 68,000 gallons of fuel oil, 1,986 rounds of ammunition from a few ammunition barges, and 1,700 gallons of fresh water from a water barge.

We left Plymouth on June 11 and returned to Normandy with the *Texas, Emmons, Baldwin,* and *Plunkett.* We arrived in France around 1830 and began patrolling at station C-31, the northeast corner of "Torpedo Junction." Here, we received bad news about the *Meredith* and *Glennon.* Both ships sank while we were gone. Then, at 2115 that evening, USS *LST-496* hit a mine and sank stern first. Not all of our losses were from enemy action, however. The next day the *Plunkett* sank a Liberty ship that didn't answer her challenge.

Herndon continued to operate off the Normandy beaches until July 2, when she was ordered to Cherbourg. In mid-July, she reported to Ireland and went on to take part in the invasion of Southern France.

Doc Peck [Lieutenant John Peck, MC, USN] writes of the invasion: "Compared to the entire, magnificent operation, *Herndon* was just a very small unit, a drop in the bucket. But I know that ever since, each and every one of us has enjoyed the satisfaction of knowing that we were there, that we participated, and that we did our best."

Quartermaster Third Class Robert E. Powell, U.S. Navy.

FIRST TO FIRE

By Quartermaster Third Class Robert E. Powell, U.S. Navy. Adapted from oral history transcript.

During World War II, I was a quartermaster third class aboard the USS *Fitch* (DD-462). In 1944, we were operating off the coast of Africa with a hunter/killer group looking for German submarines when we were called back to Casco Bay, Maine. At the time we didn't know why they called us back in the middle of the operation, but we loaded up and headed for Belfast, Ireland. After being there for about three days, we went to Plymouth, England and soon realized we were there for the big invasion of France.

On June 5 it was raining hard and we were aware that the invasion was on, but then it was called off, and so we spent the rest of June 5 turning back all the small landing craft already out in the English Channel. I really felt sorry for all of those soldiers in those small landing craft because all you could see was their helmets, with the spray flying over the front of the boats. I knew that they were probably very sick and wet.

By the time we got back to England, it was time to head back out again, for the invasion was then to happen on June 6. My battle station was "sky lookout," so I was able to keep track of what was going on. Early in the morning, while it was still dark, a couple of landing craft loaded with soldiers pulled up beside our ship and our captain told them to head for the beach. These were the men who assaulted the small islands which are just east of the Cotentin Peninsula. As it turned out, there weren't any Germans there, but we did find out that quite a few of the men were either injured or killed by mines.

By daylight we were to take positions on the firing line, just off the beach at Normandy, and as daylight broke we could see the Germans shooting at us with small arms. Fortunately, they didn't have the range. On the ship we had depth charges at our stern that had telephones to a seaman on the bridge. And they [the sailors at the depth charges] asked the fellow on the bridge, "How are the Germans doing?"

He said, "Oh, they are doing lousy. They're shooting, but they aren't coming anywhere near us."

He had no sooner said that than a big shell exploded right near our ship, sending up a geyser of water. At that point, a fellow on the other end of the line said, "How are the Germans doing now?"

I could tell you they were doing pretty darn good.

With that first shot at us, we started maneuvering, at a fast speed, making all types of turns while we started shooting back with our four 5-inch guns. As sky lookout, I was able to see the shells hitting the water where we would have been if we had not made a turn. We were told that if we got hit, we were supposed to run up on the shore so we could still keep firing in order to do the job that we were sent in to do as the decoy. As we pulled out, the destroyer *Corry* took our place but was sunk by a mine [see next story]. We went back to save her men, firing from one side while lowering our life boats from the other side.

About this time, as we were picking up survivors, the battleship *Nevada* and the cruiser *Quincy* opened up on the Germans. At this point the Germans weren't worried about us any more; they were more worried about the battleship and the cruiser. They stopped firing at us and we stopped firing at them while picking up survivors. Now the shells were going over our heads, both ways.

One of the survivors that we picked up from *Corry* happened to be a fellow from my home town, and he lived right up the street from me. When his ship got hit, he hurt his arm. I found out later that he broke a bone in his wrist and ended up with a Purple Heart.

We took the survivors back to the other transport ship that would take them back to England and then we asked for further orders and they said they didn't have any. This pretty much confirmed what we had heard, that our main mission was to go in there and draw the fire until we no longer could do that. As we were heading back to the transport ship, several ships dipped their flags to us which made us feel very proud.

We headed back to England the next day to pick up more ammunition. The guns had fired for so long that the paint peeled right off the guns and the deck was full of cork that evidently came from the shells or the powders. The following two weeks we were mostly guarding the transports in the bay there, from the E-boats and planes. We had planes come over every night while we were there. This concluded our Normandy duties, so we headed from there back down to the Mediterranean to take part in the invasion of Southern France. It was quite an exciting story.

We didn't realize it at the time, but we were the first American ship to fire on France in the invasion of Normandy. I feel this makes us quite distinct in the annals of history, and I am very proud of that. [Ed.: According to *Fitch*'s log, the destroyer opened fire at 0535 after coming under fire from shore batteries. Although *Quincy* fired two minutes after *Fitch*, *Quincy*'s shots are considered to have officially initiated the shore bombardment.]

Lieutenant (Junior Grade) Howard A. Andersen, MC, U.S. Navy

SAVING LIVES ABOARD A SINKING SHIP

By Lieutenant (Junior Grade) Howard A. Andersen, MC, U.S. Navy. Adapted from "D-Day at Normandy with USS Corry *(DD-463)," unpublished manuscript.*

USS *Corry* (DD-463) left Norfolk in late April 1944, escorting a munitions convoy to England. I was the medical officer aboard. After stopping in Belfast, where I bought some Irish linens for my wife, our convoy then proceeded to Plymouth, England, where *Corry* stayed for about three weeks. After being told that we might be going on a hazardous mission, I drove to the nearest medical supply depot, which was in Exeter, about forty miles northeast of Plymouth, to obtain extra medical supplies. On one occasion while we were waiting for the "real thing," *Corry* sailed toward France with several other ships but turned around after a few miles in the English Channel. Other groups of ships occasionally did the same thing—made false starts as though an invasion of France might be imminent.

On the afternoon of June 3, 1944, *Corry* left Plymouth, following a zig-zag course and escorting some LSTs and other slow ships. While underway, we were briefed on our mission and destination—Utah Beach on the Normandy coast of France. Landings were to be the morning of June 5, but on the morning of June 4, the operation was postponed because of bad weather. We had to pass the message to several smaller ships that had not received word of the postponement and advised them to turn around and return to, or at least toward, England.

Later that day, however, the decision was made to proceed, and D-Day was reset for June 6. *Corry* resumed its zig-zag course toward France and other ships did the same, so that from the air, the advancing convoys must have appeared to be disorganized. *Corry* arrived around 0200, June 6, at its destination between the Normandy beach near Sainte-Mère Église, France, and the Ste. Marcouf Islands, which were one or two miles farther out into the English Channel.

Land bombardment by Allied planes during the night and early morning was awesome. We could almost feel the reverberations out in the Channel where we were. In addition, the Germans sent out star shells, which burst into bright lights, dropping very slowly and illuminating the entire area. We were certain the Germans detected us off shore, but they gave us no indication of it. The "fireworks" on land and sea were so spectacular that no one slept that night.

The mission of the *Corry* was twofold: (1) to escort the slow, flat-bottomed ships, such as LSTs, and (2) to fire at designated targets on Utah Beach with its four 5-inch guns (two fore and two aft). We had left the LSTs about five miles away from the Normandy shore and had proceeded to our station. Our two sister destroyers were about a mile away, one on either side, with the same mission as ours but with different targets on shore.

H-Hour was 0630, and *Corry* was to start firing at H–40 minutes (0550). At dawn (about 0520), however, the Germans discovered our ship and opened fire on us; our crew returned the fire and began bombarding our designated targets on shore. An American plane laid a smoke screen, which protected our sister ships but not *Corry* and left us exposed to the Germans like a sitting duck. Later we were told that the plane assigned to lay the smoke screen had been hit and destroyed before it could finish its task.

Naturally, we attracted a great deal of attention from the German shore batteries. After they had found the range, small shells began hitting our ship; so our captain ordered "full speed ahead and a hard right rudder." During this maneuver, while I was in the wardroom helping a shipmate who had a large gash on his left shoulder from shrapnel, a huge explosion occurred below us in the forward fire and engine rooms. Boilers exploded, and the ship was literally separated into two parts, held together only by the superstructure. We had collided with a submerged mine. I was blown to the opposite side of the wardroom and landed on my backside but was not hurt because of good padding.

Since all power was off, I established my dressing station outside on the deck. My two corpsmen had been stationed fore and aft, but both came to midships where I was and where most of the casualties were brought. The three of us applied splints on men who had fractures (one with fractures of both lower legs, one with a fractured leg and thigh, one with a fracture of the thigh, and others with incapacitating injuries). Several men had burns from swimming in burning oil or were scalded by hot steam escaping from ruptured boilers.

We lifted others who had been injured into a lifeboat and one raft. Working on the deck below the lifeboat before it was lowered, I noted a dripping liquid on my forehead, and I discovered the dripping was battery acid. The force of the explosion had blown out the plugs in the lifeboat suspended above me and had ruptured the batteries so that the acid leaked down on me, but I had no serious burns. Later, the absence of plugs in the bottom of the boat turned out to be important for our casualties, because they had to bail out sea water from the boat, using their helmets.

I remember not being the least bit frightened or concerned about not surviving. I do remember being indignant with the attitude that "they can't do this to me and my friends!" I remember seeing no one who exhibited or expressed any fear, although one man who was not injured knelt and prayed next to me while I was trying to take care of the wounded. Though I respected his religious faith, I had work to do and had to ask him to get out of my way.

Later, planes dived down at us, and I remember wondering whether they might strafe us, but in a few moments I recognized them as friendly craft just encouraging us to "hang in there." Most of them were British Spitfires, and I saw not one German plane that day. I was grateful for the course in recognition that our group had been given on the way across the Atlantic. We had been shown silhouettes of planes and ships—both friendly and enemy—in gradually decreasing times of exposure and had been tested at one-fiftieth of a second exposure. When we had objected that the exposure time was impossibly short, the instructor showed us a pinup picture for one-one-hundredth of a second, and no one had any trouble recognizing Betty Grable. He made his point.

On the night of June 5 the communications officer attached to the *Corry* had showed me the large mail sack of documents concerning the entire D-Day operation. He had been ordered to put lead bars in the bag so it would sink to the bottom and not fall into enemy hands if the ship were sunk. He did not think the lead was necessary, so I explained that it would float if the contents were lighter than a similar amount of water. He did not buy my reasoning and did not put in the lead. After the ship was hit and was sinking, he lowered the bag into the water. When it floated, he lifted it up and tied it to the ship's stanchion (railing) so that it would be pulled down with the ship. His sheepish grin and glance at me was refreshing. Each of us was trying to do what was necessary before we had to leave the ship.

Corry was hit at 0633, and I was told that the ship went down in ten to twelve minutes. The water on the deck of the ship was knee-deep before the last casualty was removed, after which I stepped over the railing into the channel, hoping the carbon dioxide pellets in my life belt would work. I squeezed them, and sure enough, the belt inflated. Our captain, Lieutenant Commander George D. Hoffman, was the last person off the ship, and I was next to the last. He had a life jacket with a large collar—a Mae West type, named for the legendary buxom actress—which seemed to me to be much more efficient in its buoyancy than the belt that I had. The belt did not hold me high enough out of the water, especially with a heavy sea.

The temperature of the water in the English Channel that day was 52 degrees Fahrenheit. The British Air Force had geared its rescue attempts for pilots who were downed in the Channel to two hours. If the pilots could not be found within two hours after entering the water (even in summer), the Air Force figured that it was useless to persist in a rescue attempt because of hypothermia. Many of us were in the water more than two hours, but probably not more than three. Some of our men who had been rescued early (that is, they were not in the last group) died from hypothermia. Cold water is tolerated better when one is wearing clothing. Perhaps more important is the fat pad—the thicker the fat pad, the more one can tolerate cold water. No question that I was pleased to have a thick fat pad.

One of our sister ships [Ed.: this was either USS *Hobson* (DD-464) or USS *Fitch* (DD-462)] lowered a lifeboat to rescue our men, but the boat had to keep circling its own ship because the command ship (the cruiser *Augusta*), located five miles back, would not give it permission to leave due to the continued heavy fighting in the area. I learned of this almost a year later when I was on Okinawa in the Pacific Ocean with the 6th Marine Division. One of our naval corpsmen on Okinawa was in that boat. Eventually, the crew was allowed to come to our area to help us. Their boat could hold only about twenty men, and each trip back to their destroyer was a mile or two from us. These trips took a long time, and before the rescue efforts were finished, a PT boat came along and picked up the last of us. I was in that group. That crew lowered a cargo net so we could climb up. Once, when three men were on the cargo net, one end gave way, and all three men fell back into the water. One man never surfaced, but we rescued the other two, who were very exhausted and nearly drowned. The PT boat picked up sixty-five of us from *Corry* and then took us to the destroyer that had rescued most of our crew members.

After all of our men had been transferred from the PT boat, I thanked an officer who had a commander's insignia on his helmet. He advised me to thank the captain, who turned out to be a lieutenant (j.g.). I asked him [the captain] who the commander was and discovered that he was Commander [later Vice Admiral] John Bulkeley, who was in charge of a squadron of PT boats. This was the same man who rescued General MacArthur from the Philippines in 1942 by dashing to shore and taking him out to a submarine [actually, an airplane].

The crew of the destroyer had given their bunks to our men whom they had rescued earlier. I went below decks immediately to assess their status. Two men were dead but had no marks on them; certainly, they must have died from hypothermia. Three or four others were breathing just two or three times a minute. My corpsmen and I lifted them down, placed them on deck, gave them artificial respiration, and injected stimulants. All survived.

The same destroyer (it was probably USS *Hobson*) took us from action to a troop transport—USS *Susan B. Anthony* [sunk shortly afterwards; see Chapter VII]—where we could care for those who were wounded, burned, nearly drowned, or hypothermic. *Susan B. Anthony* took us to Falmouth, on the southwestern tip of England, where dozens of men were hospitalized. We arrived at the hospital in Falmouth about midnight on June 7 (D+1), about forty-two hours after *Corry* was sunk, and I spent the rest of the night getting the rescued men settled and talking with hospital doctors about their care.

On the morning of June 8 (D+2), those of us who were not hospitalized were taken by train to Plymouth, which was about fifty miles to the northeast of Falmouth. Sitting up in the train, I had my first sleep in more than seventy-two hours. After a few days in Plymouth, we went by train to Roseneath, Scotland, about thirty-five miles down the firth of the Clyde River northwest of Glasgow, to a camp where we stayed for three weeks, awaiting transport to the United States.

While at Roseneath, I examined all of the remaining crew and made new health records. I noted several crew members who had crops of boils, the cause of which I do not know to this day. Although large quantities of oil had leaked from *Corry*, the oil was soon diluted by the rough sea. Were the boils caused by the oil, or were they possibly due to the hypothermia that many had suffered? I must admit that I have not pursued the possible reasons since that time, but it was a very real observation.

From June 12 to June 30, daylight was long. While in Roseneath, I recall playing baseball and other sports at midnight without needing electric lights. To leave camp, we needed Navy uniforms. The uniform that I was wearing at the time the ship was sunk was oil-soaked (including my underwear) because I had carried men who had been swimming in burning oil below the main deck. Uniforms were not available for purchase in Scotland, so I got khaki coveralls from the supply depot, but such clothing was not acceptable for leaving camp. I scrounged an official shirt from one man and borrowed pants from another on two or three occasions so I could visit Glasgow. Once, a small group of us drove to Loch Lomond (about twenty miles north-west of Glasgow), and I climbed Ben Lomond. On the shore of Loch Lomond, we found a small shop which made its own woolen cloth, and I bought woolen material for my wife. All the linens that I had previously bought in Belfast had gone down with the ship.

We came back to New York City aboard the *Queen Elizabeth* (85,000 tons compared with 1,750 tons for our destroyer). There were six thousand men aboard the ship on our trip, whereas going eastward to Britain, the ship usually carried as many as twenty-two thousand men on each crossing. The "Queens" (*Queen Mary* and *Queen Elizabeth*) traveled without escort because of their speed of approximately forty knots. The maximum speed of the *Corry* was only thirty-five knots, and destroyers were known as fast ships. The "Queens" used a different course each trip so that enemy submarines could not easily lie in wait for them. When the ship docked, I went ashore in New York City in the same khaki coveralls that had been issued to me in Scotland. Needless to say, I bought new uniforms as soon as possible.

My corpsmen and I were awarded Bronze Star medals for our services:

> For heroic service as medical officer attached to the USS *Corry* when that vessel sank as a result of a mine explosion and German gunfire during invasion operations in the Bay of the Seine, coast of France, June 6, 1944.
>
> Courageous and selfless in the performance of duty, Lieutenant (j.g.) Andersen remained to the last aboard the sinking vessel, working desperately to save the wounded even though the word had been given to abandon ship.

Despite the gruelling strain of continuous shelling from hostile shore batteries during the subsequent prolonged period in the water, and although suffering from exposure, he carried on valiantly for another thirty hours in his steadfast and tireless ministration to the injured. . . .

The entire experience in the waters of the English Channel on June 6, 1944, after the sinking of the *Corry* and the death of many friends had a sobering, maturing, and lasting effect on myself and on many of the ship's crew.

During the fiftieth anniversary celebration of this event (1994), President Clinton was aboard a ship that anchored over the spot where *Corry* rests on the bottom of the Bay of the Seine in the English Channel. He gave a short talk about the *Corry* and then laid a wreath in the water in honor of those who perished. Evidently, it was the first ship to sink during Operation Overlord. [Ed.: *Corry* was the first of six ships to sink off Utah Beach on D-Day.]

Lieutenant Commander Harold J. O'Leary, U.S. Naval Reserve (Retired).

A DESTROYER DESTROYED

By Lieutenant Commander Harold J. O'Leary, U.S. Naval Reserve (Retired). Adapted from "My Experience at the Normandy Invasion," unpublished manuscript.

I was the chief quartermaster aboard USS *Meredith* (DD-726), a new, ten-week-old destroyer. We were the escort commander for a group of LSTs that we were accompanying to the landing at Utah Beach. We arrived at our designated landing area on the morning of June 6, 1944, and provided gun support while the landing craft steamed onto the beach. We were then ordered out to the English Channel to intercept German E-boats that were reported heading for the invasion sites. We patrolled all night with no action and then proceeded back to the area of the cruiser *Tuscaloosa* and her support ships, which were providing gun support for the troops ashore. *Meredith* fired sporadically at targets of opportunity throughout the day.

That night *Meredith* was ordered to take station on the port quarter of the *Tuscaloosa* (four destroyers were stationed around her to provide protection from enemy planes).

On June 8, shortly after 0100, a German plane attacked *Meredith*. It fired a radio-controlled bomb that hit her at the waterline between the stacks.

I was plotting in the chart room and checking bearings with the navigator who was plotting in the CIC [combat information center]. When we were hit I was thrown off the stool on which I was sitting and landed in the corner of the chart room. I laid there until the vibrations from the explosion ceased. At first I thought that we might have accidentally dropped a depth charge that went off at a shallow depth. However, when the ship started to list to starboard, I knew that we were in trouble. I ran to the ladder leading up to the pilot-house, but as I was ascending the ladder, a deluge of water came down and I thought I was too late and that we were already submerged (actually it was a tremendous ball of water that was blown into the air and dropped down on the bridge).

I subsequently got out on the bridge to see what was going on and what assistance I could render. It was apparent that we were in big trouble. The guy wires, halyards, and all sorts of debris were all over the bridge and all communications to and from all departments were out. I then realized that the SECRET chart that I was working on was still on the desk in the chart room. This was the grid chart that showed the German gun installations and the assigned positions of all our ships, including the cruisers, battleships, and our command ship (USS *Ancon*). I went back down to the chart room, rolled up the chart, put it in the waistband of my pants, and returned to the bridge.

After about half an hour, the captain gave the order to abandon ship. Reports from the various departments had indicated that our watertight integrity was lost and our list had worsened to the point that the starboard deck was awash.

Meanwhile, whaleboats and two PCs [patrol craft] came alongside to provide assistance. I looked for members of my bridge gang and for my buddy, Brady Bryan, a chief machinists' mate. I found him in a state of shock, strolling aimlessly along the port deck. He had dived down into his engine room after he escaped and rescued four men. He was later awarded the Navy Cross and promoted to warrant officer.

Bryan and I climbed aboard the *PC-1236* with about one hundred other survivors and were transferred to the *Tuscaloosa*. I immediately asked to see the intelligence officer onboard, gave him the SECRET chart that I was carrying, and requested a receipt. We stayed aboard until she ran out of ammunition and then proceeded back to Plymouth, England. At that point, the intelligence officer gave me back the chart and asked for the return of his receipt. I subsequently turned over the chart to the intelligence officer ashore.

Meredith didn't sink immediately. Salvage crews and tugs attempted to tow the ship to shallow water, but at daybreak a German bomber attacked the area and dropped a two-thousand-pound bomb alongside *Meredith*. The ship broke in two and went to the bottom.

Meredith sustained casualties of thirty-five killed and twenty-seven wounded.

Gunner's Mate Second Class James A. Jones, U.S. Navy.

DEAR DAD

By Gunner's Mate Second Class James A. Jones, U.S. Navy. Adapted from unpublished correspondence.

At the time of the Normandy invasion, Jones was a gunner's mate third class aboard USS Harding (DD-625), stationed off of Omaha Beach. Jones's General Quarters station was on the forward, centerline, 20-millimeter, anti-aircraft gun located behind and above the number two 5-inch gun and in front of and a little below the bridge. This vantage point gave Jones a nearly unrestricted view and field of fire of about three hundred degrees. The following letter was written by Jones to his father on June 27, 1944.

I am going to write the story of the invasion of France as I saw it from where I was on the high 20-millimeter gun in front of the bridge. I had about the best view of anyone on the ship, and could hear a great deal of what went on on the bridge. I will draw some maps to show about where we were, and the approximate location of many of the things we shot at, and some of the places we were in the greatest danger. I will not be able to send this until I get back to the U.S. but am writing it now so I will not forget many little incidents which make it interesting.

I think it would be best to start about five days before D-Day itself. At that time, we were anchored outside the breakwater in Portland, England, standing our regular condition watch. There was little to see except there were about fifteen large PAs [APAs; attack transports] and God knows how many small landing boats. All went well the first two days and nights, but on the third night GQ (General Quarters) was called at about 0100. I got to my gun and saw lots of firing, most of it on the beach, and two aircraft came close in the dark. Two bombs lit off our starboard bow and on our port quarter almost at the same time. They did not hurt us, but damaged a destroyer on our port quarter slightly. In about half an hour, it was all over and we went back to bed.

The next day at dawn I was awakened by a loud explosion and ran topside to see what it was and found that the Germans had mined the harbor in the night. All day, we could hear them [the mines] explode every half hour or so. By good luck, none of the APAs was damaged at all. All went well 'till that night, when at 0100 we again had GQ, and this time only one enemy plane was shot down and no bombs or mines were dropped. In about an hour, we went back to bed and slept well 'till morning.

This made D-18 hours, but we still did not know for sure when it was to happen. All that day, we worked on the guns and saw to our life jackets, gas masks, and foul weather gear on our GQ stations. Starting at about 1730, we hoisted anchor and got under way and the APAs started to come out. Landing craft had started leaving at noon the same day in large groups of about fifteen to thirty in bunches. At about 1900, the captain made a speech saying that this was D-Day and that we were going into one of the greatest adventures of our life and wished us all the best of luck in the coming operation.

At 2000, about H-9.5 [ed.: H-10.5], we went to GQ and made our final preparations for the battle. All paint and burnable material were thrown over the side. All fire hoses were broken out, and all damage repair equipment was broken out. Extra projectiles were piled in handling rooms and hoists filled with powder, and all water-tight doors closed and dogged tightly. I broke out 20-millimeter magazines for my gun, in addition to the eight magazines in my ready box. I loaded my guns and all other 20-millimeter crews did the same. The 40-millimeter guns put a dip in the loading tray so all they had to do was press the firing pedal. The 5-inch gun had the breech plugs open. Shells were loaded in the top and bottom of the hoist, and powder in the tray and scuttle, and everyone settled down to wait for H-Hour to come.

It did not get dark until nearly 2300, and I could see a long part of the invasion armada as far as you could see, and all of it was around us. I could hear the TBS [talk between ships] speaker telling us what to do from the flagship. The word came that the *Harding* was screening the invasion armada across the channel just behind the minesweepers following lines of small, lighted buoys.

Time out to say who was there besides us in the warships. The battleships present off of Omaha were *Texas* and *Arkansas*; the cruisers present were *Augusta, Tuscaloosa* [Ed.: *Tuscaloosa* was operating off of Utah Beach], *Glasgow* (English), *Montcalm* (French), and *Georges Leygues* (French); and the destroyers present were: *Baldwin, Thompson, Satterlee,* and *Harding.*

We sailed on through the night without any interference at all, and about two hours before dawn got into our position about eighteen thousand yards off the French coast and waited for the dawn to come so we could start firing. This was about H-2, and at this time over the coast a terrific air bombardment was taking place. The air over the coast was red with anti-aircraft bursts and tracer fire. There were lines of bursting bombs and a long streamer of fire from a burning plane was seen every minute or so. Some exploded on the way down, others exploded after they hit. It was a very awesome thing to see. The time was getting short, now about H-30 minutes, and we started to move slowly forward toward the beach and closed steadily from eight thousand to three thousand and then quickly closed to nineteen hundred yards.

Then dawn was at hand and you could see the coast rather dimly. One of the battleships opened up with her guns, but not before a

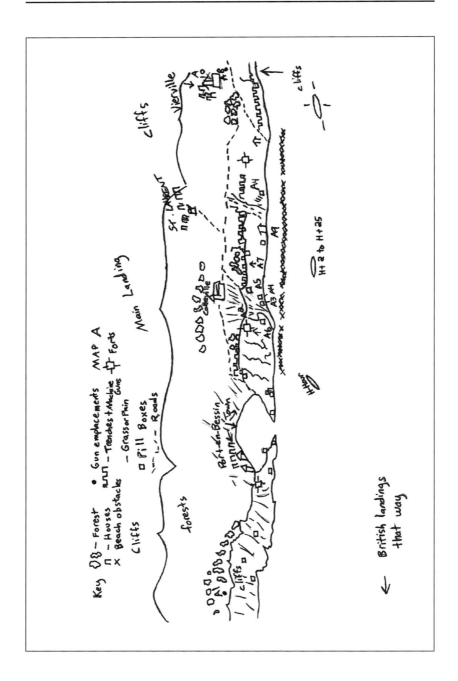

German shore battery far to our left opened up, sending shells bursting ahead of us, then behind us, and then over us. I thought that they would hit us for sure, but they did not [see Map A, point A1]. All ships present opened fire on them, and in about a minute, they were knocked out of the fight. We then shelled our assigned positions of A2, A3, A4, A5, and helped on A6, where we were until H-Hour. During this time we shot up about four hundred rounds of 5-inch ammunition and we eventually closed the range to about six hundred yards from the beach, which was point-blank range for our guns. We later found out that we were the closest to the beach of any one of the ships.

At H+28 minutes, we were called back out to the flagship to take aboard Rear Admiral Cook and Major General Hardy. At about H+3, we returned to our position and waited until H+4 to open up on the trenches [A7] and blast-out machine gun nests along with the other ships. In that district, all ships were firing at targets of opportunity. At this time, our men were still on the beaches and had advanced only in the valley that we had shelled. They were pinned down and a gun from A8 was knocking out landing barges right and left, and dozens of them were burning on the beach. The gun went on firing for nearly four hours before some ship finally got it.

At H+10, our men started to advance and slowly fight their way to the positions of A7 as well as some other sectors, but were held up by a fortified house [A9] which we shot at. The firing kept up intermittently at targets of opportunity until about H+15. In some points, our troops were a mile or better inland, and landing operations were going well. From H+15 to H+19, we were intermittently shelling some targets before moving to a new position. About two hours before dusk, we got word to open fire on target A10, which was a tall church steeple in Vierville which had machine gun nests in it and spotters for the shore battery. We opened up with the 5-inch guns. The first salvo hit the top and cross, and every salvo after that went down about ten feet. The general said that it was the most beautiful piece of destroyer gunnery that he had ever seen.

We laid to that night still at GQ. Little happened except the Germans came over and laid mines and hit one ship with a flying bomb. The ship sank three days later. I shot at a burning German plane that was headed in at us from dead ahead, and at about five hundred yards, it turned to one side and missed us. I think I hit it with about half a magazine.

The next day we went down the coast a little ways [see Map B]. Our troops had driven inland and about three miles at most points, and we were pushing down the coast. The way we went, we were about the only ones in this section this day, and these targets were ones missed in the first days of bombardment. We patrolled up and down the coast here on the first part of the morning. First, we fixed on pillboxes B1, B2, and B3, and then shelled trenches B4 and B5. Then, I was looking through glasses I had borrowed from gun number 2 and spotted pillbox B6, which we knocked out quickly. The men in the gun director spotted personnel in trees [B7] and we strafed them with 40-millimeter machine guns and ran them out [Ed.: 40-millimeter guns were anti-aircraft guns.].

At about noon, our troops came up to about line B8. We then moved to the Pointe du Hoc area and relieved the destroyer *Satterlee*, which was helping the Rangers. Then in contact with a Ranger fire control party, in B10, we shelled B9 because the Germans had them in a cross fire from that sector. We then shelled a pillbox in B11 and destroyed it, allowing the Rangers to advance to where it was located [shaded spot on map where they were when we started]. We then put our landing party ashore to help the Rangers guard their prisoners. Our boat [one of the *Harding*'s ship's boats] was damaged and destroyed, but no one was hurt [B12].

A short time later, a bigger boat came up with orders to bring out the wounded. It came back with a dozen German prisoners and a group of wounded Rangers. The Rangers came aboard for chow and to keep from getting themselves wiped out. One of them told me what had happened was that the English ship that had landed them had showed up late, and the Germans were standing there waiting for them and just rolled hand grenades down on them as they climbed out. Of the 400 or so men, 250 reached the top of the cliff and another 50 were killed taking the three forts [B13]. They then dug in on the line I have marked with gray and held that position.

The destroyer that we had relieved had not done so well and left, leaving about 130 men (some of whom were wounded) to hold the

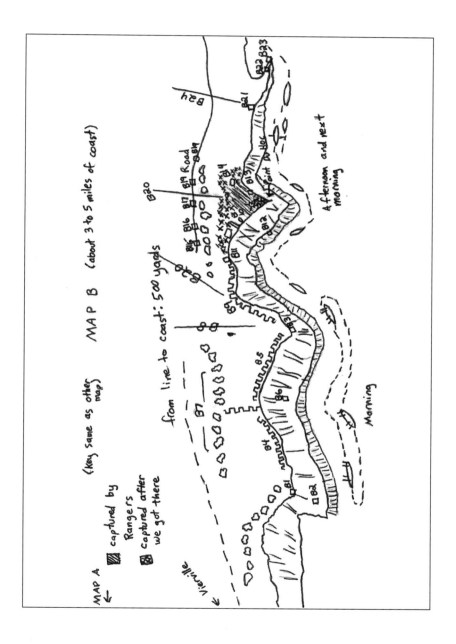

MAP A

MAP B   (about 3 to 5 miles of coast)

(Key same as other map)

captured by Rangers

captured after we got there

from line to coast: 500 yards

Afternoon and next morning

Morning

Vierville

Germans in check. He said that every time that we shot, we hit our target right on, and that this had rather demoralized the Germans for a while. He said that the Rangers looked upon us as guardian angels, and every time we came in on a firing run, they said, "Here comes Blondie again to knock out a few more." (We have a picture of Blondie painted on our stack to identify us.)

About this time, two bigger boats full of prisoners came out and a couple of companies of Rangers went into the beach. We soon got orders to shell target B14, which was a long storehouse. We fired rapid fire for two minutes and there was little left but the foundations. Later, a Ranger told me that they shot down thirty Germans running from the house, and there were some killed in it. They then advanced to the dotted line [area with XX in it], which they captured after we started the shelling.

We then started shelling targets B15-16-17-18-19, and a Ranger told me later that we got one with each salvo. He said that he had never seen anything like it; the targets just seemed to disappear one after the other, about every five seconds. We sent food, cigarettes, candy, water, and everything we could to make it easier. I don't think there was a man on the ship who would not have gone to hell for those men and I think they felt the same way about us. They were being reinforced at regular intervals and the going got easier. The Ranger major recommended the ship for the Presidential Unit Citation, but I don't know if it went through or not [Ed.: *Harding* did not receive a Presidential Unit Citation]. By this time, our troops had advanced down the coast to line B20.

As we went in on our firing runs, we were strafed by German machine guns and rifle fire from B9 and B11 until we backed down. I could hear them go over my head and bounce off the side of the ship. We were sure scared, but we had no way of seeing them to shoot back.

During all this time, a German gun had been shelling us part of the time and coming pretty close some of the time. It seemed to be a kind of random thing, but I guess he finally gave up or somebody hit him or something.

I saw some German soldiers and they were in good shape and had good clothing, but were scared to death of the Rangers and did not know what to make of our men who were guarding them. We all

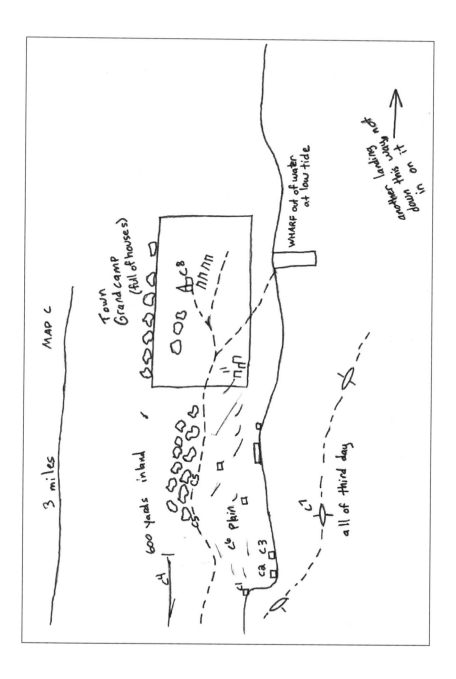

looked pretty ragged, dirty, unshaven, and very mad, plus we had our rifles and tommy guns cocked with the safeties off, so we could just as easily shoot them as look at them, and they knew it.

I have a couple of stories about the Rangers, told to me by one of them. There were two automatic rifle men who worked together and had fought together the first day and shot ten Germans each. Then one of them got killed and the other went half crazy and would yell: "Come on you dirty !#*&*, come and get me!"

Every time one would stick his head up, he would shoot them down, and when this particular Ranger left, he said this man had several Germans to his credit and, although he was wounded, was still going strong. Another time, five Rangers captured ten Germans in a dugout and just went in and got them. Another Ranger who had been wounded on the beach was shot at by a machine gun. He did not stop until he had killed every man on it. These were just a few of the things they did. They undoubtedly are the bravest men I ever saw. They did not give a damn for anyone or anything and their one ambition was to kill more Germans.

That night the Higgins boat brought out our landing party. Luckily, no one had been hurt, and the Rangers said again and again that our gunnery was what had saved them. As we lay to that night, the German bombers came over again and laid mines which sank another destroyer. A destroyer escort and three or four smaller ships did not get a chance to shoot at them. During the night, our troops joined up with the Rangers at point B20, and were about ten miles inland at the farthest point.

The next morning, we were down the coast a little farther [right side of Map B and left side of Map C]. We started that morning by shelling pillboxes B21-22-23 and we believed that we knocked out a German gun battery. Our troops advanced to line B24. About an hour later, we fired on C1-2-3 pillboxes, knocked them out, and then ceased firing for about two hours while our troops advanced to within two miles of Grandcamp. We started a flanking movement on line C4 as far as it goes. At about 1000, we got word there were troops on the road [C5]. We started firing rapid fire and had fired about one hundred rounds when some Germans ran into the open [C6] and we strafed them with machine guns. Forty men at this time were about eight hundred yards from the beach and firing all their guns and closing. When we were about seven hundred to five hundred yards offshore, we ran aground and stopped immediately. We went aground at C7 at 1600. We backed off, but it ruined our sound gear [for detecting submarines] and both screws were damaged so we could only make ten knots. This was about noon and we laid off after that and shelled targets inland a little.

We received orders to shell the town of Maisy and we started shooting first one gun, then the other, at irregular intervals at men and troops in the town and at the church [C8], which was a German spotting post. Our fire was very effective, because our troops were three miles from the town and a half-hour later, they had the town and there were lots of fires and smoke. We shot several phosphorous shells which covered large areas with burning phosphorous.

The pillboxes C9-10-11-12 were not occupied. I guess the Germans decided it was suicide to stay in them as they were right in the open. We stopped firing and soon darkness fell. The Germans came over and bombed the ships again and hit one that I know of. The next day we left for Plymouth, England, and lay there for five days in dry dock.

During the fight, we shot up 2,154 rounds of 5-inch ammunition and 2,500 rounds of 40-millimeter and 20-millimeter ammunition. On the first map [A], we shot at all the numbered targets. Some, probably others, I could not see or hear about. On maps B and C, we shot at some targets listed and others which I could not see or hear about. As luck would have it, no one was hurt in the eighty-five hours we put in over there. There are many things I left out, but that is the general way it all came off.

We were complimented by the High Command on our shooting. We did the best shooting done there the first three days. We were recommended for the Presidential Unit Citation by the commander of the Rangers. We were and are still classed as the best destroyer in the Atlantic Fleet.

USS *Herndon*'s port side is manned and ready for action on D-Day. *(Angus S. Schmelz photograph)*

Sailors hose off the *Herndon*'s red hot guns. *(Angus S. Schmelz photograph)*

USS *Fitch* (DD-462) at sea. *(U.S. Navy; National Archives)*

USS *Corry* (DD-463) before D-Day landings. *(U.S. Navy; National Archives)*

USS *Meredith* (DD-726) at sea. *(U.S. Navy; National Archives)*

I saw an LST hit a mine and tear itself completely in half. The middle section of the ship just disappeared with about 300 boys on it. I was there trying to drag scared, mutilated, and half-dead kids out of the water into my boat. Two hours later there was no more to be done. We went to a ship and ate a big supper. Somehow appetites seem unaffected by horror.

IV
BEACHED WHALES

The key to the success of the Normandy invasion was the massive amphibious assault launched by the Allies against the German held coast of France. Fortunately for invasion planners, a special breed of amphibious ships and craft had been developed early in the war and was already battle-hardened by 1944. These flat-bottomed craft were designed to beach themselves, off-load troops, supplies, and weapons, and then return to sea. Amphibious ship and craft types that took part in the invasion included LCCs (landing craft, control), LCIs (landing craft, infantry), LCMs (landing craft, mechanized), LCSs (landing craft, support), LCTs (landing craft, tank), LCVPs (landing craft, vehicle and personnel), and LSTs (landing ship, tank). Vast numbers of Allied amphibious craft participated in the invasion: 250 LCIs, more than 900 LCTs, 480 LCMs, 1,100 LCVPs, and 230 LSTs.

The seagoing LSTs (many of the other craft had to be carried by ships to the invasion site for off-loading) were especially important in bringing the men and matériel from England to France throughout the invasion. These ships made hundreds of trips across the channel, going back and forth so many times that crew members lost track of the number of round-trips they had made. The flat-bottomed ships rolled sickeningly even in a calm sea, and during the week before the invasion, when troops were kept on the ships, their holds stank of diesel oil, backed-up toilets, and vomit.

Crewed by about ten officers and one hundred enlisted men, LSTs carried far more than their name suggested; they could haul troops by the hundreds, jeeps, cranes, ammunition, supplies, casualties, and yes, tanks. Although nicknamed "large slow target," these ten-knot, diesel-powered ships with their high freeboard were so essential to the war effort that when invasion planners faced a shortage, Winston Churchill exclaimed: "The destinies of two great empires . . . seemed to be tied up by some Goddamned things called LSTs." Despite their regular channel crossings and participation in all aspects of the Normandy invasion, only five LSTs were lost, none on D-Day.

In the accounts that follow, we leave the Navy's great floating arsenals, board a slow, ungainly, amphibious craft, and touch the sands of Normandy for the first time.

Water Tender Second
Class Fred W. Norton,
U.S. Naval Reserve.

AIR RAID IN WEYMOUTH

By Water Tender Second Class Fred W. Norton, U.S. Naval Reserve. Adapted from unpublished manuscript.

I was on *LST-317* during the invasions of Sicily, Italy, and Normandy.

Our flotilla was in Weymouth Harbor prior to the invasion of Normandy. One night, the German planes got in behind our [aircraft] formation coming back from Germany and after a few bombs in the harbor, General Quarters was sounded. I got up to my guns with pants in hand. My trainer strapped me in and I was prepared to shoot the German plane going between us and the full moon, when the trainer advised that we were not supposed to shoot and give away our position.

After U.S. Army personnel were loaded onboard, a *Life* photographer came aboard and took pictures of our crew and the soldiers. When we headed across the Channel for France, there were minesweepers ahead of us, clearing a path and marking it with red and green buoys.

We landed at Omaha Beach, Normandy on D-Day at H-Hour. Following D-Day, we made twenty-five trips across the Channel, sometimes bringing back severely wounded soldiers who were treated en route by doctors and medics. One time, we beached the *LST-317* at high tide. As the tide went out, we sat high and dry and the beach. This allowed the troops to drive out on dry land, but we felt like sitting ducks. Nevertheless, we made it off, and eventually came through the war in good shape, with God as our co-captain.

Lieutenant Commander Osgood H. Hilton, U.S. Naval Reserve (Retired).

DON'T FORGET THE TIDE!

By Lieutenant Commander Osgood H. Hilton, U.S. Naval Reserve (Retired).
Condensed from LCDR Osgood H. Hilton, The Kid from Vallejo: An Autobiography *(Vallejo, California: Privately printed, 1995).*

Hilton's ship, USS Ancon *(AGC-4) was the amphibious force flagship for the Omaha Beach assault forces.*

In preparation for the invasion, I and a fellow officer were assigned to a British naval intelligence school at South Meade near Wimbledon for training in top secret operations. Each of us had a team of four U.S. Navy yeomen assigned to us for the work we were to do. I soon discovered that all of my yeomen were highly trained in German. One held a Ph.D., one had an M.A. in German, one was a Lutheran minister who delivered his sermon each Sunday in German, and the last one was a very young yeoman who had just graduated *magna cum laude* from the University of Wisconsin with a B.A. in German. So I was now commanding officer of the U.S. Navy "Y" Team No. 1.

Officers and men trained separately, but all were given final exams after a month of training. Passing successfully, I was given the choice of duty aboard the USS *Texas* or USS *Ancon*. By this time it was fairly clear that an invasion was imminent, but no one seemed to know where or when. I knew that the *Texas* was a battleship, but didn't know that the *Ancon* was the headquarters ship for the invasion. I chose *Ancon,* and when reporting aboard her, was delighted to find that the Navy had simply painted the former passenger liner battleship gray and placed a lot of electronic equipment on her so that she could be a command ship.

Ancon was just under fifteen thousand tons and almost five hundred feet long. I was pleasantly surprised to be assigned to an outside cabin with a private bath and another lieutenant as my roommate. I was even more surprised to learn that I had to wear my dress blue uniform throughout the invasion, because the British had no other uniform in northern waters. Khakis and greens were not allowed. Best of all, the large dining room had not been altered at all, so the officers on the ship ate all their meals at linen-covered tables served by mess stewards.

From the time I joined USS *Ancon* in May 1944 until she sailed for Normandy at midnight on June 5, Weymouth Harbor underwent several night attacks by the Luftwaffe. The enemy planes dropped land mines on the harbor, hoping to hit any of the ships there, but all of the mines fell harmlessly into the water.

Just before sailing on June 5, [author and war correspondent] Ernest Hemingway came aboard the *Ancon* along with a contingent of Rangers who were destined to cross Omaha Beach and scale the steep cliffs where the inland side of the beach ended. The Germans were entrenched on the top of this cliff, so the Rangers lost more than half of their number. Hemingway got into an LCI from the *Ancon* just prior to H-Hour and went ashore with the Rangers.

Also, a few days before sailing, King George VI came aboard the *Ancon* to review the officers and men. While walking on deck a bit ahead of his entourage, the King noticed a door slightly ajar. He pushed the door open a bit wider only to have a U.S. sailor push him back out again, saying, "I'm sorry, sir, but you haven't been vetted" (cleared for top secret information). It was later reported that the King had complimented the admiral on board for the devotion of his crewmen.

At Normandy, *Ancon* dropped anchor about two hundred yards offshore and stayed in the same position until she returned to England on June 28. Late on D-Day, George Hicks of ABC was broadcasting to the United States from one of the gun turrets of the *Ancon*, interviewing the gunners. Suddenly, one of them shouted that a JU-88, a Nazi dive-bomber, was heading directly for the *Ancon*. The crew went to work at once with their anti-aircraft weapons and succeeded in shooting the plane down. They saw the German pilot parachute from the plane and land in the water where he was picked up by a U.S. destroyer escort.

Admiral J.L. Hall aboard the *Ancon* sent orders to me to leave *Ancon* at once to find the ship with the German aviator on board and to interrogate him. Early on the morning of D+1, I clambered over the side of the *Ancon* in my dress blues and got into an LCVP, a craft not much bigger than a whaleboat and operated by a coxswain handling an outboard motor. There were already two other officers in the craft when I climbed aboard, but they were wearing what looked like Army apparel. They were, however, naval officers and one of them was a lieutenant commander, so he out-ranked me.

After a short period of seeking the destroyer escort in vain, the lieutenant commander told me that he and his fellow officer were supposed to go ashore. He told me to let them off ashore and then I could come back out and take all the time I needed to find the destroyer escort. I told the coxswain to head into shore and we tied up at the stem of an LCI which had been hit and was leaning heavily to port. The two officers scrambled across the LCI to the beach.

Then the coxswain came up to me, saluted, and asked if it would be all right for him to step ashore for just a few minutes so he could tell his grandchildren that he had been ashore on D+1. Without thinking, I told him it would be okay and then told him that I would accompany him. No sooner were we on the beach, however, when I realized my mistake. I knew that the tide in Normandy runs in and out faster than anywhere else in the world except for the Bay of Fundy. So, when I looked over the LCI, I saw that the tide had run out so fast that there was eight feet of sand behind the LCVP. I told the coxswain that since he was the skipper of the craft, he would have to wait for the tide to come in before taking the LCVP back to the *Ancon*.

I then walked up the beach about fifty yards where I found an Army DUKW [an amphibious U.S. Army vehicle commonly called a "duck"] operating. So I asked for a ride back to the *Ancon*, and the Army personnel operating the DUKW were glad to do so.

Fortunately for me, the destroyer escort that I was looking for had left for England the moment it picked up the Nazi aviator, so I would never have caught up with it anyway. The admiral knew this by now, so I was off the hook. The next day, the lieutenant commander who had gone ashore ahead of me came back to the *Ancon* with a bullet wound in the buttocks. When he applied to the admiral for a Purple Heart, the admiral told him that he had had no authority to go ashore, so he would never get a Purple Heart from him (the admiral). I never did hear whether or not the lieutenant commander was court-martialed for this faux pas.

Back in England on June 28, I and my team of enlisted men arrived just in time for comprehensive attacks by V-1s and V-2s. We got used to using the London bomb shelters. One of my men was walking across Hyde Park one afternoon when he heard a V-1 coming, looked up, and saw it not too far away. Almost automatically, he quickened his pace. An elderly lady walking with a cane stopped him and said quietly, "Don't worry about that one, young man. It's headed for South Kensington."

I and my men fully expected to be sent home now that the invasion was over, but the captain in London told us that our job wasn't over yet and sent us by rail to Plymouth. Here we boarded the USS *Bayfield* and were transported by sea through the straits of Gibraltar to Naples in Italy to prepare for the invasion of Southern France.

The members of U.S. Navy "Y" Team No. 1 received a Navy Unit Commendation about a year after the invasion for their efforts in Normandy.

Warrant Officer William T. Potts, Jr., MC, U.S. Navy (Retired).

COMFORT AND SOLACE?

By Warrant Officer William T. Potts, Jr., MC, U.S. Navy (Retired). Adapted from unpublished manuscript.

From the looks of things in Plymouth Harbor, it was obvious that the Allies were massing for an invasion of the continent. It was now April 1944 and we forty-two medical personnel had done nothing but eat and sleep since we came aboard the USS *LST-494*. For the most part we stayed in a berthing compartment, only coming out to eat and view the scenery.

LST-494 had one permanent pharmacist's mate first class named Reidt who had a small, one-room sick bay. In civilian life Reidt had been an undertaker. At night, in a swap for a little 190-proof alcohol, Reidt would get a tenderloin, and he and I (also a pharmacist's mate) would cook it in the sick bay on a hot plate after we had plugged the cracks around the door so other crew members could not smell the cooking. We did this because ever since the soldiers had come aboard, the food had been terrible, as it always is when troops are aboard.

Late in April 1944 we took on a full complement of GIs with vehicles and set sail from Plymouth. On the night of April 28, 1944 off the southern coast of Devon, very close to land, German E-boats got in amongst us. LSTs *507* and *531,* fully loaded with troops and gear, were sunk. In the excitement of that attack one LST depressed its 20-millimeter guns and raked another of our LSTs. It was a real screwup and we knew it the next morning. Thirty-two Navy medical personnel were lost on the two LSTs, including Dr. Tiffany V. Manning and my good friend Chief Pharmacist's Mate Lloyd L. Witten, USN. *LST-494* was fortunate in that we suffered no losses at all. That night, 749 soldiers and 197 sailors died; twenty-six percent of the sailors were medical personnel.

Shortly before the invasion of Normandy, our medical group was augmented by the reporting aboard of Lieutenant Louis Kalodner of Baltimore, an experienced physician. Then an Army surgical team, consisting of a major and two GIs, reported aboard. The major sought me out immediately and asked how much ninety-five percent grain alcohol I had on board. I told him sixteen half-gallons. He said, "Chief, take care of it—it's for drinking purposes only."

Throughout the invasion and until he left us shortly afterwards, the major stayed in his stateroom in his long underwear. Once he came out to tend a wounded GI and performed what appeared to be a laparotomy to repair intestines damaged by shrapnel, but he butchered the soldier from Vidalia, Georgia. I could not bear to watch. Then it was back to his bunk.

We were due to hit Omaha Beach at H+12, but were delayed by unexpected resistance. We evacuated only a handful of wounded at Omaha Beach, probably because so many died there. On D-Day, I was hit in the face with a small piece of shrapnel, possibly from our own guns since anti-aircraft fire was coming down like rain. Outside of that I suffered only tension for about twenty-four hours a day. The first night at Omaha Beach German planes did come over, and Doc Kalodner and I were kneeling, treating an American sergeant who had a bullet wound in his shoulder, when a near miss rocked our LST. We both looked at each other and said nothing.

Then it was back to Plymouth, keeping our bow on the mast of the LST ahead of us to avoid mines, loading up again with men and gear, and back to Normandy. This time we hit Utah Beach, the other American beachhead closest to Cherbourg. Eventually we also landed at the British beaches of Juno, Sword, and Gold.

I believe we had air cover of some 10,000 aircraft over the beaches. On return from bombing missions our aircraft were not supposed to fly over us, but some chose to do so. Our crew, who were very undisciplined, would open up on them with our 20-millimeter guns. One youngster, a survivor from the USS *Maddox*, which had been sunk in the Mediterranean, would open up at night when he heard small boat engines, thinking it was aircraft. When his ship had been sunk, officials had shipped him to Normandy, instead of sending him back to the States.

For thirty-three days I did my sleeping during the day and we tried not to get stranded on the beach with our bow doors down at night. The English Channel has thirty foot tides and once we beached you could eventually walk one hundred yards or more behind the ship. It was several hours before the tide swung around enough to permit us to get off the beach.

One day at Juno Beach, a British *Dido* Class cruiser was sunk by a torpedo manned by a German sailor. The ship settled but its superstructure was still visible. We picked up the Free Polish sailors who were manning the cruiser and they came aboard dragging suitcases filled with vodka. We supplied the grapefruit mix. In no time at all it seemed that everyone on our LST was "under the weather." The Poles were on the tank deck singing and playing guitars. The harbor master wanted us to move, but our skipper and the crew were so incapacitated that we could not get underway for several hours.

On one of our trips back to Plymouth I bought a bottle of Old Angus Scotch for sixteen dollars from a Limey sailor. I was lucky it was scotch, because some of our crew made the same deal with British sailors and it turned out to be tea, and they were out sixteen dollars. I waited until nightfall and then sat on our bow door nipping my precious scotch when, lo and behold, I saw a figure coming toward our ship. It turned out to be Bill Wayner and he joined me in our quiet party. However, the tide was coming in, and when he left he had to wade through surf to his LST. I learned later that the tide was chest high when he got to his LST and he had to be hauled aboard.

Chief Boatswain's Mate
Daniel J. Coyle, U.S. Navy.

LSTs: ALL IN A DAY'S WORK, PART I

By Chief Boatswain's Mate Daniel J. Coyle, U.S. Navy. Adapted from unpublished manuscript.

The D-Day and H-Hour originally set for June 5, 1944 was postponed for twenty-four hours (June 6 at 0630) because of rough seas. My ship, USS *LST-281*, spent June 5 in Condition II [anti-aircraft readiness] until 1800 when General Quarters was sounded. We arrived in the invasion area about 0300 on June 6 and put boats off, one of which took a Naval Combat Demolition Unit ashore. The other five boats hauled soldiers from transports.

At this time there were flares all around us and on the beach. Battleships were firing their guns, and cruisers and destroyers shelled the beach constantly while we manned our guns.

Later in the morning, the Rhino barge that we had towed across the channel tied to our bow and we off-loaded about half of our cargo. [Ed.: Rhino barges were pontoons assembled in 175-foot barges with detachable outboard motor units. They were used for unloading cargo ships and LSTs.] We also made several attempts to tie up to a sinking LCT to off-load its cargo, but every attempt ended in failure. The LCT was eventually towed to the beach, and we suffered a busted elevator winch, a broken ramp chain, and two holes in our port side.

While we were still anchored there, LCIs, LCTs, and other small craft brought casualties aboard (Army and Navy personnel). The fleet minesweeper USS *Chickadee* transferred a number of badly burned men from the *Osprey*, which had been sunk by a mine the previous day.

That evening, I saw another convoy of LSTs and LCIs come across the Channel. Overhead, hundreds of planes were flying to bombard the continent. We retrieved four of our boats, but two had been sunk on the beach. Fortunately, all six boat crews were okay, although one man was hit by a machine gun bullet in the heel.

All that night tracers lit up the sky, and we saw at least five planes go down. One plane had crashed near us during the day, and a destroyer moved in to pick up the pilot, who had managed to bail out. After 2400, there was very little action.

The next morning, June 7, we watched more bombers flying overhead. We finally secured General Quarters and set the anchor watch after approximately forty hours on our guns and battle stations, all the while eating Army rations. We had a dirty ship and a dirty crew and much of the ship was ruined, but it wasn't half as bad as it was for the hundreds of casualties that we were carrying.

Coyle and LST-281 *made a total of ten crossings of the English Channel in support of the Normandy landings.* LST-281 *later saw action in the Pacific theater.*

Radioman Second Class Earl O. Blair, U.S. Naval Reserve.

LSTs: All in a Day's Work, Part II

By Radioman Second Class Earl O. Blair, U.S. Naval Reserve. Adapted from unpublished manuscript.

As a radioman second class aboard USS *LST-284*, I participated in the D-Day invasions of Normandy and Southern France in Europe and served in combat operations against enemy forces on Okinawa Gunto in the Pacific. My LST received three battle stars for Normandy, Southern France, and Okinawa.

In May 1944, after sixteen days of rough Atlantic seas the good ship and its crew arrived in Europe and sailed to various English ports. Underway on June 5, 1944, from Brixham, England with several other LSTs, we were loaded with troops and equipment for the June 6 Normandy invasion. We arrived in the transport area (Utah Beach sector) and lowered four boats for detached duty on shore. We came along USS *YMS-352* and hoisted nineteen casualties aboard and ten by sling from LCVPs. Enemy planes strafed the beach and explosions resulted from charges presumed to be rockets. We then hoisted two sinking LCVPs aboard for salvage and unloaded more casualties from DUKWs via slings. Finally, we received survivors of USS *Meredith* (DD-726) from DD-638 [USS *Herndon*].

After transporting all of the above to Portland, England for unloading, we returned through the Channel to the Omaha Beach sector (Dog White Beach). Intermittent attacks from enemy planes caused our ship's gunners to open fire, but I do not know if they hit anything successfully.

USS *LST-284* made eight trips across the Channel to and from English ports, loaded with Army and Navy wounded plus tank deck loads of German prisoners, the latter for English prison camps.

After the beaches were secured, USS *LST-284* participated in the invasion of Southern France and later saw duty in the Pacific. USS *LST-284* returned stateside from many Pacific operations in late 1945, and was decommissioned on March 13, 1946, and struck from the Navy list on June 19, 1946. On December 11, 1946, she was sold to the Southern Shipwrecking Company for scrap, after travelling a total of 58,895 nautical miles during her World War II service.

Lieutenant Commander
Wilfred P. Lawless, U.S. Naval
Reserve.

THE FRUITS OF PLANNING

By Lieutenant Commander Wilfred P. Lawless, U.S. Naval Reserve (Retired).
Adapted from "The Normandy Invasion," unpublished manuscript.

As commanding officer of the USS *LST-310*, I took part in all of the
European invasions of World War II, including Sicily, Italy, and Normandy. I was overwhelmed with the logistics of the Allied invasion
of Normandy on D-Day, June 6, 1944. The code name for this operation was Overlord.

The massive invasion fleet included more than forty-four hundred
ships and landing craft. With the fleet came fifteen hundred tanks
and eleven thousand fighters, bombers, transports, and gliders. The
ships approached the five invasion beaches—Utah, Omaha, Juno,
Sword, and Gold—through twelve channels that had been mine-
swept.

The exact landing point was a closely guarded secret, combined with much subterfuge to confuse the Germans. The Germans were convinced it would be Calais and kept their 15th Army in that area. The invasion date was based on considerations of tide, wind, and light, but bad weather on June 5 forced Eisenhower to defer it to the following day. During the night, one British and two U.S. airborne divisions were dropped into the dark French countryside behind German lines in a massive parachute-glider assault designed to secure and hold bridges, roads, rail-lines, and airfields for the Allied advance. The amphibious landings began at 0630. The Americans landed on Utah and Omaha beaches; British and Canadian troops landed on Gold, Juno, and Sword. On "Bloody Omaha" the troops were exposed to the German gunners on the cliff. With awkward and slow assault boats, the troops were sitting ducks, and Omaha casualties numbered over two thousand.

Many soldiers never reached shore, drowning under the weight of heavy equipment carried in knapsacks on their shoulders. They were released from the ships' small boats, each of which carried thirty-six people toward the shoreline.

Following D-Day, we continued to make numerous Channel crossings, always under heavy shell fire, especially when passing near the Guernsey Islands en route to Cherbourg. Because of the vast network of planning and control of personnel by General Eisenhower, my respect and admiration for him and his staff knew no bounds.

Signalman Third Class
Robert E. Farrington,
U.S. Navy.

TOMMY ATKINS WADED INTO HELL

By Signalman Third Class Robert E. Farrington, U.S. Navy. Adapted from oral history transcript.

I was stationed aboard *LST-528* and was assigned to the British beachhead at Gold, Juno, and Sword beaches in the British assault area from June 6, 1944 to July 26, 1944. The efforts of the officers and crew of *LST-528* enabled the ship to carry out forty-four channel crossings in support of the invasion.

Assigned to an LCVP as a signalman-gunner, I made landings at all three beachheads. Afterwards, I decided to write down what I saw in a poem. It is dedicated to the men of the 4th Winnipeg Rifles in remembrance of their ordeal in the Juno Beach area mine field. "Tommy Atkins," by the way, was the British equivalent of "GI Joe."

Proudly through the night the British guns roared,
As all hell broke loose off the Normandy shore.

95

Ships by the thousands anchored off that beach,
Were safely beyond the eighty-eights' reach.

The small boats were loaded with machines and men,
And the engines groaned amidst the din.
Whilst above decks a British chaplain was forgiving sins.

Machine guns chattered and mortar fell,
and Tommy Atkins waded into hell.
He met the Hun under the rockets' red glare.
Lunging and stabbing, smelling death in the air,
Fix bayonets and at 'em again,
May the devil take those who hope to stop us, men,

The Hun retreated, the battle lost,
And God only knows the price it cost.
Away from the beach, on top of a hill,
Tommy Atkins is standing, standing so still.
Away from the beach, the sound of war passed,
Tommy Atkins is gone, and there's peace at last.

I returned to the British beaches on the fiftieth anniversary and visited the cemetery where the boys of the Canadian 4th Winnipeg Rifles are entombed. I placed a Canadian flag and an American flag on the grave of an eighteen-year-old boy. As I did so, a veteran came up and asked me if the deceased was a friend of mine. I got up from where I was kneeling, looked out over the graves, and replied, "They were all my friends." [Ed. Bob Farrington died in September 1997 while this book was being prepared for publication.]

Boatswain's Mate Second Class Everett E. Hatley, U.S. Navy.

FOULED ANCHOR

By Boatswain's Mate Second Class Everett E. Hatley, U.S. Navy. Adapted from oral history transcript.

I was a boatswain's mate second class on *LCT-517*. We sailed from Plymouth and when we got to the beach it was about four o'clock in the morning. We dropped anchor. The anchor would not hold, and we finally found out that there was about a two-thousand-pound round rock hung in the anchor. It took us about an hour-and-a-half to get enough rope tied around it and get the rock off. By that time we had to go on into the beach. So, we carried in our group.

I was the one who got the rock off the anchor. And that was something I will never forget, because they gave me a round of applause after I got it off. To get the rock off the anchor, I had to take about thirty feet of line and wrap it around; like these women do when they have flowers that they hang up in rooms. I tied up the rock to the top of the anchor where the winches stick out and then lowered the anchor there, by myself, and pushed it off. And by the time I got it off the anchor, the line broke. All the soldiers and sailors were really happy to see that thing go. That was the first unforgettable experience we had at the beach. Then we landed on the beach at 0645.

During most of this time, the large ships were firing on the beach. The sounds were devastating to our ears. My ears still ring today.

Gunner's Mate Master Chief Lewis W. Moyle, U.S. Naval Reserve.

A Burning LCI

By Gunner's Mate Master Chief Lewis W. Moyle, U.S. Naval Reserve. Adapted from oral history transcript.

I was a gunner's mate second class aboard USS *LCI(L)-555*. We departed for the beach from Plymouth, England on June 5, had to return because of the rough weather, wound up in Weymouth, and then finally left from Weymouth to our beach. We landed on Dog Red Beach, discharging our troops. We had our starboard ramp shot away and we lost some soldiers in the deal but, fortunately, our crew members weren't injured.

While backing off the beach, we got a signal to go over to the adjoining beach and attempt to salvage an LCI that was stranded. We went over and the *LCI(L)-553* was up on the beach. It seemed like we spent an eternity, but I guess it was an hour or so, trying to pull the craft off the beach. All the while, we were under fire. The *553* eventually caught fire and started burning, so they decided to abandon ship. We returned to the transport area and they decided that we had to go back to England to get a new ramp because we couldn't discharge our troops fast enough with one ramp. So that was the result of D-Day for us on the *LCI(L)-555*.

Lieutenant Commander Jacob Brouwer, U.S. Naval Reserve (Retired).

NEAR MISS

By Lieutenant Commander Jacob Brouwer, U.S. Naval Reserve (Retired). Adapted from "The Captain and the Commander," unpublished manuscript.

Finally, during the first week in June, hundreds of landing craft which teemed with men and were loaded with battle gear crawled out from harbors and rivers. We formed up in locations prescribed by the convoy diagrams. As I held down my seat on the conn of *LCI(L)-513*, I was fascinated by the unfolding spectacle. The ships appeared to be a gigantic, twisting dragon. Our small ship, at reduced speed, floated in a procession of LCIs.

Top Secret orders from the Supreme Allied Command had sealed us from the outside world. As a thirty-two-year-old ensign, I had attended an overall planning meeting with admirals and generals, as well as key persons in civilian positions. We had studied charts; invasion plans were highlighted and reviewed. Each of us returned to his ship with detailed secret orders. We were told not to open them until a code signal was sent to us via radio.

Bad weather postponed D-Day from June 5 until June 6. Our huge, waiting armada treaded water in the channel for twenty-four hours. We mustered our crew and read them a pep message from General Eisenhower. The scene was a lot like a coach sending his team into a game. We gave an overall description of invasion plans and wished our men well.

The real thing had come at last and as dawn broke through a cloudy sky on June 6 our ship stood sloshing in enemy waters, within sight of the distant shore. All men topside including me were weighted down by awkward, sticky, anti-gas clothing. Gas masks hung from our necks, ready to be slipped on at the first sign of a Nazi counter-attack.

Somewhat awed, and wondering what the day would bring, my gaze swept the distant shores where Hitler and his regime had ruled the past four years. Impregnable Europe, the land of the goose-step, lay shrouded in mystery.

Isolated gunshots reported from far away. With startling suddenness, formations of American planes zoomed from behind us and swept down the beaches dropping bombs that, crackling like firecrackers, intensified a thousand times. Bobbing on the restless waters around us floated a whole city of ships.

Navy "Big Berthas" [battleships] belched fire and smoke and seconds later the air reverberated with deafening explosions. Rows of small amphibians, a variety of flat-bottomed boats, sliced into the wave-lashed beaches. Rocket boats a few hundred yards offshore arched trajectories of fire into Nazi fortifications. German howitzers spit lead at us from beyond the low coastal hills.

In a way it looks pretty, I thought. It was well organized and orderly with precise rows of ships and barges.

Welch, the executive officer, stood next to me on the bridge.

"I'd say the Nazi wall is cracking, wouldn't you?" I shouted, over the commotion.

"Shore looks like it a'right. B'gorry, ain't it somethin' now, skipper?"

Operations orders had us scheduled to beach at 1030, four hours after the first shot. We sat, idling, in formations of threes, waiting. A control ship lined us up like race horses. Then our ship lunged forward towards Utah Beach.

Another command ship blinked a message, halting us temporarily. Messages seemed to come from several directions, helter-skelter. The last one spelled out:

"Do not beach, unload to LCMs."

A small vessel pulled up on each side. Scramble nets were flung over the sides. Our engineers, doctors, and specialists in electronic equipment lowered themselves down the nets. They sloshed ashore to secure the beach. Men and vehicles landed without opposition.

As captain, I was in charge during the landing. All semblance of order disappeared. We drifted shoreward. The beach appeared crowded. Our orders were to retreat ten miles to the transport area, but I had an urge to tarry long enough to survey what action existed on shore. Mortar fire from behind a hill made a pattern of splashes which roiled the ocean. Slowly I nosed our ship ahead to see more.

"You're taking chances," Welch sang out in an excited voice. "Get the hell out of here. We've got orders to get back to the staging area right away, you know. This is downright dangerous territory. Let's get out."

Commander Carbone's group flagship splashed directly ahead of us, almost on the beach.

I waved at Welch and pointed at Carbone's ship.

"Look. The old banana boat captain is curious, too."

Welch only frowned, so I headed our ship back out to sea.

Carbone turned his ship back too, so I followed him into deeper water. Barges roared past us, going the opposite direction, churning into the landing strips. Our conning tower, exposed and circular, made an excellent observation platform for me. It had a 360-degree view.

A warming sun evaporated the early morning clouds. Welch, Spigoni, and I studied the beach with our binoculars. Jeeps and tanks, with their human cargoes, seemed to be spilling out on the sands without trouble. Bustling small craft retreated from the shore line and puttered back to large ships for troops which now were landing in an uninterrupted procession. From my vantage point it appeared that the invasion was going well.

When we arrived at the transport area, about ten miles from the action, our glasses could no longer make out the details on shore. Formations of bombers winged in toward the mainland. Shelling from large naval vessels continued, raising bursts of smoke around us.

In the afternoon Carbone rounded up a group of LCIs, using blinker messages, and we headed back across the channel to England. The invasion had left us with a sense of excitement. Several men and officers remained topside, talking, laughing, wondering how the big game was going. The ship's radio announced a second big invasion at the Omaha beachhead, and described strong German resistance. We had been relieved and were thankful about the ease of our Utah landings.

As our small group of ships crept away in the evening shadows, with a wind rising, the sounds of shore batteries diminished and normal ship activities resumed. The drama of Normandy was lost in indistinct distances.

Ships stood on the ocean like toys in the shrinking transport area. We could still see Navy cruisers, like black cats, spitting fire at Nazi planes. Our anti-aircraft guns sent trajectories of light into the darkening sky as we sought to chase the angry marauders. We felt defenseless and alone, a small band of ships in the darkness. We stole away with a sense of relief into the obscurity of the channel night.

The excitements of that day took their toll and my exhausted body longed for the sack. Young Spigoni had the watch and relieved me.

I was nicely tucked into bed, warm, comfortable, and about to drop off when the jangling of General Quarters bells and sirens jarred me awake. The fearful drone of a plane sounded overhead. It was swooping down on us. Painfully and automatically, I jumped into my clothes.

"Now, what the hell is going on?" I mumbled. I grabbed my helmet and life jacket. I rushed to the bridge to hear Spigoni still screaming over the public address system.

Never had I seen the young officer so agitated. He flapped his arms wildly, while shouting in strident tones. "The dirty sonovabitch almost got us. Christ, that was too damn close for me." He breathed hard, his face strained.

"Did you see that plane dive straight for us? That damn ship in front of us showed a blinker light. The German saw it, dropped right down through the cloud cover. Skimmed down our whole row of ships. Did you hear the explosion? The bomb dropped off the port side, only a couple hundred yards from the ship ahead. Boy, what a close call that was!" His words were rushed.

"Let's secure General Quarters, Spigoni," I advised. "We'd only give away our position by opening fire. He won't be able to find us in the darkness anymore. I just hope every ship remains blacked out now."

Nobody showed another light. The planes remained well above cloud cover. We could see faint lights off in the east, where Nazis dropped flares in an attempt to expose ships lying off-shore at the Normandy beachhead.

The incident held center stage around the wardroom table in the morning. Spigoni was still excited when he woke up.

"It all happened so fast, by God, just like a nightmare. The German plowed right down over us. So close you could have hit him with a rock." He recounted the details again.

We all agreed with Spigoni that this had to be our closest call yet.

By mid-morning our ships pulled into Portsmouth harbor, stringing into the Calshot docks. Along the banks five or six badly shot-up LCIs had already been pulled up out of the water awaiting repairs. Being at home in England gave us a warm, safe feeling. We had survived D-Day.

Captain Morris G. Ness, U.S. Naval Reserve (Retired).

SALUTING WITH BOTH HANDS

By Captain Morris G. Ness, U.S. Naval Reserve (Retired). Adapted from unpublished manuscript.

At about 1400 on D-Day, I arrived offshore in the anchorage area off Omaha Beach on the USS *LST-54* with plans to unload our Army personnel and a variety of vehicles that day. Due to the confusion, bad weather, and the German resistance, all time tables were set back, causing us to be at anchor all night. After being at our guns and General Quarters until the wee hours of D+1, I flopped on my sack until about 0700, when I was awakened by the captain shouting at me from the bridge to report there immediately. He had received a message from the USS *Augusta,* which was anchored nearby and was the flagship for Operation Overlord. *Augusta* wanted a small boat officer and crew to report to the flagship immediately. The small boat was an LCVP—usually used for initial assaults. Operation of the LCVP was my special training.

I finally scared up a crew amidst the confusion of personnel and vehicles. We lowered the boat from a davit and started for the *Augusta* in cold and very rough water. After climbing a rope ladder, I was met by Admiral Kirk who was in charge of the entire U.S. Navy operation for the invasion. With him was a small group of high-ranking officers. I had never seen an admiral or a general before—I felt like I should be saluting with both hands. After some brief questioning of my knowledge of the various beaches, etc., he ordered me to take General Bradley (the highest-ranking field general in the European theater) directly to "Easy Red" beach (Omaha Beach was divided into approximately nine different beaches). He pointed out the area directly under a particular barrage balloon and the specific contour of the hill that ran along the coast. I wonder how many times I said "yes, sir" in that short episode. At that time I was what was usually called a "bare-assed" ensign, the lowest grade an officer can be.

After successfully getting the three passengers (Bradley and two aides) boarded into a bobbing, wobbly boat, we started for the hazy shore. At this time I would guess we were about eight to ten miles from shore. The words of Admiral Kirk kept ringing in my ears: "Do you understand? I want you to go directly to that spot."

Generals made me uneasy, but were not quite on the same level as admirals—who scared the hell out of me! Because of the rough water and strong wind, almost nothing was moving onto the three-and-a-half mile beach. Because of a strong easterly tidal current, I kept my attention on our destination. Soon, a mortar started landing shells on the starboard side of the boat. Then the shells began alternating from port to starboard. They were zeroing in on us, but I was still very concerned with the image of the admiral pointing to that specific spot on the beach. Many boats had hit the wrong beach on D-Day. I had heard the admiral tell Bradley that all of their glasses would be focused on us all the way in.

We started some zig-zag maneuvering, but as the shells narrowed us in more and more the general eased over to me and said, "I think we should go parallel to the beach for a while." We did so immediately, but I worried what that pointing admiral was thinking of as he looked at us through his glasses.

As soon as the shelling stopped, I immediately headed for Easy Red. However, the persistent mortar started again to zero in on us. Now I had this feeling that I was a pawn between a general and an admiral because I was not sure the admiral could see exactly what was happening. I stepped down to the deck and asked the general, "Any instructions, general?" After taking a look at the last splash, he said to again go parallel with the beach. When the mortar stopped, we turned in and finally hit the beach on Easy Red near the E-1 exit.

We hit what I assumed was a sand bar and Bradley and his aides waded ashore. He instructed me to wait there and said he would return in about an hour. He wanted to make a personal assessment of the progress and speak with General Gerow. I walked in with them and when I got back to the boat, the crew showed me the flooded deck. We had hit one of the numerous underwater obstacles near shore. Fortunately this one was not mined. Before seeing the damaged boat, I had planned to retract from the beach and stay off shore within easy sight of the beachmaster. The tide at Omaha Beach would rise and fall about twenty-four vertical feet. Horizontally, this meant the tide would go out about three hundred yards every six plus hours. The beach was littered with everything from wrecked vessels and equipment to dead bodies and a few German prisoners. I went back to shore and got into a foxhole with the beachmaster. He had been through the invasions of Sicily and Salerno and was not at all confident that we could keep our foothold on Omaha. At one time even Bradley was contemplating withdrawing from Omaha.

I asked the beachmaster to signal the *Augusta* to send in another boat because mine was partially sunk. After about an hour, Bradley and his aides returned and I directed the boat to come in. My crew and I stayed to see if we could possibly get the boat temporarily sealed so we could get it off in the next high tide. We were unable to make the LCVP seaworthy.

To make a long story short, I arrived back on my ship later that same day. The next day, while I was on a ship to shore trip, my skipper received orders to leave with a convoy departing for the United Kingdom.

I never did get back to my ship again. After several other episodes, I was integrated into operations and later worked with the port directors and base headquarters. The Overlord plan called for landing about twenty-four hundred tons of material on D-Day. Actually, less than one hundred tons was landed. However, we were told that Omaha Beach eventually became the biggest port in the world from a standpoint of tonnage. Six months later I was in the small contingent of three officers and about twenty-five men who moved out to stay on an LCI and officially close USNAB-11 (U.S. Naval Advance Base-11). It was Alpha and Omega for me—I was at Omaha the first day and the last.

Boatswain's Mate Second Class Gordon B. Lease, U.S. Coast Guard.

LUFTWAFFE NUISANCE RAID

By Boatswain's Mate Second Class Gordon B. Lease, U.S. Coast Guard. Adapted from unpublished manuscript.

I was a boatswain's mate second class aboard USS *LST-381* during the invasion of Normandy, France in 1944. On June 13, during our second trip to Utah Beach, we landed and began off-loading vehicles as the tide receded. At about dusk, we retracted from the beach and made a turn to starboard. As we turned, however, our ship overran a pontoon causeway and we were unable to retract.

Around midnight, the German Luftwaffe visited the area and dropped a string of four bombs, two of which exploded near our ship. The explosions blew approximately fifty shrapnel holes in the port bow ramp control room and "air conditioned" the crew's head near the starboard quarter. None of our crew was injured, and we were able to retract the ship from the causeway with the next full tide.

Our ship continued amphibious operations for another two weeks. Upon entering dry dock at Barry, South Wales on June 29, over one hundred shrapnel holes were discovered in our hull and repaired. We completed fourteen round trips to the Normandy beaches during the period between June 6 and early September.

Lieutenant Edwin H. Lemkin, U.S. Navy.

THE UNTOLD STORY OF THE ROCKET BOATS

By Lieutenant Edwin H. Lemkin, U.S. Navy. Adapted from oral history transcript.

I went through Little Creek, Virginia [an amphibious training center], and as an ensign, I was taken up to Solomons Island, Maryland, where we became the first rocket boat group. We had thirty-six of us at the beginning and the highest ranking officer was an ensign, that's how new it was.

The rocket boats [LCS(R)] were approximately thirty-six to forty feet long. We had an ensign and a crew of six on each one. We carried twelve rockets in racks. We also carried our main batteries amidships, which were twin .50-caliber machine guns, and we had a .30-caliber on the stern.

We crossed the Atlantic on an LST by means of a five-week convoy up to Iceland and all the way over to England. We disembarked from the LST in Wales and were taken by train to Plymouth. We stayed at Plymouth quite a while, training until our boat arrived.

After that we patrolled the channel, guarding small convoys up and down the English Channel, including a short stint at Slapton Sands. We were at the far reaches of the exercise [Exercise Tiger; see Introduction] and never knew anything about it until many years later.

Before the invasion we were sent back to Weymouth, and from there we were loaded aboard an LST and dropped off on D-Day about five miles off the beach. Then we were attached to the scouts and raiders, who had gone in the previous night in boats like ours and in small, inflatable boats, to help the UDT [underwater demolition teams] disarm the hedgehogs [mined obstacles].

We went in ten minutes before H-Hour. Right behind us were the amphibious tanks—unfortunately we know what happened to them. I think only one reached the beach. We fired our rockets about fifty yards off the beach. Our fire control was not accurate, but I guess we made a lot of noise anyway.

Fire directed at a destroyer also hit us and put a big hole in our bow. We kept the boat going for several days and reported to the beachmaster as directed and asked him what we should do. He told us to pick up bodies. We picked up some and then we didn't know what to do with them. He said to bring them to the yellow zone. We went to the yellow zone, but they didn't want the bodies, so we put them back in the water.

After several days we sank. I had a .50-caliber ammunition chest aboard filled with silk stockings, perfume, lipstick, and chocolate bars, anticipating a great welcome from the French ladies. When my boat went down, I lost that ammunition chest. It was probably my greatest loss in the war. This has still been a cause of laughter for the last fifty years among the few people who knew about it.

My crew was taken off by one boat, and I was taken off by another ship and eventually assigned, along with those American officers and crews who had lost their boats, to Juno and Gold beaches. We reported to the *George W. Woodward,* headquarters ship for Americans serving with the British assault forces. We were on the British beach for several weeks, helping with their small boat operations. A lone German would come over almost every night and try to drop a few bombs. It was sort of a last gasp on their part.

Eventually, I shipped back to the States. I would say this as far as Normandy is concerned: I am the last one that I know that is alive who was in that operation. I have never found any sign of anybody else. We had approximately twenty-one rocket boats on that beach and every one was sunk, as far as I know, and I don't think there is anybody else living. So, I only give this little report because there is no one else to do it as far as I know. I eventually ended up as executive officer on an LSM, hit every island in the Pacific and ended up in Japan. The war was quite an interesting experience.

Signalman Second Class
Charles F. Tague, U.S.
Navy.

STRANDED BY THE STORM

By Signalman Second Class Charles F. Tague, U.S. Navy. Adapted from oral history transcript.

At the time of the Normandy invasion, I was a signalman third class and a member of the gunfire support group, which consisted of approximately twenty-five hundred boys and men who came to Roseneath, Scotland, to take over twelve British ships. My ship was *LCF-18* (landing craft, flak), which was commissioned into the U.S. Navy in December 1943.

At that time, we trained for a brief period in the Firth of Clyde and then proceeded south to our home port of Falmouth, England. While at Falmouth, we participated in many practice landings, including the assault exercises held at Slapton Sands in Devon during April 1944 where we lost three LSTs from an attack by German E-boats [Exercise Tiger; two LSTs were sunk and a third was heavily damaged].

111

On June 3, 1944, we departed Falmouth and sailed the English Channel, under heavy seas, until the night of June 5, when we pulled into Portsmouth. We remained there for less than an hour, and at approximately 0100 on June 6, we were ordered to proceed to France. We had practiced so many landings that we were not sure that this was the "real thing" until we saw two ships go down after hitting floating mines.

Four of our ships were scheduled to be off Utah Beach and eight off Omaha Beach. Our ship was with the Utah Beach contingent. At approximately H-Hour, we lost one of our four ships. It hit a German acoustic mine and sank within thirty seconds.

Our main assignments were to assist in protecting the landings from German air raids and directing other landing craft onto the Beach. At H-Hour and during the remainder of the morning there were no air raids, but we did experience shelling from the shore batteries.

During the afternoon of June 6, two low-flying planes came in on the western side of Utah Beach and dropped "skip-bombs" that landed in the water, skipped onto the beach, and hit an ammunition dump. The planes made a second pass and this time, we were ready for them. We believe that our 20-millimeter guns brought them down; the two planes went over a hill on the beach and we never did see them come up. The next day we were told that the planes were shot down.

We continued directing other landing craft onto the beach, always concerned about the floating mines, until the big storm of June 19. We were anchored approximately one thousand yards off the beach when our anchor chain broke, and before we could get underway, the ship was washed up onto the shore. The beach scene was catastrophic, with hundreds of craft shipwrecked and destroyed by the storm. Our ship was seaworthy, but unable to get off the beach until July 8, when we were successfully towed free and returned to England to decommission our ship and return it to the British.

I then returned to the United States and after a short leave, shipped out on an LSM that was on its way to the Pacific and the invasion of an island called Okinawa.

A stern view of USS *LST-317* and USS *LST-318* moored together in a North African port. *(U.S. Navy; National Archives)*

USS *Ancon* (AGC-4) (foreground), amphibious force flagship, with landing craft and the French coast in the background. *(U.S. Navy; National Archives)*

Troops and crewmen aboard a Coast Guard–manned LCVP as it approaches the landing beaches on D-Day. *(U.S. Coast Guard; National Archives)*

USS *LST-310* (foreground; with barrage balloon on deck), beached for off-loading, is one of the landing ships in this famous picture taken in the invasion's aftermath. *(U.S. Coast Guard; National Archives)*

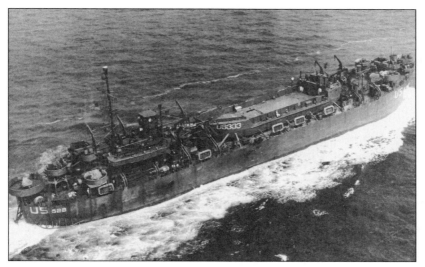

USS *LST-528* at sea. *(U.S. Navy National Archives)*

Landing craft (USS *LCT-199*, USS *LCT-555*; USS *LCT-638* [British], *LCT(A)(5)-2421*, and LCVP from USS *Thurston* (AP-77) on Omaha Beach shortly after H-Hour, amidst piled supplies and dead soldiers. (*U.S. Navy; National Archives*)

USS *LCI(L)-553* and USS *LCI(L)-410* land troops on Omaha Beach during the initial assault. This photograph was taken shortly before *LCI(L)-553* was hit by two shells. *(U.S. Navy; National Archives)*

An LCM brings wounded American soldiers alongside a transport for evacuation from the combat zone on D-Day. *(U.S. Coast Guard; National Archives)*

RADM Alan G. Kirk, USN, watches the Normandy landings from USS *Augusta* (CA-31). *(U.S. Navy; National Archives)*

RADM Alan G. Kirk (left), USN, RADM John L. Hall, USN (center), and LTG Omar Bradley, USA (right) inspect the invasion beaches. *(U.S. Navy; National Archives)*

An LCS(R) makes fast to another off Normandy. *(U.S. Navy; National Archives)*

The ocean is tremendous . . . and powerful. So powerful it makes our ship minute in its insignificance. If there were a thousand ships like this, or ten thousand, they would still be a ridiculous manmade impudence on all this gorgeous, churning immensity.

There are those long twilights here now. The sky is billions of miles away and you feel very much alone. The water stretches away forever. The ships sit alone in the water, each in its own pool of aloneness— It's big and empty and very quiet. The emptiness comes off the water and crawls right into you.

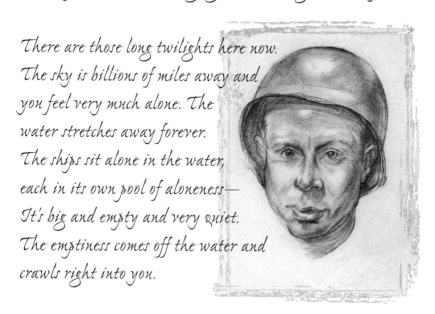

V
UTAH'S PROMISE

Utah was one of the five beaches on the Normandy coast selected for Allied landings, and one of two under U.S. jurisdiction. British and Canadian forces were responsible for Gold, Juno, and Sword beaches; the Americans were responsible for Utah and Omaha beaches.

Like the landings at the Canadian and British beaches, the landings at Utah were spared the worst of the devastation, although the heavy surf and surface currents complicated the landings. A strong current caused the first assault wave to land several hundred yards from the intended spot. Fortunately, that part of the beach proved to be lightly defended. Under the leadership of former President Theodore Roosevelt's eldest son, Brigadier General Theodore Roosevelt, all subsequent waves were ordered to land at the new location. Navy Underwater Demolition Teams (UDTs) sustained casualties, but rapidly removed obstacles from the beach.

Shore fire control parties, working with the infantry, allowed U.S. Navy ships to provide outstanding fire support for ground forces throughout the day. By nightfall, American troops had established a solid, defensible perimeter and Admiral Moon, commanding Utah's Naval Task Force U, declared the assault a success.

Lieutenant Nathan S. Irwin, U.S. Navy.

UNDER COVER OF DARKNESS

By Lieutenant Nathan S. Irwin, U.S. Navy. Adapted from oral history transcript.

On June 6, 1944, I was a member of an NCDU—Naval Combat Demolition Unit. We did the underwater demolition work on Utah Beach just prior to the first wave of the invasion. We crossed the Channel in LSTs and disembarked about 0330. It was dark, it was cold, it was windy, and water was splashing all over. We had to go over the side of the ship down cargo nets and load about a ton of explosives into our small LCVPs. We shoved off about 0400, milled around in the assembly area, and then headed for the beach right at the crack of dawn. Fortunately, the resistance was light. There was firing, but we were able to get to the beach and get to work and by eight o'clock we had our section of the beach fairly well cleared. This was on Utah Beach. Luckily, I was assigned to Utah Beach—because we lost 40 percent of our men over at Omaha. Our casualties on Utah Beach were approximately 10 percent.

We had to get in early in the morning because the tide was out and the obstacles were exposed. We had about an hour-and-a-half before the tide would be starting to come in, so it was imperative we get our work done before that tide came in and covered up the obstacles. We went back again later in the afternoon when the tide went out again and cleaned up a section of the beach that we weren't able to get to in the morning. We stayed on the beach about six days, living in a pillbox and then we were ordered back to England.

[Ed.: According to Walter Karig, *Battle Report*, Vol. 4, the Omaha Beach NCDUs received the Presidential Unit Citation and the Utah Beach NCDUs received the Navy Unit Commendation.]

Motor Machinist's Mate First Class George I. Johnson, U.S. Navy.

THE VIEW OFF UTAH

By Motor Machinist's Mate First Class George I. Johnson, U.S. Navy. Adapted from oral history transcript.

When USS *PC-1252* left New York City bound for England, we were escorting a convoy of tug boats. Each tug was pulling two barges which I assumed were partially sunk later to make docks for ships to unload at shortly after the invasion. It took us twenty-three days to cross the Atlantic. One day we were traveling at two knots ahead and losing three knots because of heavy winds and bad weather.

USS *PC-1252* was used a lot during the war for escorting convoys, chasing subs, and preventing submarine attacks. We escorted many convoys up and down the coast of the English Channel prior to the invasion. On one trip we picked up a number of deceased in the English Channel, and I never saw any significance in it until this trip [1994 Normandy reunion] and now I have a strong suspicion that some of the people that we picked up were from Exercise Tiger. We picked them up for over a week and at the later stages, they were so decomposed that it was difficult to get them aboard. The primary thing they were looking for, after the bodies became so decomposed, was the dog tags for identification purposes.

When we left port on June 4, we had immediate orders to throw all the paint aboard over the side because the captain said that if we went into combat, the paint would burn readily and he was trying to prevent as many injuries as possible.

Our role in the invasion was to lead a flotilla of landing craft which did not have navigational equipment. When the invasion began, they followed in our wake across the English Channel. We went in to fifteen hundred yards off the beach at Utah Beach and dropped anchor. We had personnel aboard who were watching the beach and, when the beach was clear, then the lights on our yardarm would change and the next flotilla could hit the beach. I stood all of my watches, including General Quarters, in the engine room and I did not see as many events as a lot of the other personnel aboard.

It seems like we were at General Quarters for several days—it was at least twenty-four hours—but I did get a chance to go topside in the late evening of June 6. While talking to one of my shipmates, I noticed in the distance something that looked like bees coming out of the swarm. As they approached we were able to determine that they were airplanes, but they were still too far away for us to know whether they were friends or foes. The airplanes passed right over our ship and we saw that they were U.S. airplanes and each was pulling a glider. They would pull the gliders and then the gliders would cut loose. The gliders would go down and then the planes would return, going back to England. Some of them had been shot up and some of them were abandoned in the English Channel. When this was done, the PT boats went out and picked up survivors.

I remember going topside, after dark on the night of June 6, and seeing the tracer bullets shoot from one side to the other. They were the greatest fireworks I've ever seen in my life. When you take into consideration that we only saw one-third of the fireworks because only the third round of ammunition was a tracer, you can imagine how much ammunition was fired that night.

Several days after the invasion, we could pick up with our radio the talk between the walkie-talkies on the beach and the walkie-talkies on board ships. I can recall hearing the walkie-talkies on the beach saying, for example, that a sniper was in the tower of the church. The next thing you know, you would hear a big round of explosions come from the cruiser. Next time the walkie-talkie would tell them how far he was off target and the cruiser would fire again. The third time they fired, the walkie-talkies on the beach said, "You got him outta there this time."

After the beach was secured, our assignment was to go out and meet convoys in the English Channel and bring them into their destination. The reason we had to do this was because the convoy channel changed constantly so that the submarines and E-boats wouldn't know where to place the mines.

When we went into Cherbourg the people were not too happy about the Americans. It was easy to understand why not, since at that time they were digging in the rubbish looking for what valuables they may have or for people who may have been pinned in the buildings. Cherbourg was heavily bombed, and when we went in the port was partially blocked due to sunken ships in the harbor. I do not know what type of ships these were, although I think that the Germans had sunk them to prevent the port from being used by the invasion forces.

We stayed on this assignment until the war ended in Europe. We first went into Cherbourg and later into Le Havre. This is where the convoys were designated to go. The convoys changed designated ports as the troops moved closer to Germany. We were scheduled to go to Germany when the war ended but we never got there. We left to go back to the States on June 6, 1945, one year from the day of the invasion. We had spent this entire time period in and around Cherbourg, Le Havre, and the various beachheads.

Lieutenant Howard Vander Beek, U.S. Navy.

GUIDING LIGHT

By Lieutenant Howard Vander Beek, U.S. Navy. Condensed from: Howard Vander Beek, Aboard the *LCC-60*: Normandy and Southern France, 1944 *(Cedar Falls, Iowa: Privately printed, 1995).*

Along with hundreds of thousands of others in the Allied armed forces, I participated in the June 6, 1944 invasion of France as a naval amphibious officer aboard the USS *Landing Craft Control (LCC)-60.*

Her duties, detailed in *Overlord*, the voluminous master plan for the assault of Nazi-held Europe, included serving as one of the two secondary control vessels at Utah Beach.

Few have seen or heard of the LCCs and their service both on Normandy's Utah and Omaha beaches, and later in the Southern France invasion and numerous Pacific invasions. Some today consider them the best-kept secret of World War II. From a distance, the little gray vessels looked much like cut-down PT boats. Constructed of steel, they were fifty-six feet in length and thirteen feet in beam. Powered by two 225-horsepower diesels, they had the capability of maximum speeds of 13.5 knots. Above and below decks much of their limited space was consumed by equipment: smoke pots, an odograph [a recording odometer], two fathometers [depth sounders], and three radio transmitters and receivers. In addition, ammunition, provisions, personal gear, and other essentials were crowded into every available space. Even the crafts' two bunks served as places to stow personal gear, equipment, and food and water, rather than providing cramped, uncomfortable spots for exhausted crew members to catch a moment's rest.

In spite of the fact that she was devoid of all comforts, those of us who served aboard her look back upon the LCC, or as we called her, "the Lily Cup Cruiser," with fondness. She provided us with what we needed most: shelter and security. We knew her well, but there were not many others who even knew of her existence. She and her purposes, for reasons obvious in wartime, were kept secret. Little wonder that today few, except for those of us who were intimately acquainted with her, remember the LCC.

Before leaving Dartmouth on June 3, we sensed what a very tiny part we and our small craft were in the gigantic armada. All around us we saw U.S. naval vessels of every size and description. More continued to enter from the sea to squeeze into assigned berths. On ships and shore, feverish activity was evident. Provisions, ammunition, gear, and, of course, the most important component of the forthcoming assault—the men of the VII Army Corps—were being taken aboard. An electrical charge of excitement surged through the moisture-laden, bone-chilling Devon countryside. Within short hours, we realized, the "this is it" message would be sent from

Supreme Allied Headquarters and we would embark on a perilous journey. We would be part of Naval Task Force U in Operation Neptune, participating in the most massive invasion of all time.

Task Force U, commanded by Rear Admiral D.P. Moon, USN, was comprised of approximately 865 ships and craft. They came in twelve separate convoys from Belfast, Ireland, and the southwest English ports of Plymouth, Tor Bay, Weymouth Bay, and Dartmouth. The groups were to converge at predetermined rendezvous points and form the great armada for the crossing to the Bay of the Seine.

The signal for us to begin the journey of over one hundred sea miles came through at 1600 on June 4. We were among the first to get underway, in order to be in the vanguard off the enemy-held beach the next morning. We moved out into the winds and waves of the English Channel. Crew members, all gravely silent, were at their stations.

The voyage seemed rough. It seemed endless. Channel weather was the worst in twenty years, so we struggled with a heavy sea and poor visibility. But somehow the *LCC-60* maintained her position up front, ahead of the large ships—silent, dark hulks crashing through the ever-mounting waves. We crew members, weary and cold from the bitter winds and raw salt spray, were silent too. There was good reason: we were acutely aware that we were nearing the Nazi-held coast of France.

Back in England at about that time, General Dwight D. Eisenhower made the decision to postpone the invasion one day, to June 6. The wireless message "Post Mike One," was received by some of the vessels in our group and relayed to others. Military personnel who had not left the security of the English coast must have celebrated that night, but those of us forging through the cruel waters off the coast of France wished, since we had gone as far as we had, that the plans could have been carried out.

I do not recall how word of the postponement reached us. Nor do I remember the trip back to the safety of port, one which must have been abusively choppy and disagreeable. I do remember, however, that we were an exhausted, salt-water soaked, and hungry crew long before we got back to England and tied up at Weymouth. And I remember even more clearly being one of the fortunate few to be invited by a kind English family into their cozy, old dwelling. They gave us a tasty, wholesome meal—something we had not had for months, and would not enjoy again for many more. They showed us to warm, soft, feather beds.

How long we slept—possibly dreaming that the postponement had been changed to a cancellation—I do not know. But it seemed that I had just fallen asleep when we were routed out. H-Hour, we were told, would be at 0630 the next day, June 6. So, with our gear and still-weary bodies, we jumped onto the deck of our little boat, got underway and re-positioned ourselves among the other vessels at the front of the invasion fleet.

The second crossing was no easier nor more comfortable than the one the day before. As we witnessed the constant beating of the unruly waters and sought to resist the sharp, salty winds, we had a feeling of being led to oblivion by our guide ship and of being followed by towering, splashing, black gargantuans.

"Why me?" must have been in the minds of each of us aboard the little fifty-six-foot craft. We may have been too young to acknowledge openly the possibility of personal disaster ahead, yet we must have realized that our dreams of the future might never reach fruition. So, in retrospect, we must have surveyed our lives' joys and accomplishments, sorrows and disappointments, and above all, warm associations with our families and friends.

I also thought—between prayers—about my future: getting back into civilian clothes and living the good life with family and friends; continuing my teaching career and probably going on to graduate school; traveling to places of my own choice (not those to which Uncle Sam decided to send me); and—most important of all—asking a young lady in Florida, Grace Alena Taylor, to be my wife.

Whatever I held in retrospect or included in dreams of the future that somber night, I know that there were survival concerns and unvoiced prayers. Both intensified an hour or so after midnight when we spotted flares or signal lights far to the starboard, well out of the invasion fleet route. We realized that they came from enemy surface vessels.

At about 0230, we entered the Utah Transport Area, a pre-designated location twenty-two thousand yards off the shore of France.

Our flagship, USS *Bayfield*, anchored there with Rear Admiral Moon and other top U.S. Navy and Army officers aboard, along with some of the attack troops for Tare Green and Uncle Red sectors of Utah Beach.

We continued beachward with the *LCC-60*, taking it through the Tare Green approach lane, astern our primary control vessel, the *PC-1176*. Despite the darkness, we attempted to match the faint silhouette of the Nazi-held territory before us with the one in our minds. Then, when a Germanized-English voice from the beach came in on our radio frequency—the speaker posing as a British Red Cross worker frantic for us to come to his rescue, we felt the first icy chill of confrontation with the enemy on his own battleground.

The relentless surf tossed us about without mercy on a briny no-man's land. Minutes lost their pace. We felt naked and defenseless. Hundreds of friendly guns on United States battleships and destroyers five to ten miles behind us were poised and silent, ready to begin their onslaught. But Wehrmacht [German Army] artilleries hidden in shore bunkers did not hold back. Their angry projectiles hissed and sizzled over and around us and, fortunately, pierced only the rising tidal waters.

Aware of the sounds of war, fellow officer Sims Gauthier left his navigation charts and came up the ladder to top deck for a momentary glimpse of what was occurring. Fraught with anxiety and fright, I somehow managed to answer the question evident from his facial expression: "Yes, Sims, this is it!"

We could only imagine the frenzied, last-minute battle preparations back in the Utah Transport Area. The hundreds of ships that had choked the waterlane across the Channel were probably setting anchor there, with the LCTs, jammed full of GIs and their battle gear, unloading men and equipment into LCVPs, the small landing craft that formed the boat waves we would later lead to the beach. Stephen L. Freeland on the *LCC-70*, our tertiary control vessel, and James A. White, on the *LCC-90*, tertiary control for Red Beach, and members of their crews were undoubtedly keeping those waves in holding formations.

We pictured in our minds minesweepers setting red-and-green-lighted dan buoys along the boat lanes and the fire support channels they had cleared. And, although we were to learn later that we were in error, we assumed that the *LCC-80,* "and *PC-1261* were to our left several hundred yards off Uncle Red Sector and that we could not see them because they were shrouded by mist and darkness.

Ahead, on the low-silhouetted beach, we could discern little activity. But we knew hostile forces were there: they continued to fire on us! In time, however, we gave their barrage little more than cursory attention. Instead, we focused on a multitude of tasks—sending, receiving, and relaying messages; making sightings; and ascertaining our position.

At approximately 0540, the real horror of battle was unveiled before us. We saw the *PC-1261,* primary control vessel for Red Beach, suddenly veer off course to starboard. Within five minutes, with the main mast down and men scrambling over her sides, she sank. She had been the victim of either a chance shell hit or a mine contact on her port bow.

A few minutes later—at 0552, the *LCT-597,* directly astern of our primary control boat (*PC-1176*), was lifted out of the water by the powerful force of a mine she struck. She sank almost immediately, taking with her four "DDs" (duplex drive amphibious tanks) that she had aboard. We witnessed the tragic occurrence from a distance of but a few yards and felt the explosion's potent shock waves course through our craft.

Then suddenly during the slowed-down minutes before H-Hour, a deafening, thunderous roar sounded behind us, then over us, then ahead of us. Our fright was thawed by an assuring feeling of warmth—a blending of relief, security, and gratitude—when we realized that the 9th Air Force and 9th Tactical Command were beginning air bombardment to soften the enemy's beach line defenses.

Soon after the pin-pointed air attack and about twenty minutes before H-Hour, USS *Nevada* led the ships out at sea in a saturating, long-range bombing of Hitler's Atlantic Wall. Over us, also at a terrifyingly low level, drenching, mammoth streaks of fire expelled by rocket launchers whooshed to shore. Tons of destructive force fell only yards before us. Quickly, violent explosions and spectacular blazes transformed the scene. Bursts of smoke, dust, and scurrying sand curtained the view. Heavy defensive batteries that had survived the pre-D-Day air strikes were being obliterated.

It was about that time when we learned what had happened to our sister ship, *LCC-80*, with officers Tom Glennon and Bob Davis and their crew aboard. Before arrival in the transport area, her screw fouled on a dan buoy, rendering her unmaneuverable. Because she was out of commission and the primary control boat for her beach had been sunk, we knew what we were to do: triple duty. So we added the assignments of the two vessels for Red Beach to those we originally had been given for Green Beach.

Remembering the exact sequence of pre-H-Hour events is impossible. Too much was happening too fast. We were so rushed and frustrated with multiplying duties that we hardly noticed dawn cast its light unassumingly upon the panorama of war. We made no attempt to distinguish the elements of the intermingled spectacle, nor did we try to interpret the sundry sounds of war that came from far and near.

Gliders had passed overhead earlier. At the time, they probably were being towed by planes or, having been cut loose from their tug lines, they were slipping silently through the air on their own, like long, dark birds of the night. Once beyond Nazi coastal strongholds, some landed safely, others crashed just beyond the beach fortifications; and still others were speared by "Rommel's Asparagus," the tall, pointed poles that the enemy had planted in the flooded coastal marshlands to raise havoc with the landing of both glider-borne troops and parachutists.

The night skies, too, must have been filled with parachutists who had been carried to their drop zones over the enemy-flooded region behind the coast. Wherever they had landed, in places as diverse as barn and cottage roofs, apple orchards, church steeples, and hedgerows, they created chaotic confusion for the Germans. We knew from our briefing sessions earlier back in England what those 'chutists were destined to do; however, we did not see them float downward from the sky to carry out their perilous tasks.

The sun rose from our left a minute or two before 0600. But low-lying clouds and billowing smoke and dust blocked out the colors it might have painted the drab French coast, thereby depriving us of its rays of cheer and hope. When daylight crept unobtrusively upon the battle site, we were too busy to appreciate the release that its subdued illumination gave us from the bonds of darkness.

I looked astern and saw what lay at sea behind us; the greatest armada the world had ever known; the greatest it would ever know. I was overwhelmed by the sight as I clung to the rail and took in the magnitude of that assembled fleet: many great, gray ships majestically poised in their positions; larger numbers of unwieldy landing vessels heaved by the heavy sea; and countless numbers of smaller amphibious craft tossed mercilessly by the waves. Above the armada, anti-aircraft barrage balloons attached to the larger ships were buffeted by the strong channel winds.

My vantage point afforded me a glimpse of but a small part of the colossal assemblage of naval vessels. Beyond my sight and to our east lay Omaha Beach, the second assault site of the Western Task Force. Off it lay a congregation of American attack ships similar to ours on Utah. Farther to the east, even greater numbers of British vessels made up the Eastern Task Force, ready to strike Gold, Juno, and Sword beaches.

What I was privileged to see from the *LCC-60* in the waters just off the Cotentin Peninsula was spectacular. How much more so it would have been had I had a bird's eye view of the expanse from France to England. Then I would have been able to see the control craft, the amphibious boats, and the minesweepers just off the invasion coast; LCTs and other landing craft farther out in the staging area; and battleships, troop ships, and supply ships in the transport area ten miles off shore. Also, from that vantage point, I would have been able to watch destroyers and smaller patrol craft circling protectively; rocket and flak barges, completely spent after projecting their devastating flames and destructive steel during the softening of the beach; and hospital ships, repair boats, tenders, and rescue craft prepared and alert to provide their services.

From a bird's-eye view, too, I would have been able to see American, British, and Canadian vessels continuing to spill out from the southern English ports. Ships large and small, they would have been laden with back-up troops, equipment, clothing, food, medical supplies, and the numerous support items which would be needed when the ensuing battle was waged.

Standing at the rail of the LCC and surveying the historic scene, I felt much like an automaton momentarily aware of human qualities. The intermix of physical discomfort and emotional turmoil I sensed defies accurate description. Stiff, heavy pieces of drab-green clothing shielded me only to a degree from the wind and salt spray, but under the protective layers my legs seemed wooden, my stomach devoid of space, my arms and shoulders heavy and burdened. Fear, anxiety, apprehension, and dread, interlaced with a myriad of unrecognizable feelings, threaded their way from my head to my toes. Slowly they were supplanted by the warming assurance of divine protection, the reassuring pounding of my heart, and the words: "This too shall pass."

I turned from the massive display of military might and glanced at my Westclox. Its hands would soon move forward to mark an historic minute: 0630, the H-Hour of the invasion of Normandy. Then, as my gaze fell upon the steel-gray deck upon which I stood, I felt the security the *LCC-60* and my fellow crewmen gave me at a moment when the world around me was at war.

U.S. Navy underwater demolition specialists and U.S. Army combat engineers were arriving at that hour to obliterate the Nazi-planted obstacles in the sea-covered portion of "Rommel's Death Zone." Thousands of mines in the that hazardous area were hidden below high tide. Some were free-floating, others were magnetized, and many were set in place. Hundreds, too, were atop the vast array of triangular, cone- and pyramid-shaped defensive devices the enemy had concocted of wood, concrete, and steel to damage, stop, or destroy the invading landing boats and tanks which we would soon lead to shore.

Earlier, shortly after both the *LCT-597* and its DD tanks and the Red Beach primary control vessel were sunk, we had gone out to direct the LCTs in Wave 1A for both Red and Green beaches to move in two thousand yards and locate three thousand yards offshore. In the calmer waters there, they could more easily discharge the DD tanks they had aboard. Moreover, the DD tanks would not be in as much danger of being swamped as they would have been at the original discharge point out on the heavy seas.

The position change was a boon for the *LCC-60*, too. The shorter travel distance helped us make up time we had lost because of the rough water we had encountered and the added duties we had taken on for our ill-fated sister vessels. Best of all, we were able to meet our critical H-Hour schedule.

By 0615, the primary control vessel for Green Beach had returned to a point four thousand yards from shore to mark her position at the line of departure. From there, the *LCC-60* led Wave 1, the first of the LCVPs, beachward, and when it reached the LCTs' discharge point, it led Wave 2, which consisted of twenty-eight DD tanks.

The DD tanks were unique to the invasion. When they followed our lead that morning, it was the first time I had seen them at close range at sea. They looked even more strange than they had on land. Wallowing through the heavy waves and struggling to keep in formation, they appeared to be odd-shaped sea monsters depending upon huge, doughnut-like balloons for flotation. In reality, inside the queer water wings were thirty-three-ton Sherman tanks, fitted with screw propellers powered by their own engines.

Once we had led the boats and tanks to within five hundred yards of the beach, we reversed our course to return to the line of departure to carry out the duties the primary control vessel for Red Beach would have had. This gave us a chance to see the GIs on the overcrowded LCVPs in the shore-bound first wave at close range. We shouted cheers, gestured support, and offered encouragement, but only a few on each boat returned our acknowledgement. Some were too busy using their helmets to bail out the seawater sweeping over the low-set craft. Others, suffering from seasickness, were bent over the boat sides. Most, however, stood pressed together—motionless, salt-water soaked, and dulled by fear and cold.

The English language does not provide a multi-faceted, precise word that alone can describe what surely must have been surging through each man's mind and body. Were one to be coined, it would include meanings embodied in such interrelated words as: bravery, weakness, trust, toughness, uncertainty, love, tenacity, determination, despair, fearlessness, fright, faith, assurance, doubt, hate, loyalty, distrust, resolution, seriousness, prayerfulness, bravado, and hope. Courageous men all, Brigadier General Roosevelt among them, those men in Landing Wave 1 would in moments ink a page in history: splashing through surf and dashing across the gray sands of

Utah Beach, they would be among the first Americans who, through personal combat, would begin the destruction of Hitler's formidable Atlantic Wall. Some would die there; many would be injured; others would fight on, to live or to die along the perilous road leading to V-E Day.

General Roosevelt and I had developed a short-lived friendship, the sort that is not unusual for individuals sharing wartime stress. I will always be grateful to him for his afternoon visits when over a cup of tea, he told me stories of his boyhood days in the White House during his father's presidency. And I can never blot from my mind an event the night before our first departure for France. I was standing on a quay looking out into the choppy Channel, pondering the imminent, uncertain future, when someone put his arm around my shoulder. It was Teddy Roosevelt.

I don't remember the exact words of our conversation, but stamped forever in my memory is his parting statement: "Well, my boy, my life is now in your hands." And I still sense the assurance he gave me when he patted me on the back and walked away. Roosevelt was the only general in the first wave of assault troops that the *LCC-60* led to the sands of Utah Beach. The next month when I read in *Stars and Stripes* that he had died of a heart attack, his words to me that night on the quay echoed and re-echoed.

Equally valiant were the men in what the Americans called "Donald Ducks," the DD tanks. They were out of our sight inside the clumsy amphibians wallowing beachward through the heavy sea swells. We knew, however, that their fears, thoughts, and prayers were as inextricably intermingled as ours. Shortly after H-Hour, they would reach shallow water, drop the canvas "bloomer" from their armored vehicles, and track out of the sea and across the sandy expanse to shatter the remaining beach strongholds. With no respite, they would then climb over the coastal rise and set out across France and Germany to engage in battle after battle until war's end.

A matter which through the years has been like a burr in the saddle for *LCC-60* crew members should be put into true perspective: assertions have been made that the first waves were led to the wrong assault point on Utah Beach at H-Hour. Individuals not on the scene to witness what really happened have written that the control craft

139

erred in determining the site. Some have even made unfounded statements reporting errors ranging in distances from one thousand to ten thousand yards.

We—the *LCC-60* and her crew, who were carrying out the duties for the ill-fated primary control vessel for Red Beach as well as our own secondary control responsibilities for Green Beach and those of the *LCC-80* for Red Beach—are the ones about whom those statements center. Because we were there, we know what happened.

Lieutenant (j.g.) Gauthier, navigation officer, *LCC-60*, had used his skills to determine the landing point. Those of us trained to recognize the beach silhouette confirmed his findings to the best of our abilities. Our sightings were hampered, of course, because in the darkness the airborne debris, spreading smoke, dust, and fog curtained much from our view. Once we had agreed upon the assault site, however, we led the waves of LCVPs and DD tanks to a position from which they could reach it on their own.

The limited visibility may have confused the LCVPs as they neared shore and took over the lead for the DD tanks. Ocean wind and strong current, too, forced them to drift in a southeasterly direction. As a result, the boats did not touch down precisely on the pre-determined spot. Instead, they came up on the beach five hundred yards or less in error. The time was 0632, two minutes after H-Hour. At intervals during the next ten minutes, the DD tanks pulled themselves up on the beach.

In his *Operation Neptune Report* dated June 26, 1944, stamped "Secret" and declassified October 3, 1960, Rear Admiral D.P. Moon, commander of Task Force U, corroborates our observation that the assault landing occurred about five hundred yards southeast of the point from which it had been planned. Writers and historians, it can be assumed, did not take time to scrutinize the information available to them. As a result, they have put into print distances that are wrong.

The slight deviation in landing proved to be extremely fortuitous. A mighty Nazi shore battery at the exact landing point had remained intact despite the earlier saturation bombardment from air and sea. If the Allied invaders had gone ashore there, the foe would have had such an advantage that the Americans might have had difficulty in getting a toehold on the continent. Instead, the altered assault site harbored less enemy resistance and fewer obstacles and mines, and therefore afforded relatively easy access. In addition, casualties were lower by hundreds than the number that had been projected for the original position.

Once H-Hour had passed, we on the *LCC-60* went on with our roles, small parts in the center of the action on the stage of the huge combat theater. Physically and emotionally exhausted, we played those roles more like robots than live actors.

Looking back today, it seems that at the time there was no doubt in our minds that when the drama ended it would be a success, not another Dunkirk. On land, on sea, and in the air, the Allied invaders carried out their assignments as they had been directed. Their guns blared on the beach and from the ships at sea; their explosives shattered enemy defenses and hurled debris skyward; their rockets ignited conflagrations from which heavy smoke rose and moved slowly southeasterly; and their aircraft dropped parachutes that sprang open to crowd the sky space with silent, floating back-up forces.

Hour trailed hour that morning as we dispatched successive waves of combatants, arms, and war equipage to the Red Sector of Utah Beach. We did so with dulled minds and desensitized bodies, for we had been cramped aboard the *LCC-60* for seventy hours (less one hot meal and four hours sleep when D-Day was postponed). Even so, I am still able to recapture scattered fragments of images and sensations I had as we threaded our craft through the vast military spectacle.

A nauseating mix of diesel fumes, gun smoke, and salt-laden air made my breathing difficult. Deafening blasts of Allied artillery fire, thunderous sounds of on-shore explosions, and plaintive whines of enemy retaliatory arms muffled my hearing. A multitude of unidentifiable rumbling, piercing, and hissing noises, along with the grinding, chugging, and splashing of amphibious craft; the unexpected spasmodic detonations of concealed mines; the last gasps, or the eerie silence, of sinking vessels; and the cries for help of the wounded and drowning—sounded and resounded in my ears.

I can recreate fairly well, too, portions of the mental snapshots I took that morning from our boat's deck: the sun-streaked American planes spewing dark blobs—each a fighting man or a load of equipment or supplies—from which parachutes opened to give them safe, smooth descent to the Normandy countryside; red, white, and blue stars and stripes fluttering over gray naval vessels; blue-black masses of smoke on the coastline which—losers in their attempts to rise and dissipate—were being pushed inland by the more powerful wind; orange flames consuming the dried grasses that topped the rise of grotesque forms being exposed by rapidly receding tide; and hundreds of glossy, multi-colored jellyfish, defenseless victims of underwater explosions, bobbing and floating on the steel-gray waves.

Other sensations were less spectacular. They affected us physically, nonetheless, and diverted our attention from the unpleasantness we saw and heard and smelled. Piercing cold numbed and stiffened us despite the early June sun's feeble attempts to warm us. The raw channel wind wafted salt spray upon our faces; waves often doused us with sea water. Our drab-green, kapok-filled jackets and long, thick trousers had become damp, heavy, and cold almost as soon as we had set out from England two nights before, a discomfort that increased as more chilling wetness soaked through the cumbersome outfits. Salt crusted on our exposed skin; we licked it off our lips. The only pleasant taste that morning was a hard piece of chocolate in our K rations [military food rations].

After the third wave landed, we observed a greater barrage of enemy gunfire than there had been when we led the first waves. Later we learned that 88-millimeter Nazi guns, perhaps not fully manned earlier, had begun dropping shells among our troops and had knocked out some of our tanks. The succeeding sixteen waves (we dispatched nineteen waves during the day) encountered only sporadic shellfire.

At 1400, we were relieved of our primary control duties for Red Beach by the *PC-484*. We returned to act as Green Beach secondary control, our original duty position. That, however, was short-lived: Lieutenant (j.g.) Gauthier and I were ordered to "report without delay to the commander of Task Force U on board the Flagship, the USS *Bayfield* (APA-33)." Such an unexpected directive unnerved us. Was our day, already too long, to be extended by further duties? Were we to be questioned about our performance, what others had done, or what we had witnessed from our vantage point so near the assault beach? Or were we to receive a reprimand because the first wave hit the beach a few yards from the pre-planned landing point?

Our LCC crew rushed us out into the Channel to the headquarters ship. With minds and bodies equally tired, we paused to salute the ensign, then the officer-of-the-day. We identified ourselves and had hardly done so when a waiting seaman was ordered to take us to the wardroom. He led us apace up and down ladders and through passageways to it.

Military men occupied chairs around the wardroom tables, except for those reserved for us; other men in drab, non-military attire, supported themselves against bulkheads or stood in the limited space. Fatigue and lack of sleep kept us from realizing that we were facing not only Admiral Moon but also many of the other top Navy and Army leaders of Utah Beach.

Once seated, Gauthier and I sensed that the assembled group had been awaiting our appearance, for Admiral Moon opened the meeting immediately. First, he graciously welcomed us and the two others he had called to the ship, officers from the surviving primary control vessel whom we had not recognized when we were seated next to them. Next, he explained that we had been sent for to report what we had seen and heard and done, beginning our accounts with descriptions of our approach to the enemy coast before H-Hour.

We felt at ease as we told our stories and answered questions put to us by the admiral and his staff. Realization of the importance the assemblage attached to what we had to say gradually dawned on us when we saw everyone was taking down our words. Those standing were taking notes too. I recognized them as war correspondents. Edward R. Murrow was the only one that I recall now. Ernie Pyle must have also been present, for I had a memorable conversation with him on an isolated spot on the beach two or three days later.

I wish it were possible to restructure the meeting now so that I could know exactly what transpired. About all I have to go on is a footnote from Samuel Eliot Morrison's *The Invasion of France*: "LT (j.g.) H. Vander Beek in *LCC-60* and LT J.B. Ricker in *PC-1176*, Reports to Admiral Moon, 6 June," in reference to what he writes about the landings.

We got up from our chairs to leave the *Bayfield* shortly after 1500. We felt greatly relieved, somewhat rested, and pleasantly warmed by both the amicable atmosphere of the occasion and the comfortable temperature aboard the ship. But we were saddened, too, when we came out on the deck: injured men, both American and German, were being lifted aboard the ship and rushed to sick bay.

The *LCC-60* was signalled to come for us, and the crew brought the craft alongside the *Bayfield*. As we were about to cast off, a young newspaper reporter jumped aboard and asked us to take him to several of the other large ships anchored in the area. Taxiing him about was one of the most pleasant experiences of the day, a complete switch from those we had had earlier. It was relaxing and enjoyable, because Ted proved himself affable and refreshing. We enjoyed his war anecdotes, and together we compared his observations of the invasion from his vantage point aboard the communications ship with those of ours from the center of the landing operations. The man was Theodore H. White, later to become a world-renowned journalist and remembered today for his series of books on the making of the president.

For the remainder of D-Day afternoon, we were given dispatch boat duties. We took officers and newsmen, and messages and materials from one ship to another. Finally, somehow, the day that had begun an eternity before back in England ended sometime before the sun set. It was then—at least for us on the *LCC-60*—that June 6, 1944, became a day in history.

I cannot attach a name to the ship that took us aboard, provided us with evening chow, and assigned us quarters for the night. Each of us chose a berth, loosened our boot strings and our stiff, heavy clothing, and stretched out. Then, with gratitude for the divine protection that had seen us safely through the interminable day, we fell asleep. If there were enemy air raids and calls to General Quarters, we did not hear them, or, put more accurately: we chose not to hear them.

Roused by reveille, we hit the deck early the next day. Morning chow over, we stood at the ship's rail and took in the continuing drama of war in the air and on the land and sea. Thick gray clouds, stirred by strong, chilling winds, canopied the area. Sounds and smells seemed far less unpleasant than they had been the previous day, perhaps because we considered them necessary elements of the on-going Allied military thrust. Flashes of color lifted our spirits, particularly those of the American flag waving majestically over the beach. Knowing that it had been raised by men whom we had led in the assault fed our pride.

Planes flew farther over the Normandy lowlands than the day before. Parachutes, attached to gear and provisions for the advancing GIs, dropped from them. Amphibious small craft and ships passed us port and starboard on their way to shore to unload tons of equipment and supplies, and hundreds of fresh troops. And, to our west, we saw something which baffled us: several large barges, loaded with long, steel pylons and huge, odd forms made of concrete, and two rusty, old freighters being pulled and pushed toward land by tugs [see introduction to Chapter VII].

Looking toward the beach, we saw changes in the silhouette. D-Day bombardment and subsequent American construction had altered many of its features. What had been a toehold on the sands twenty-four hours earlier had been transformed into a massive landing site and beehive of military activity.

We felt good: we were rested to a degree, and we were no longer filled with the numbing tenseness of fear and uncertainty. But there were moments when our moods sobered and we stared down into the dark water and were silent. Images of what we had so recently gone through forced their way into our minds. We struggled to blot them out with dreams of what we hoped would happen to us within the next few days. After all, our invasion duties were over; we had done what we had come to France to do. So we visualized written orders to sail back over the channel to the security of Shapter's Field in Plymouth, England. And, still fantasizing, we saw a ship ready at a British port to rush us back to the United States.

Dreams we had of going home were shoved aside by our prayers for others who had been in the invasion. Some were Navy men, less fortunate than we, whose hardships had begun in the beach waters on D-Day and would go on for weeks until full military control of Normandy could be established. Others were the soldiers who had hit the beach and overcome the enemy there, had crossed the ridge and slogged through the marshlands, and then had started out on the first miles of the hundreds along which they would battle until the war in Europe ended. Still others were men from all branches of the service whose names already appeared on casualty lists: the captured, taken to Nazi prison camps; the injured, suffering in field medical stations, sick bays, and British hospitals; and the perished, awaiting eternal resting places beneath single white crosses set in symmetry on a verdant expanse along the Normandy coast.

We had not yet had an opportunity to set foot on France. Eager to do that and at the same time see what was happening on land, some of us found a way to get ashore. There we ran across men we had known back in the United States and England, and swapped invasion stories with them. We watched as prisoners-of-war were processed before their incarceration within temporary, open-air, barbed-wire pens set up on the ridge above the beach; examined some of the silenced Wehrmacht artillery, immobilized tanks, and shattered defense posts and strongholds; and looked over new American construction and stood by as men and machines built still more. Our greatest curiosity, however, centered upon what was happening farther down the beach. The old ships and strange structures we had seen being towed toward land earlier were being put into place near shore. We started to walk over for a closer look when a couple of us hooked a ride on a jeep about to turn onto a sandy passage that served as a beach access.

The lane led to a narrow country road which ran between hedgerows, along narrow parcels of farm and grazing land, and past orchards, peasant cottages, barns and sheds. Picturesque as the countryside was, its serenity and beauty were blemished by such scars and vestiges of war as ripped parachutes hanging from the limbs of apple trees, wide pits from exploded bombs, shattered gliders, burned and wrecked farm buildings, upended Panzer tanks and American vehicles, gashes in thick shrub and stone wall borders of fields, strewn personal belongings of men who would never again need them, and bloated bodies of cows on fresh, green pastures.

We drove on, reaching Ste. Mère Eglise shortly before noon. The townspeople were celebrating in the streets and singing, cheering, and waving small French and American flags. We learned that an hour or so before, our fighters had cleared the town of the last of the Nazis who had occupied it. We were welcomed with hugs, kisses, and flowers as if we had been a part of the feat.

A sudden burst of applause in the nearby churchyard drew us there to see what was happening. A shopkeeper, more fluent in English than I was in French, volunteered information with both words and animated gestures. A Yankee parachutist, he told us, had just been lowered from the church steeple. The man's chute, the Frenchman explained, had been caught on the spire, and he had hung, playing dead, for more than a day, tricking the Germans too involved in battle with the American invaders.

The jubilation continued and in the midst of it we were invited by a family to their modest cottage for the noon meal. The potage of fresh vegetables, along with thick slices of oven-fresh bread and a glass of grape wine, was the finest French cuisine that I can ever expect to have. After our expressions of gratitude for the fine food and warm hospitality, we embraced our hosts, scrambled into the jeep, and made our way back to Utah Beach.

We discovered that while we were inland, the pair of obsolete ships ("corncobs") had been sunk in line near shore. A breakwater and an outer seawall were being built by setting the concrete forms in pre-determined order to make a "gooseberry," a sheltered anchorage for landing craft. Five were being set up, one for each assault beach, while the two mulberries were being assembled at other points along the coast.

My curiosity took me up the gangway of one of the old ships, the SS *Robertson*. Part way up, I knew that I had made a mistake. I met Lieutenant Commander D.D. Dunn, with whom I had become acquainted during the briefing sessions at Dartmouth. He greeted me with unexpected enthusiasm.

"Lieutenant Vander Beek!" he exclaimed. "You are the man I have been looking for. Now that your big job is over, I have an easy one for you right here on this ship. You are going to run it, starting right now. Don't worry about your gear. You can have it later."

First I was a deck watch officer, but within hours I had the dubious honor of being the ship's executive officer, with Tom Glennon from the *LCC-80* coming aboard as first lieutenant on June 23. "Running the ship" simply meant being a quasi-innkeeper as the outdated vessel was used as on-shore quarters for Army and Navy top brass and other important individuals. Satisfying their demands for top-quality accommodations on such a dilapidated crate was impossible, and I often took verbal battering.

Ironically, I was a scarred veteran of "sunken ship duty" when temporary duty orders, dated June 8 (my birthday), were delivered to me. Sent by the commander, Task Group 127.4, they directed me to proceed and report to the U.S. Naval officer in charge, SS *Robertson*, the ship on which I was already the executive officer, so I was ordered to report to myself!

The month I was aboard the *Robertson* had its share of unpleasant moments. Duties were the most trying during nighttime hours when some of the high-ranking officers, military observers and consultants, journalists, and occasional notables who were aboard insisted on food and comforts even the Ritz could not have provided. Night after night, too, the Luftwaffe, intent on bombing the gooseberry area, approached and sent us to GQ. At any hour of the night, shell fire and explosions occurred near us and near vessels that had sunk—often victims of mines that had eluded the minesweeping units. The most taxing and trying experience of all was sitting out the violent three-day storm that rushed in from the channel on June 19 and challenged the gooseberry's invulnerability.

Pleasant times on the *Robertson* were usually during the daylight hours, when the skeleton crew and I could relax and brush aside our ennui. Our morning chores over and those quartered on the ship away for the day, the men and I could fill our time with what we wanted to do. We read whatever was available, wrote letters we would not be able to toss into the mail bag for weeks; had heated sessions of hearts and gin rummy; and most enjoyable of all, we caught up on lost sleep.

Some days I took walks on shore. One morning I was on a narrow beach access lane when I realized a weapons carrier had come up behind me, suddenly. I jumped into the roadside brush to let it pass. "Get out of the way, you SOB!" With that directive, I became one of the thousands given that epithet by General George Patton.

Soon afterwards I strolled out onto the beach and had a much warmer encounter. The khaki-clad man, heating soup in a helmet he had propped over a struggling flame, appeared to be a lonely GI. He disregarded my introductory small talk and began to question me about my part in the invasion. When he pulled out a note pad and began to jot down my responses, I checked his shoulder patch. He was no ordinary soldier; he was a war correspondent.

"M'gosh!" I exclaimed. "You must be Ernie Pyle!" He conceded in a dry, matter-of-fact manner that he was. Later, after the war and after his death in April 1945 on tiny Ie Shima off the coast of Okinawa, I read a collection of Pyle's Scripps-Howard columns and his book, *Brave Men*. I trust that I was not imagining that a few of the lines seemed familiar. They took me back to that chance meeting with a kind, warm, mild-mannered human being for whom I had had immediate affection and respect.

On July 9, a naval messenger came to the *Robertson* to deliver an envelope marked S-E-C-R-E-T. Inside was a letter from the naval officer in charge, Utah Beach. He informed us that he had received a dispatch from England which read: "*LCC-60* scheduled to leave area X return without delay Lieutenant (j.g.) T.J. Glennon and Lieutenant (j.g.) Howard Vander Beek of *LCC-80* and *LCC-60*." The letter detached us from our temporary duties and directed us to comply with the intents of higher command. *LCC-60* had another invasion to attend to, this time in Southern France.

More than fifty years have now passed since I volunteered and served in World War II. Time-dimmed, long-repressed memories of that period in my life, ranging from the gratifying to the unpleasant, have surfaced in recent years. Therefore, it was with a mix of eagerness and reluctance that I returned with other veterans to London, Plymouth, and sites along both sides of the English Channel where we trained for and took part in amphibious warfare five decades ago.

During the two weeks of stirring events commemorating the 1944 Normandy invasion, the expressions of gratitude and manifestations of esteem shown us by the British, French, and other Europeans were overwhelming. Grateful as we were, we were humbled by thoughts of those living and dead not at our sides who were more deserving than we to be shown such homage.

Observances great and small allowed us to pause for profound contemplation. Wreath-laying ceremonies amidst the white crosses set in the green grass of the American cemeteries in Brittany and Normandy and at monuments to fallen leaders stirred our emotions. The magnificent D-Day observance on June 6 evoked many reflections of happenings on that date half a century before.

The most momentous experience for me, however, took place during a solitary stroll on the gray sands of Utah Beach. As I gazed pensively out upon undulating waters through a gossamer mist, mental images of the *LCC-60* and the seamen aboard her enacting their roles in a theater of hostility appeared. Then, gradually, the haze disintegrated, the ashen skies slowly changed to azure, and the billows calmed to gentle ripples on a silver-blue sheet.

In the soft caress of an early June breeze, I felt the reassurance of his warm and comforting touch.

Chief Pharmacist's Mate Quinten S. Coyer, U.S. Navy.

Vanishing Major

By Chief Pharmacist's Mate Quinten S. Coyer, U.S. Navy (Retired). Adapted from "Some Thoughts of D-Day," unpublished manuscript.

On June 6, 1944, I was a chief pharmacist's mate with the 2d Naval Beach Battalion. Early that morning I was on an LCI off Utah Beach on the coast of Normandy. We had come to England from North Africa in November 1943, where we had participated in the invasion of Sicily on July 10, 1943.

Our outfit was quartered in a camp near the town of Fowey in Cornwall, England. While we were there, we made practice landings. We were attached to the Army 1st Engineers Special Brigade, and were a part of the exercise in April [Exercise Tiger] that was conducted off the coast of Devonshire to rehearse for D-Day. German E-boats attacked part of the force, sinking two LSTs and damaging a third. Eight hundred Americans were killed.

On about June 3, we were told where we would make the landing in Normandy and proceeded to board an LCI. The sea was very rough the day and the night before the landing. On the morning of June 6, we went over the side of the LCI into an LCM and headed for the beach. The LCM took us closer, but it was a long walk to reach the beach. Shells were exploding in the water. It was the longest walk I ever took. There were tanks sitting on the beach and nothing was moving. It looked like utter confusion.

A short distance from the water was a sea wall about three to four feet high. We set up our aid station next to this wall. We were safe from the exploding shells there, but had to go out and carry and help the wounded to the aid station. After a while, the engineers blasted a hole in the sea wall and the tanks moved inland.

One of our men, a signalman, had been hit by a machine gun or machine pistol across his waist. One of the bullets had hit his canteen and the bullet was still inside the canteen. He died before we could evacuate him back to a ship. All we could do for the wounded was give them morphine, put on sulfa powder, and bandage the wounds. The more serious cases were given plasma. It was late in the day before we could evacuate any of them.

Thank god for the Spitfires. What a beautiful sight they were. They kept an umbrella over us and I never saw a German plane that day.

We were exhausted, but did not get much sleep that night. Early the next morning an Army major suddenly appeared at our aid station. He was dressed in a clean uniform and looked as if he had just stepped out of an office. He demanded to know who was in charge, and the guys all pointed to me and said that I was.

He said, "I want this placed policed up immediately!"

Just then, the German guns opened up, and shells began exploding nearby. He took off, and we never saw him again. Needless to say, we did not do any policing up.

And so ended D-Day for us on Utah Beach.

Commander Walter H. Preston, U.S. Naval Reserve.

"CAN DO"

By Commander Walter H. Preston, U.S. Naval Reserve. Adapted from "A Part of My Life in World War II," unpublished manuscript.

World War II was in full swing when in April 1943, I received my commission as an ensign in the Navy's Civil Engineer Corps—to be with the Seabees [CBs; the U.S. Navy Construction Battalions]. Following several months' training at Camp Peary, Virginia, I and others received orders to report to the 1006 Construction Battalion Detachment, currently located in southern England and preparing for the invasion of France.

After traveling on a tanker in a convoy to England, we were stationed in Plymouth, on the southern coast. Plymouth had been badly damaged by bombing during the early part of the war. In the central part, no standing buildings could be seen for blocks. Here, the 1006 C.B. Detachment Seabees were busily engaged in assembling strings of steel Navy Landing (NL) pontoons that were being tied together to form various types of floating structures to be used as tugs, Rhino ferries, and floating piers (causeways). The men knew that they were preparing for an invasion of France.

In March 1944, I was transferred for a month to Falmouth. I continued my training in landing troops there and then went to Fowey in Cornwall for about three months of fabricating pontoon structures and training others in our operational techniques.

We knew that D-Day was approaching and were assigned special arms, clothing, and equipment for that cross-channel job. German troops were expected to use poison gas against invading troops, and we were each issued chemically-treated coveralls, socks, and a gas mask. Only work clothes were to be used on the far shore. My dress uniforms and personal belongings were left at Fowey. We all wore steel helmets with a hard, plastic liner. Around each of our necks was a string or metal necklace from which dangled two stainless steel identification tags.

On D-Day, June 6, we headed slowly out of Salcombe Harbor into the English Channel. We were not part of the first wave. It wasn't until the next day that I first saw Utah Beach ahead in a haze. Standing on the deck of our LST, I witnessed a massive armada of hundreds of ships and small landing craft. Dozens of silver barrage balloons floated in the air above the ships to prevent strafing attacks by the enemy. I also saw a long line of about twelve cargo ships that appeared to have been sunk. I thought the German shore batteries had been on their mark, but later learned that these old ships had been purposely floated into position and sunk to form a breakwater in the shallow Bay of the Seine.

A mile or more to the west loomed the battleship USS *Nevada.* A flash of fire spurted from its 14-inch guns and three black specks sped through the air towards shore, exploding once they had found their mark. Later, on the beach, I saw an unexploded 14-inch shell lying in the sand near our work area. A slender wooden stick with a red flag had been placed in the sand next to the shell as a warning.

As our LST neared the shore, we boarded landing craft and maneuvered our causeway string onto the beach. Other pontoon strings were being grouped together with ours to form a pier that extended from the beach out into the water. Our steel pontoon piers were finally positioned in a configuration 28 feet wide and 350 feet long. They were sunk into position by allowing seawater to enter the pontoons through open seacocks. At low tide, if we wished, we could move the pontoons by opening the seacocks, draining the pontoons, and re-positioning them.

The causeways started operation as soon as they were in position on D+2. Fortunately, we were not hampered by enemy aircraft or gunfire until the next day when a shell landed next to one side of the pier. No one was hurt but we were alarmed. A U.S. Army tank came up the beach and sped off toward an area of German resistance. After that the only sound of gunfire came from a long distance away.

Overhead we saw large groups of Allied bombers flying from England to make bombing runs inland. Following the bomb drops, great clouds of black smoke rose into the air. Once, two fighter-bomber aircraft appeared over the bay. They spread apart, then like two football backfield runners doing a reverse play, one dove downward from the left, dropping his bomb. The other dove downward from the right and likewise dropped his bomb. They had apparently hit an enemy ammunition dump, and the explosions and smoke clouds lasted for hours.

I only saw two enemy air actions, as the Luftwaffe had been almost completely silenced before the invasion. Two days after our arrival, an enemy fighter plane, being chased by an Allied aircraft, dove down through the cloud cover. The German rose back into the clouds, but the Allied fighter continued downwards. Our anti-aircraft gunners fired at and hit the Allied plane, but as it crashed into the bay, I saw the pilot parachute to safety. He was picked up by a small U.S. Navy boat. The German plane escaped. Then, two days later, we heard the drone of an airplane after dark. Although we weren't strafed or bombed, we found a small, unexploded, incendiary bomb the next day in a pasture near the beach.

The first night I was ashore I slept on the ground under a truck. I wore chemically impregnated overalls and had my gas mask, sea bag, and weapons nearby. Our food consisted of K rations; water was supplied from jerry cans. The following day, a tent and folding cots were set up in a cow pasture near the beach. While living on the beach, I soon found out that steel helmets were one of our most useful pieces of equipment. Not only did they serve as head protection, but they also made great wash basins when filled with water. Though I didn't see it myself, other Seabees told me that they had cooked meals over a fire with theirs. Once, behind our beach, I even saw a soldier milking a cow into his steel helmet!

There were hundreds of ships in the Bay of the Seine. One caught my interest in particular—it was a cargo vessel with a huge reel amidships that appeared to extend forty feet into the air. The ship was moving slowly towards shore from the channel as if it were laying cable. After the war, I found out that the ship was actually laying a two to three inch aluminum pipeline to deliver gasoline from England to our forces in Normandy. [Ed.: Known as PLUTO, (PipeLine Under The Ocean) the pipeline delivered over one million gallons of gasoline a day when it was completed.]

To help protect our equipment and men from German strafing attacks, silver colored barrage balloons were tethered to many ships and landing craft. I was told that their connecting lines consisted of lightweight steel cables intended to entangle low-flying airplanes. Thus, pilots would be forced to fly higher, limiting the effectiveness of any attack. Those big silver balloons dotted the sky over the bay during the early weeks of the invasion.

About a week after D-Day a terrific storm hit our landing beaches [Ed.: June 19; almost two weeks after D-Day]. Heavy winds and high waves delayed landing activities for two to three days. Fortunately, the Army had enough men and equipment on the Cherbourg Peninsula for their offensive action. The storm threw our pontoon causeway in disarray, and we had to re-float the assemblies and set them up again for the operations to continue. Large ships and landing craft rode out the storm in the bay or channel or returned to England. Over 115 small craft and barges, however, were cast upon Utah Beach. Many were irreparably damaged. Salvage work continued for weeks after the storm.

German prisoners of war who had been captured on the Cotentin Peninsula were marched down the beach in groups of one or two hundred by U.S. Army soldiers. Most were from east European countries. Dressed in gray uniforms with heavy overcoats, they were held in wire compounds awaiting transfer to England. Their leather belts had been removed from their trousers and stacked outside the compound as a precaution against use as a weapon.

During that period, the Seabees learned of a large cache of Calvados (alcohol made from distilled apple cider) that the Germans had secured in a tunnel between Utah Beach and Cherbourg. They found it and appropriated a good supply, pouring it into jerry cans. That evening, samples flowed, resulting in a merry time for the finders and their many guests. One of our lot, becoming excited, shouted: "I'm on an invasion and haven't fired a gun. I have to fire my gun here!" He pointed it at the ground and pulled the trigger. To the best of my knowledge that was the only shot fired by our Seabees in the invasion.

When the Utah Beach area was secure and safe from German guns, landing craft were brought onto the beach for unloading as the tide receded. LCTs, LSTs, and LCIs ran up onto the beach sand, their flat bottoms sitting soundly on it. Once the tide had gone out, their bow doors were opened and ramps were lowered. Vehicles drove safely onto the beach and goods were unloaded. On the next incoming tide, the ship re-floated, pulled off the beach, and headed back to England.

Stories have been told for years about how our Seabees could build anything and accomplish all sorts of tasks. This is true. Not only could our mechanics, riggers, equipment operators, and all the rest do their jobs in an outstanding way, but their accomplishments showed up in other ways as well.

For example, once a carpenter's mate asked me if I'd like a barbecued steak for dinner. How could I resist after eating K and B rations? When I asked where the steaks came from, he answered, "One of the ships in the bay." Seabees had visited the ships with amphibious small craft. He grilled those steaks to perfection over a makeshift grill. That was one of my most memorable dinners.

Although personal cameras were not permitted at our training base in the U.S. or overseas, I noticed that many of our men had cameras and film with them. Accordingly, I had left mine at home, but in one of my letters home, I asked that my Leica camera be sent with some 35-millimeter film. Around June 20, my camera arrived in a sack of mail via an LST from England. What a wonderful break! General Eisenhower and those other top brass whom I'd never seen would have to excuse me. Discreetly and judiciously, I took photographs of our beach operations, ships on the beach, German prisoners, German defensive structures, and French towns.

On the evening of July 4, 1944, I was returning to our camp after spending part of the day touring the Cotentin Peninsula. The sky was darkening after sunset and an occasional stream of tracers zipped across the sky. Then a big gun sounded. As the sky grew darker, more guns were fired. When darkness settled, the sky was ablaze with tracers from anti-aircraft guns and brilliant flashes from bigger guns lit the horizon. The booming and cracking of guns of all sizes broke the quiet. The gunfire, however, was not directed at enemy forces. The invasion had progressed for a month, and there was no enemy nearby. Rather, the spectacle was a colossal July 4 gala. For an hour or more, the night was lit up with a tremendous celebration that, for all I know, was done entirely with live ammunition.

An LCC like Vander Beek's leads landing craft to the beach in the invasion of Southern France. *(U.S. Navy; National Archives)*

Army troops aboard an LCT just prior to landing. *(U.S. Navy; National Archives)*

A weapons carrier departs from a landing craft and moves through the surf towards Utah Beach. Its anti-aircraft gun, pointed skyward, is ready for instant action. *(U.S. Army Signal Corps; National Archives)*

U.S. Navy 2d Beach Battalion members rest after initial action at Utah Beach. *(U.S. Navy; National Archives)*

A U.S. Navy Hospital Corpsman with the 2d Beach Battalion writes a letter in a Normandy beachhead bunker, June 11, 1944. *(U.S. Navy; National Archives)*

U.S. Navy 2d Beach Battalion members on Utah Beach. *(U.S. Navy; National Archives)*

U.S. Army trucks moving from LCTs onto pontoon causeway built by the Seabees. *(Walter Preston photograph)*

German Army prisoners being held in an enclosure on Utah Beach. The Navy landing craft on the left had floated onto the beach at high tide. *(Walter Preston photograph)*

Young men dying seems to me somehow the greatest tragedy. I know that death serves only to accentuate the love of living we both share so dearly. The bridge between is so quick, so complete, so final that you finally stop thinking of its terrible proximity.

You cling rather to pulsating life. Your laughter is a little quicker, your thinking is a little less shallow, your energies and ambitions fired with a new urgency.

VI
OMAHA'S WRATH

Twenty miles to the east of Utah Beach the American forces had to contend with an offensive nightmare: steep cliffs looming directly behind an almost featureless beach. Thirty minutes of naval bombardment did not destroy the German defenses, and lethal fire greeted the American invaders as they stumbled ashore. Landing craft were sunk, many amphibious tanks foundered in the rough seas, and men perished as they plunged from the relative safety of their landing craft into the hail of awaiting machine gun and shell fire.

Those soldiers who made it to the beach huddled behind obstacles, and organization disintegrated in the face of the brutal fire. The Navy provided relief in the form of reinforcements and demolition teams, who, when a rising tide forced them to abandon their mine clearing, joined with the infantry to help them fight. Few Army artillery pieces or tanks had made it successfully to shore. So, as was the case on Utah Beach, close fire support from offshore naval ships was instrumental in allowing the U.S. troops to gain a foothold and begin their inland advance. American casualties numbered twenty-five hundred on the first day at Omaha, and by evening U.S. soldiers had progressed only one mile inland from the beach.

Nearly one-fourth of the Allied troops landing on Omaha and the other beaches were engineers. These engineers were responsible for everything from managing the flow of landing craft, traffic, and goods; to destroying mines, obstacles, and barbed wire; to assuring access to the hinterland from the beach. Attached to the Army's Engineer Special Brigades (ESBs) were U.S. Naval Beach Battalions which, in addition to assisting with the aforementioned duties, also coordinated communications between the beach and the ships, repaired boats, performed hydrographic duties, and established first-aid stations. On Omaha, the Navy's 6th and 7th Beach Battalions were "in on the action," as many of the following stories relate.

Although the German defenders put up a stiff resistance, they were surprised by the attacks. The Germans had expected the Allied invasion to come farther north and not when the weather was so uncertain. Slow responses by the German leadership—Rommel was at his wife's birthday party, Hitler was asleep when the invasion began, and two Panzer divisions were held up for a full day—compounded Germany's surprise. By nightfall on June 6, all five Allied divisions (150,000 men) had disembarked on the five, Allied-held beaches.

Seaman Second Class
Jackson Hoffler, U.S. Navy.

THE YOUNGEST MAN-OF-WAR

By Seaman Second Class Jackson Hoffler, U.S. Navy. Adapted from unpublished manuscript.

My most memorable experience during my World War II military service was the landing on Omaha Beach during the invasion of Normandy. I had enlisted in the summer of 1943 at fourteen years of age. [Ed.: Like many underage veterans in World War II, Hoffler lied about his age in a patriotic bid to help the war effort.] In June 1944, I was still fourteen, and believe that I was the youngest combat sailor present at D-Day. I was a gunner on an LCVP.

On June 6, 1944, we carried troops and supplies to the beach all day. All that night I shot at parachute flares being dropped by German aircraft, to extinguish the flares. On June 7, we carried troops and supplies to the beach and brought wounded back to the ship. Late that evening, my LCVP struck an underwater obstacle and sank; it had been loaded with ammunition.

My ship (*LST-512*) had already left the beachhead, so from that time on I served with the beachmaster and the 6th Beach Battalion. We moved supplies across the beach to the forces inland. My most memorable experience during this time was the removal of a young soldier who had been caught in and killed by the propeller of an LCM. I had to put a sand bag over his head so I did not have to look in his face. The dead were everywhere. I shall never forget seeing vehicles driving over bodies, and I remember grabbing another sailor and having him help me move about twenty bodies so that the trucks wouldn't run over them. I shall always remember those long days and nights on the Normandy beachhead.

I was wounded twice during this period, on June 9 and July 4. After being wounded, I was placed in an Army hospital and, after recovering, finally returned to my ship. My medical records were kept by the Army as they moved inland, and my captain had me court-martialed for being AWOL. They were going to put me on bread and water for twenty days, but instead I was sent to a Navy hospital in England for further treatment. They transferred me stateside, where I was to receive the Purple Heart. Plans went awry, however, and I was transferred to a patrol torpedo craft in the Pacific and soon after, was given an honorable medical discharge at age fifteen. I did not receive the Purple Heart. Fifty years later, despite my best efforts, I have still not received that medal.

Pharmacist's Mate Second Class Fred Camp, U.S. Navy.

SAVING LIVES ON A RED BEACH

By Pharmacist's Mate Second Class Fred Camp, U.S. Navy. Adapted from "Operation Overlord," in The Bugle: Newsletter of the American Legion *(June 1994).*

I returned half a century later to the Normandy beaches. As I gazed out over the water all I could hear were the sounds of spiraling sea gulls and shouts of laughter by little children on the beach below. The battle images of that first Tuesday in June have vanished for the most part. The sight of terrifying obstacles, battered hulks of landing craft and burned out tanks are no more. It all has a clean and sanitized look to it. You begin to question if this was the spot where you landed or whether it was fifty yards farther down.

I landed with the third group of Army Engineers. My job as a Navy medic was to set up an aid station to treat and evacuate the wounded.

The engineers' job was to clear the beach of anti-tank traps and mines set up in checkerboard formation. This would ease the way for artillery and tanks landing in succeeding waves. They managed to clear a few lanes but this was pitifully inadequate to allow sizeable quantities of heavy equipment to be brought in. Three waves of infantry and engineers found themselves pinned down under a hail of machine gun, mortar, and artillery fire from German fortifications on the ridge. Oncoming waves of men and equipment behind us found themselves blocked by men ahead of them.

Only a few days before we had been briefed in a circus-size tent in England by a be-medalled British Army colonel stating that "every grain of sand will be turned over twice before the first wave hits the beach." It was a little past 0900 and I wondered where he was and what beach he meant.

That was the plan but someone forgot to tell the Germans. Field Marshal Erwin Rommel in charge of the defense was said to have told his men: "When the invasion begins our only chance will be at the beaches where the enemy is always at his weakest." Three German infantry divisions were stationed there as well as the crack 21st Panzer Division which had only days before arrived in the area and was positioned by fate along the crescent of the Normandy beach sector.

By noon the water's edge had turned red as American dead floated in and out with the tide. As with all deadly conflicts, individual acts of heroism were abundant. I heard a sergeant yell to what was left of his platoon, "We're getting killed on this beach, let's go inland and get killed." My mouth went dry and I couldn't swallow. The "Limey" colonel with the medals was nowhere in sight as I recall.

At the end of the "longest day," I remember being bone-tired and I sat down for the first time on a blood-stained stretcher. I cried.

Evacuating the wounded was a slow and risky process as shell fire continued to rake the beach. Toward afternoon it became more intermittent and the transporting of the injured to the waiting ships offshore improved. We did what we could—administering plasma, bandaging, and injecting morphine from disposable packets in our pockets. Our medical officer, Dr. Ralph Hall, was hit with shrapnel in his leg shortly after we landed. One of the medics from our ship looked at me and with a thin smile said, "I hope we live at least 'till noon." I kept repeating the 23rd Psalm or what I could remember of it. It helped.

General Omar Bradley, who viewed the landing from the flagship USS *Augusta,* was to state decades later: "Even now it brings me pain to recall what happened there. I have many times returned to honor the valiant men who died on that beach. They must never be forgotten. Nor should those who lived to carry the day by only the slimmest of margins."

Of the five D-Day beaches, Omaha Beach would be remembered as the site of the worst losses. In recognition, our unit was awarded the *Croix de Guerre* by France for valor under fire.

As the hours wore on, the low-flying planes poured rocket fire into the fortifications while destroyers continued to fire at the ridge. A breach was at last effected with men and equipment pouring through it. They were the U.S. 1st and 29th Divisions.

There is an elegant American cemetery on the bluffs above Omaha Beach. More than nine thousand white marble headstones stand row on row. Inscribed on a semicircular wall in the cemetery's Garden of the Missing are the names of 1,557 men whose remains were never recovered or were unable to be fully identified. It is a sad and still place to visit. You almost have the feeling you know them all but of course you do not.

Is there some meaning to all this? Here are my thoughts:

- A small number of brave men can make a large difference;
- Men usually fight better in a good cause;
- Morale is essential to victory;
- Nothing helps morale like superior firepower and a measure of luck;
- War is very cruel and wasteful;
- The good die young; and
- God forgives us and understands we felt we had to do what we did for our nation, our people, and our future generations.

A wall in the cemetery chapel bears the following inscription: "Think not upon their passing—remember the glory of their spirit." I can never forget.

Pharmacist's Mate Second Class Frank Walden, U.S. Navy.

WOUNDED WITH THE 6TH

By Pharmacist's Mate Second Class Frank Walden, U.S. Navy. Adapted from oral history transcript.

I was attached to Company C-7 of the 6th Naval Beach Battalion as a hospital corpsman to treat wounded on Omaha Beach. We were attached to an engineer unit and we stayed on the beach until everything came in and out. I was eighteen years old at the time and I was scared to death.

Although it seemed like one of our many training runs, I think that when we saw bodies floating in the water as we approached the beach, we realized this was to be the real thing. We relied on our training to take over, which it did. During the course of the day I was wounded around 1500.

At the time I was wounded, we were pinned down all day and couldn't really do our jobs. We were lying there and a couple of Army medics came by with a fellow on the stretcher. The Germans started to shell the beach, and the medics set the stretcher down and an 88-millimeter shell went off and wounded them. Virgil Mount, Corpsman in the 6th Naval Beach Battalion, and I jumped up to treat those two and that's when Virgil was killed and I was wounded. My good friend Don Burroughs was also wounded.

Because our beach was closed and we had no way to evacuate, I walked down to the next beach and made it onto an LCT and then to an LST. The LST took me back to England and I was treated there in the hospital and was sent home in September.

Lieutenant Commander Joseph P. Vaghi, U.S. Naval Reserve (Retired).

BEACHMASTER ON EASY RED

By Lieutenant Commander Joseph P. Vaghi, U.S. Naval Reserve (Retired). Adapted from "D-Day: Easy Red Beach, Normandy," unpublished manuscript.

At the outset, permit me to define what a beachmaster was and what his duties were. A beachmaster was like a traffic cop at a very busy intersection. All sorts of activities took place around him; and it was his responsibility to establish and maintain order. The beachmaster controlled all the traffic coming onto the beach—men and material—and arranged for all movement from the shore to the ships at sea. It was the beachmaster's responsibility to establish radio communication between the beach and the ships at sea. Beachmasters were responsible for rendering medical aid to injured personnel until they could be evacuated to the ships offshore and for maintaining radio communications from ship to shore. In addition, they provided hydrographic assistance to incoming landing craft, instructed them where to land, placed markers, and performed minor boat repairs.

The beachmaster for each sector of the various beaches—of which Easy Red was one sector—was responsible for all activities between the low tide mark and the high tide mark. The rise and fall of the tide amounted to some eighteen to twenty feet twice a day in the English Channel. Our 6th Naval Beach Battalion was responsible for most of Omaha Beach.

I was the beachmaster of Easy Red Sector on Omaha Beach, Normandy. I was a platoon commander of Platoon C-8 which was one of the nine platoons in the 6th Naval Beach Battalion. The Battalion was composed of three companies: A, B, and C. Each company in turn was composed of three platoons, which consisted of three officers and forty-three enlisted men. My platoon, C-8, was one of the three in C Company. The landing craft that my platoon was assigned to for the crossing of the English Channel was landing craft infantry (large) *LCI(L)-88*.

A secret report by Lieutenant H.K. Rigg, the skipper of *LCI(L)-88* to the Commander in Chief, United States Fleet of July 12, 1944 contains this statement: "This vessel beached on schedule at 0735, 6 June, the first LCI(L) on Easy Red Beach." Platoon C-8 of the 6th Beach Battalion arrived in France at 0735, British Double Time on June 6, 1944, one hour and five minutes after H-hour.

My platoon, along with the commander of the 6th Beach Battalion, Commander Eugene Carusi, USN (a Naval Academy graduate), some Army personnel, and A.J. Liebling (a writer for the *New Yorker* magazine), were aboard the *LCI(L)-8* when it beached on Easy Red, some five hundred yards from the dune line of the beach. Our ship kissed the sands of Normandy when the tide was at its lowest. The distance was so great because of the tidal variation, as noted above.

According to Liebling, who reported all the details of the landing, I was the first person to leave the LCI(L) after beaching. The craft had ramps on each side of the bow for purposes of discharging the passengers. Shortly after I left the craft, the right ramp was blown away by an enemy shell which caused numerous casualties, both on the craft and in the water.

D-Day, needless to say, was a day of memorable events. I shall attempt to recount a few that were extraordinary. These events occurred along that sector of the beach known as Easy Red Beach, which was assigned to our platoon.

The beach was cluttered with thousands of beach obstacles strategically placed by the Germans to thwart an invasion attempt. A Navy Underwater Demolition Team (UDT) had landed prior to our arrival and was successful in clearing away some of the obstructions, so as to permit movement onto the beach by the various landing craft assigned to this and other beaches.

My first awareness that what we were doing was real was when an 88-millimeter shell hit our LCI(L) and machine gun fire surrounded us. The Germans were in their pillboxes and bunkers high above the beach on the bluff and had an unobstructed view of what we were doing.

The atmosphere was depressing. The top of the bluff behind the beach was barely visible; the sound of screeching 12-inch and 14-inch shells from the warships USS *Texas* and USS *Arkansas* offshore were new sounds never heard by us before; the stench of expended gunpowder filled the air, and landing craft with rocket launchers moved in close to the shore and spewed forth hundreds of rounds at a time onto the German defenses. The sea was rough. Purple smoke emanated from the base of the beach obstacles as the UDT prepared to detonate another explosive in the effort to clear a path through the obstacles to the dune line—this was the state of affairs as the platoon made its way to the dune line, oh so many yards away.

Using the obstacles as shelter, we moved forward over the tidal flat, fully exposed to machine gun fire. We finally reached the dune line. All of C-8 including Commander Carusi and his staff made the long trek of five hundred yards safely. God was with us! Three days later, however, Commander Carusi took a bullet through his lung and had to be evacuated. A great leader to be sure.

Having reached the high water mark, we set about organizing ourselves and planning the next move as we had done so many times during our training period. The principal difference was that we were pinned down—with real machine gun fire—with very little movement to the right or the left of our position and absolutely no movement forward.

Because the UDT had opened four gaps through the underwater obstacles onto Easy Red (the designated gaps were numbers 11, 12, 13, and 14), most of the personnel and vehicles came ashore on my beach. As a result, we were very crowded, and became "sitting ducks" for the enemy fire.

I believe the most dramatic event that I experienced that morning was when an Army officer came to me and asked that I, as the beachmaster, pass the word over my powered megaphone that the soldiers were to "move forward." The men of C-8 have speculated that the officer was Colonel George Taylor, who landed at 0830. Taylor is reported to have said: "There are only two kinds of people on this beach—the dead and those who are about to die."

After I gave the order, an Army sergeant pushed a "Bangalore" torpedo through the barbed wire at the top of the dune, exploded it, and opened a gap in the mass of barbed wire. He then turned to his men and said "follow me." He did not order his men forward, but he led them, which was the sign of a leader. The men rushed through the gap onto the flat plateau behind the dune line to the base of the bluff, a distance of some fifty yards or so through heavily-mined areas. Many lost their lives or were seriously wounded.

Once the sergeant's heroic act was accomplished (the first penetration of Hitler's Atlantic Wall), the Army began its offensive against the Germans. As the GIs began to attack the German strongholds and began to fan out into the countryside, the Battle of Normandy was now underway.

As a component part of our C-8 platoon, our communications section established contact with our control vessel offshore and reported all conditions on the beach as furnished by our company commander, Lieutenant George Clyburn, our battalion commander, Commander Carusi, and elements of the 5th Engineers Special Brigade, to whom we were attached. Because we were sending so many messages via radio, it was later reported to us that the Germans had "zeroed in" on our radio frequency and proceeded to pinpoint our exact location.

As best I can recall, it was midmorning when an Army First Aid man came to the area on the beach where I was standing and attempted to roll a dead soldier off a stretcher. I told him not to do that, but to take hold of the other end of the stretcher and that together we could place the body away from the area where trucks and jeeps were passing for travel to the openings in the German defenses.

As I bent down to pick up the stretcher, a very large explosion occurred. I was momentarily stunned; and when I regained my senses, I discovered that my clothes were on fire. After regaining my bearings and extinguishing the fire on my coveralls, I noticed that a jeep close by was burning. I turned to one of my men and told him to come with me. We went to the jeep and removed two five-gallon cans of gasoline and a number of boxes of hand grenades. I was concerned that if those two elements were to explode, more deaths would occur in addition to those who were already dead due to the explosion. Amin Isbir, seaman first class and the oldest man in my platoon (born in 1909), was killed instantly by the explosion. Prior to leaving England for D-Day, Isbir confided in me that he would not come back alive. How prophetic!

As beachmaster, I had the awesome responsibility of being very much intertwined with the overall aims of the landing operations, and the safety of the lives that would be affected by my orders. At one point, I ordered Seaman First Class Jim Gately to go out some distance in the turbulent waters to assist a soldier who was floundering while pulling a large weapon ashore. Gately followed my orders, only to come back and report that he had been hit by machine gun fire in the shoulder while giving assistance. His expression said, "I did what you told me to do." He was evacuated later in the day.

Another incident that I remember was when an Army bulldozer reached a point some twenty to thirty yards from the high water mark when suddenly, I noticed there was no operator on it. I ran out to the "dozer" and after a few moments got it running and started toward the beach. I had not travelled more than ten to fifteen feet when one of my men ran up to me and reported that Commander Carusi wanted me off the bulldozer. "I was more valuable as a beachmaster than a bulldozer operator" was the message. A short time later we did get the "dozer" off the beach area. I think it was humorous because I always wanted to operate a bulldozer, but this day I was denied the opportunity.

Perhaps the most touching moment, in a sad way, was when a young soldier lay dying on the beach. I bent over him and told him to hang on and that I would send help. Dr. Jim Davey, Lieutenant (j.g.), MC, of my platoon administered morphine which relieved some of the pain, but shortly afterwards he died. I shall always regret that I did not get his name. He was so young and so dependent on us to help him.

The word D-Day indicates the day of the landing, but to the men of the 6th Beach Battalion, it meant at least three twenty-four hour days that became one long day. Each night at dusk, German planes would strafe our beach with gunfire, causing much anxiety and some casualties. Seaman First Class John Hanley (from Boston) was hit in the leg by a strafing plane while jumping in a foxhole and had to be evacuated.

The evening of the first day, our communications section sent repeated messages to the control vessel at sea that the Army was in desperate need of "bazooka" ammunition to repulse an expected counter-attack by German tanks. As it turned out, we did not get the ammunition nor the German counter-attack. We also experienced the fear and anxiety of a gas attack. An alarm was sounded indicating the presence of gas. All of us without exception ran to retrieve the gas masks that we believed would never be used. As luck would have it, the warning was a false alarm.

On D-Day, a college classmate of mine, Ed Gallogly from Providence College, Rhode Island, came to shore. He saw me and said, "Hi, Joe . . . what the hell are you doing here?" Ed later became Lieutenant Governor of Rhode Island.

The greatest satisfaction that the men of the 6th Naval Beach Battalion experienced was that we were the welcoming committee for the thousands and thousands of men who came ashore over our beaches and fought their way to ultimate victory over the German war machine. Among those we welcomed were Lieutenant General Omar Bradley, who came ashore on Easy Red near the E-1 exit to inspect the Normandy beaches. [See also CDR Morris Ness's account in Chapter IV.]

Following the Normandy operation, many of the Beach Battalion sailors served in the Pacific and took part in the Okinawa D-Day landings.

Joseph Vaghi was later awarded the bronze star for his heroism in removing the gasoline and explosives from the burning jeep, thereby preventing further injuries or deaths. All members of the 6th Beach Battalion were awarded the Croix de Guerre *with Palm by the Provisional Government of the French Republic.*

Journalist A.J. Liebling's articles on the Normandy invasion appeared in the July 1, July 8, and July 15, 1944 issues of The New Yorker.

Seaman First Class Robert
Giguere, U.S. Navy.

FIGHTING WITH THE GIS

By Seaman First Class Robert Giguere, U.S. Navy. Adapted from "My Personal History of 6th Beach Battalion," unpublished manuscript.

With my parent's permission, I enlisted in the Navy on my seventeenth birthday: June 10, 1943. After attending boot camp at Newport, Rhode Island, I was sent to Camp Bradford, Virginia. I was assigned to the 6th Beach Battalion, and was then sent to Fort Pierce, Florida, where I was trained in demolition. I think this was the start of what is now the Navy SEALS [Ed.: Navy commandoes].

We were sent back to Camp Bradford, then on to England in the fall of 1943. We were put in a camp at Swansea, Wales. This was the start of the 5th Engineers Special Brigade. We all carried packs and rifles and lived and trained with the Army. Finally in spring of 1944, my company was put with the 16th Infantry, 1st Division. We conducted maneuvers with them in southern England.

On the evening of June 5, 1944, we pulled out of Weymouth, England on *LCI(L)-85*, following other LCIs. This LCI was Coast Guard-manned. On board we had Platoon C-9 of the 6th Beach Battalion, a medical attachment of the 16th Infantry, 1st Division, and engineers of the 37th. We were part of the 5th Engineers Special Brigade.

I was below lying in my bunk and could not sleep, so I put on all my gear, took my rifle which was an old Springfield .30-06-caliber rifle, and went top-side. I really can't tell you what time it was. I was hungry and seasick as hell. A friend, Clare Mason, came top-side a while later and we talked about what was going to happen. As we stood there talking and getting wet from the spray of the bow, the battleships started firing. You could see the flash of the guns and see the projectiles going through the air and watch them explode on the shore.

As it was getting light I could still see we were following one LCI after another. As we stood there, there was a loud explosion in our forward compartment. We had just come out of that compartment where most of C-9 was quartered. Smoke came pouring out the compartment door along with a lot of my buddies who had been hurt real bad. We had medical men from the 16th Infantry with us, and they began helping out with the casualties.

The Coast Guard starting putting the fire out. I know at least three were killed in the compartment and twelve to fourteen wounded. All of them were from Platoon C-9. We were told we had hit a mine. Having no watch, I don't know what time it was, but I did notice we stopped following the other LCIs that were headed for shore.

That was when all hell broke loose. We were getting hit from everything. The machine gun bullets hitting the side of the *LCI(L)-85* sounded like hail hitting a tin roof. My friend, Clare Mason, was hit in the left arm. I put a tourniquet above the wound to stop the bleeding as the LCI hit bottom. The port ramp dropped, the Coast Guard linemen started for shore, and a lot of men started to follow. The starboard ramp would not drop all the way; it had been hit.

I said good-bye to Clare Mason, took off my pack and left it, blew up my life preserver, and ran down the starboard ramp into the water. It was up to my armpits as I began to work my way towards shore. There were very few of us that came off that starboard ramp. As I looked back, the LCI was backing off the beach; it had not been fully unloaded.

As I was working my way towards shore, I felt something like a bee sting on my left shoulder. I put my hand on it and felt blood and kept on going until I found a steel obstacle I could hide behind to dress my wound. As I lay there dressing my wound I could see machine gun bullets kicking up the sand as they were spraying the beach.

After they passed me, I ran as fast as I could to the high water mark and looked for a familiar face, but could not find one. I did not know what beach I had landed on. I think it could have been Fox Green, as I found out later. After lying there a while before regaining my composure, I ran out to help some of the wounded to shore. I had never seen so many wounded, dying, or dead. I had never seen such a mess: trucks, jeeps, tanks, halftracks, burning everywhere. The first wave was still lying at the high water mark. A big gun emplacement in back of the anti-tank ditch was shooting down the beach at men and tanks, and creating a lot of trouble. One hundred feet in back were two machine gun emplacements that were about fifty feet apart and were shooting over our heads at men coming in.

After crawling around and looking for guys in my platoon and finding none, the thought went through my head that I would not come out of this alive. Then I thought I saw somebody I knew. It was Amin Isbir of C-8. I asked if he knew where C-9 was; he said he didn't know. As I left going towards the east, I heard a loud explosion. Years later I heard that he had been killed.

As I lay there, word came down from the infantry officers that we would probably get killed here on the beach. They were hollering for "Bangalore" torpedo men and demolition men so we could blow up the barbed wire that filled the anti-tank ditch and start moving. I didn't know what to do at the time, so being a demolition man, I went to see if I could help. Two infantry men had already put the pipes under the barbed wire. The second man set it off and blew a path through.

I was asked to crawl through, so I took all my equipment off and the Army officer gave me two hand grenades. I think he thought I was an infantry man. I crawled through the opening and along the outer ridge towards the big gun emplacement. Everything was in my favor—there was a lot of smoke and I could keep down low enough so the machine guns shooting over the banks could not see me. I crawled on my hands and knees a long ways, until I was right under the opening of the gun emplacement. At the right moment I threw the two grenades I had with me into the opening. The guys from the other side of the anti-tank ditch also threw grenades over at me and I pulled the pins and threw them in as well. In all I must have thrown six to eight grenades and then got the hell out of there in a hurry because a destroyer was coming in to start shelling the gun emplacement.

As I was crawling back, I experienced the awful ordeal of having those 5-inch guns shooting over my head. After I had crawled back towards where I started from, I picked up my equipment and an Army officer took my name and told me I had earned recognition for decoration.

The shelling from the destroyer just about buried the two machine gun emplacements with sand and dirt. So an officer, or a sergeant, started through the anti-tank ditch. I remember him saying, "Watch out for mines; step in each other's footsteps if possible." He led the way. There were around fifteen of us, I think. On the way, we threw grenades into the machine gun nests to make sure they were knocked out.

In back of the machine gun emplacements, we found a path and followed it up through the bushes to fields with hedgerows. It was along one of those hedgerows that one of the scouts ahead passed the word—"German patrol." He gave me two hand grenades and told me to run down to the corner of the field and when he waved, to throw the grenades over the hedgerow. As the German patrol came down the road and passed the opening, the leader waved his arm and I threw the grenades over the hedgerow. As the patrol backed up, the BAR [Browning Automatic Rifle] men opened fire on the Germans. We inflicted very heavy casualties on the patrol.

We crossed the road and headed for Colleville. There were five French underground people hiding in the basement of the church of this town. They came with us and showed us where some of the Germans were and where we could be safe until reinforcements came up.

Late that afternoon American infantry patrols were starting to come in great numbers. I knew I had to get back to the beach to help out and I told the officer that I was a Navy man and had to get back to the beach to do my job. So I, the five French underground people, and some of the walking Army wounded went back to the beach. I was still looking for my outfit going up the beach, when I was blown up by mortar or artillery. I must have been knocked unconscious because when I came to, I was in the 40th Army Hospital in Cirencister, England. It was June 10—my eighteenth birthday.

Until five years ago, I never knew what happened to my shipmates in C-9, and it really bothered me. So, it was really nice when they started having reunions and I was able to meet some of the guys that went through the same things that I did. It was wonderful to meet Lieutenant Karl Hines after fifty years and find out what happened to the rest of the platoon.

I received the *Croix de Guerre*, Silver Star, and three Purple Hearts. One of the Purple Hearts was earned on Okinawa, April 4, 1945.

Boatswain's Mate First Class Herbert W. Goodick, U.S. Navy.

FROM *LCI(L)-85* TO OMAHA

By Boatswain's Mate First Class Herbert W. Goodick, U.S. Navy. Adapted from oral history transcript.

I was with the 6th Beach Battalion, Company C, Platoon 9 on Omaha Beach. The most memorable part of my experience on D-Day was going in on the beach [Fox Green] on *LCI(L)-85* which was commanded by the U.S. Coast Guard. We landed and proceeded to the beach at an early hour. When we hit the sand, one of the sailors from the Coast Guard [Gene Oxley] went in on the beach with an anchor and a line for the beach battalion sailors to follow to the beach.

After we hit the beach and the ramp was lowered, we had to go in hand over hand on a rope prepared by the Coast Guard man [Oxley]. The time was H+15-30 minutes and six men actually made it to the beach on the first landing. There were approximately twenty-six sailors on the *LCI(L)-85* and the survivors came onto the beach by other means later in the day.

This was when I found out the *LCI(L)-85* had been hit by German 88-millimeter batteries from shore, and when backing off Omaha Beach, also hit a mine. The LCI then proceeded out to a hospital ship to unload wounded and dead and was scuttled later in the afternoon.

We dug in a foxhole and stayed on Omaha for nineteen days, leaving to return to England, then back to the States. Following leave, I was sent to Long Beach, California, to join USS *Merriweather* (APA-203) for duty in the Pacific Theater.

Returning to Normandy for the fiftieth anniversary on June 6, 1994, I retraced my steps along Omaha Beach. Viewing the beach from the German batteries above, I realized how fortunate we were to have made such a successful invasion.

Chief Yeoman William
Garwood Bacon, U.S.
Naval Reserve (Ret.).

FIVE MEN AND A RAFT

*By Chief Yeoman William Garwood Bacon, U.S. Naval Reserve (Ret.).
Adapted from unpublished manuscript.*

On May 15, 1944, after nine months of intensive beach battalion
training from Camp Bradford, Virginia to the English coast, we left
for our marshalling area for the invasion of France. As the trucks—
loaded down with battle-clad men and tons of medical, communications, boat repair, and hydrographic gear—rumbled noisily out of
the strangely quiet and vacant camp, the feeling of "this is it" was evident on the grim faces of the veterans of previous invasions and on
those of older but inexperienced men. We could all sense that this
was not just another dry run; it would be the test for all the training
and individual initiative we possessed.

As we careened crazily down the narrow country lanes of Devonshire towards our unknown destination, some of us started to sing

186

some old songs to break the tension. Since most of our battalion consisted of young men averaging about nineteen to twenty years old, it wasn't long before our entire company of trucks and jeeps was yelling away lustily on such refrains as "Marching Along Together," "Caissons Go Rolling Along," and a beach battalion song some of the boys had composed a few months before. It was a relief to get rid of the pent up energy caused by weeks of waiting. Everywhere the British gave us the "V" for victory sign and they too seemed aware that "something was up." They had been waiting a long time for this occasion.

We finally arrived at our marshalling area, which was located on a large estate outside the city of Dorchester. Training continued; then, towards the end of the second week, officers began briefing their leading petty officers as to their assignments on the so-called "maneuver." Following briefing and training, on June 1, we were broken into groups called "boat teams," which were composed of both Army and Navy personnel, and loaded onto trucks. Once more it was evident to all of us that the "maneuver" was soon to begin. Our boat team consisted of 220 men, 41 of whom were from our 7th Beach Battalion. The balance was composed of infantry, engineers, MPs, and medics.

In an overcrowded port, we clambered aboard the USS *LCI(L)-92*, designated by the Army as USS *LCI(L)-531*. We were assigned to the number 3 hold, numbers 1, 2, and 4 being occupied by Army personnel. Once aboard, no one was permitted ashore for security reasons. We had been informed that we would not be in the harbor more than three days. Our quarters consisted simply of bunks stacked four high in rows so close together that it was impossible to go between them while clad in battle togs. As we scrambled down the ladder, we shrugged out of our packs, gas masks and ammunition carriers and carried them in our hands along with our weapons, in order to squeeze back to our assigned bunk. We felt reasonably certain we would be there for a couple of days anyway, so everyone settled his mind to that fact.

From June 1 until the afternoon of June 4, we spent our time playing cards, reading, passing rumors, eating our K, C, and D rations in shifts up on the open deck, and waiting to use the limited supply

187

of water in the two wash basins on the ship. Considering that so many men were crowded with their equipment into such a small space, there was little or no bickering or arguing. On the morning of June 4, a Sunday, services were held on the open decks. Few if any failed to whisper a solemn "Amen" to the prayers for guidance and protection in the great undertaking which we were about to experience.

Shortly after noon, I went up on the bridge with a pair of borrowed binoculars. I could see that many of the ships had left the harbor and others were getting up steam, including our own vessel. The scuttlebutt [rumor] passers were all sure that June 5 would be D-Day and that we were going to shove off soon. However, around four o'clock the ships shut off their motors and by morning of June 5, the harbor seemed full again with ships of all descriptions. They had been turned back by the storm, and the invasion was postponed until the next day. On June 5 at 1700 our flotilla of LCIs got underway. We were permitted to remain above decks until black-out time. As far as I could see, on both sides of the ship as well as fore and aft, there were ships, ships, and more ships.

Despite all that lay ahead, we somehow were able to sleep after our boat commander read us Eisenhower's speech. Some of the ship's crew gave occasional reports of huge armadas of airplanes passing overhead toward the French coast for the apparent purpose of softening up the "Jerries."

Around 0600 on June 6, the big guns of the Allied fleet began a mighty barrage on the invasion coast. Shortly afterwards, we began filing topside again for our morning ration of food. We all ate something because no one knew when we would eat again. Everything seemed to be going smoothly and very few of us inexperienced men could shake off the feeling that this was just another maneuver. Around 0630 the Allied sea monsters, belching forth their message of death, suddenly ceased firing as abruptly as they had begun. We dipped our mess kits in the cold, greasy water in an effort to clean them, took another hasty glance at the smoking and blazing shoreline, and ducked through the hatchway leading down to our quarters.

According to our schedule, our craft was to land on Dog White Beach at H+100 minutes (0810) through a fifty yard passage cleared by our demolition men. Our ship's crew were veterans of North Africa, Sicily, and Salerno and promised us they would get us ashore somehow. At 0755, with only fifteen minutes left before our scheduled landing, no shots had been fired on us and we were rapidly approaching what seemed and proved to be an impassable barrier. Nowhere in sight was the promised cleared passage.

Finally, with only a few minutes between us and our appointment with fate, our LCI veered sharply to the right and headed directly for the right flank of Dog Green beach. Some three hundred yards to the right of us, another LCI was drifting aimlessly, riddled by 88-millimeter shells. A machine gun was mercilessly cutting to ribbons any floundering troops who had managed to jump clear of the smoking and burning hull. On our left, among the obstacles, I could see two or three LCMs half sunk or overturned by shell fire or mines. Only one hundred yards from the first row of obstacles, it was still quiet—too damned quiet. I spoke briefly with my Executive Officer, Lieutenant Commander Southward, who was standing by the number 3 hatchway forward, and then eased myself back to a position of readiness beside the rubber raft of supplies that I and four others were tasked with bringing to shore.

Suddenly and without warning, a blast shook our sturdy little craft from stem to stern. A sheet of flames shot up thirty or forty feet into the air through the number 1 hold, directly forward of the conning tower. A fire broke out below and smoke poured out of the gaping hole torn by the mine. As if the explosion were a pre-arranged signal, the Jerries opened up with everything, 88s, mortars, and machine guns. Terror seized me as I witnessed the burned and bleeding men frantically rushing and stumbling past me, trying to get away from the blinding fire and smoke. I fought off weakness in my knees and struggled to keep my mind clear. Then I heard a voice yell: "For God's sake, somebody cut that blankety-blank line!" There, against the rail in the thickening smoke, I could see Johnakin slashing at the lines holding the rubber raft against the conning tower. Haines cut the remaining strands, and with the appearance of Artz and Bemiss, we dropped the raft over the side.

As Johnakin tied the raft's stern line to the LCI, I climbed over the side, dropped the remaining seven or eight feet, and landed on all fours in the pitching and rocking craft. Haines made fast the bow lines and I braced my knees against the gunwales to prevent my being pitched overboard while catching the radio sets and medical packs my shipmates began dropping to me. Artz leaped into the other end of the raft, and together we managed to catch all of the gear safely and stow it as compactly as possible. Next came our personal gear—packs, tommy guns, ammunition and canteens. Finally, Haines, Johnakin, and Bemiss dropped into the loaded craft. We began to paddle towards shore, some 150 yards away. Machine gun and rifle bullets whined past our ears or plunked into the water near our raft as we pushed our way through the iron and wooded ramps and poles, to which were wired teller mines. As we reached the surf zone, I marveled that we had not yet been dashed against a mine or riddled to pieces by gunfire.

We slipped off the raft into the cold water and pushed it in front of us to shore. We dragged the equipment to the water's edge. From our position to the three foot seawall was a scant thirty yards of open beach, already littered with dead and dying soldiers and unused weapons. Destruction and chaos enveloped the entire area. Troops were dug in and still fighting from the beach. It was even tougher than we had anticipated. All of this took just a matter of seconds to observe. I did not know just what to do next.

As we dragged the last bit of gear out of the raft, Johnakin yelled, "Hey Bacon, do you think we could make it out to the ship again? Some of those wounded guys will never make it ashore." "I'll give it a try if you will, Johnnie," I replied. So while Haines, Bemiss, and Artz pulled the unit's gear away from the water's edge to the shelter of the seawall, Johnakin and I quickly tossed our packs, tommy guns, and helmets on the beach and crawled around behind the raft to catch our breath before starting out. "Wow!" Johnakin cried, as a bullet ripped into the water where he had just been. "Those blankety blank blanks mean business!" A couple more bullets plunked into the water nearby and we began crawling backward out in the deeper water, keeping the raft between us and the beach. Bullets continued to whiz near us, but we finally managed to fend our way out through the barriers and obstacles to the side of the ship. In a few moments, some fifteen or twenty wounded or non-swimmers were crammed into or hanging on the outside of the raft. We all managed to reach the shore once again, where several able-bodied men helped take the wounded to the protecting seawall and administered first aid wherever possible.

"Safe for the moment," I shouted to Haines, some ten feet away. "Where is my gear?"

"Here is your helmet and pack, but someone grabbed your gun and ammunition," he answered.

I muttered something unprintable under my breath and crawled out of my foxhole long enough to pick up an unfired carbine lying useless beside one of the countless bloody forms littering the beach.

The rapidly rising tide and stiff breeze had by now swung our LCI around broadside to the beach, and it was slowly drifting through the obstacles towards shore. There were still some survivors struggling in the water, trying to reach shore. I could see two apparently uninjured soldiers about ten feet apart wading through the choppy sea in my direction. Just as it appeared that they would make the beach, I heard that already familiar and dreaded whooshing sound that an 88 shell makes as it zips through the air overhead. Wham! It burst so close that the concussion blew the men sideways under water. One staggered drunkenly to his feet with a stunned expression and then gave a hysterical scream, grabbed frantically at his face as blood spurted and poured down his face and the front of his jacket from a head wound. The mingled expressions of surprise, pain, fear, and bewilderment that he showed were indescribable. His buddy came up unhurt, and yelled "For blank's sake, take hold of yourself!" This seemed to snap the wounded man out of it momentarily, and together they stumbled past the breakers on the beach.

The amphibious tanks were holding their own with small arms fire, but the deadly accuracy of the 88 fire forced them to change their position on the beach occasionally to avoid being blown apart. Every time they changed positions, it compelled those of us dug in close to that particular tank to move with the tank.

Since most of our group were some twelve hundred yards to the right of our assigned beach, we took advantage of a lull in artillery fire to gather all the radio and medical gear we could carry. We began our trek along the beach, a trek that lasted some ten hours instead of the planned thirty minutes. We crawled under coils of barbed wire and twisted our way through wooden ramps and barriers washed ashore. Whenever the enemy opened up with artillery or small arms fire, we ducked behind burned out tanks or dug fox holes. At one protected point on Dog Red Beach where the situation was desperate, Lieutenant Carpenter, who was in charge of Dog Red Beach, requested that our beach battalion send a message to the flagship asking for supplies and men on our beaches. A radioman and I put a waterproofed radio set number 609 together, which we had been lugging along with us. After trying unsuccessfully for about an hour, we finally got a call through. All of us were beginning to shiver as the cold wind whipped through our water soaked clothes.

The Allied planes flying overhead with their wings and fuselages plainly bearing five newly painted black and white stripes were very reassuring, as we were quite vulnerable to air attack. Occasional broadsides from nearby cruisers and destroyers gave strength to the fainthearted.

My assignment was to locate my commanding officer to help set up our command post, so I asked permission from Lieutenant Carpenter to go further down the beach to search for him. Leaving my pack in my foxhole, I picked up my carbine and started down the beach. The seawall at this point was about three feet high, so I crouched low, ran about ten yards and hit the dirt for a few seconds. In this fashion, I covered some two or three hundred yards without mishap. The Army chaps I questioned on my way had not seen any members of my battalion.

I got up again for the umpteenth time and dashed another few yards. Suddenly, I found myself in the midst of about fifty or seventy-five men, all prostrate on the sand. Thinking that they were lying there, held down by gunfire, I threw myself down between two soldiers and buried my face in the sand. Suddenly, I realized that there was no rat-tat-tat of a machine gun or rifle bullets whining overhead, so I lifted my head cautiously and looked about. The sickening sight that met my eyes froze me to the spot—one of the men I had dropped between was headless, the other was blown half apart. Every last one of them was dead, apparently blasted and battered by 88s or machine gun fire during the assault wave. Directly in front of me, there was an opening in the seawall through which this murderous fire had probably come. Although the Jerries responsible had undoubtedly met the same fate, I did not wait around to find out. In seconds flat, I leapt up and put considerable yardage between me and that spot.

I continued my search for another one hundred yards without success. I then holed up behind a protecting bank for a few minutes to decide my next move. Concluding that my commanding officer had either hit the wrong beach or was among the missing, I turned back and retraced my steps to Lieutenant Carpenter's small group without mishap.

It was noon now, and we could see that the outgoing tide had left our LCI lying broadside to the beach in about two feet of water. Several men volunteered to go back along the beach and go aboard the craft for whatever food or other useful supplies they could find. Johnakin led a small group aboard her and threw down a few cartons of self-heating soups and some blankets to a couple of us. We broke open a carton of soup for noon chow and used the blankets to help keep some of the wounded men warm. I was one of the lucky few who had saved his D rations [chocolate bars], so we divided the three bars equally among six of us to ease our hunger. Our four beaches were closed to landing craft until the tide receded [1500].

Taking advantage of the receding tide, about eight or ten men from our demolition unit began scurrying around amongst the obstacles, hastily stringing wire in preparation for blasting open a passage through which landing craft could pass undamaged when the tide rose again later in the day. Just as they seemed to be finished and were grouped together fixing the detonator, a shell landed right in the middle of the group, sending mangled bodies flying in all directions. Some three or four did not get up and it was all that a couple of others could do to hobble, with the aid of their luckier shipmates, out of sight behind a wrecked and overturned LCM.

By 1800 the entire beach (thirty yards wide at high tide) was a mass of men, supplies, and equipment. All were waiting for the moment when the two roads leading off our beaches to Le Moulin and Vierville would be cleared of mines. According to invasion plans, these particular roads were to have been cleared for traffic by H+12

(1830). Then, the Germans opened up again with a terrific barrage. Many of us were speculating just how prepared we were going to be for a German counter-attack, since in our briefings we had been informed that mobile Panzer units were only eight or nine hours away from our strategic strip of beach. To make matters worse, the tide was already on its way again, and within an hour or two would cover most of the area occupied by the mounting mass of vehicles and supplies.

During the heavy bombardment we sought cover in the only direction possible, "good old mother earth." We used hands and feet to push the stones away from our bodies and dug ourselves down into our hastily formed fox holes as far as possible. A wounded soldier and I ended up sharing a fox hole. The shells kept coming closer and closer, methodically blasting the cluttered beach every few yards. The last ones that I remember hearing showered us with loose stones and small fragments of metal and debris.

BLAM! Something exploded in my head, making crazy patterns of dancing lights. My head swam and my entire body seemed to vibrate; everything continued to whirl, but with the fading of the grotesque flashes of blinding lights and tremors through my body, I opened my eyes to find everything black. From far away, I could hear my fox hole buddy asking, "Say mate, are you hit?"

My limbs seemed paralyzed and it was all that I could do to slowly mumble: "I don't know—I think so—maybe it's a concussion."

Now I began to feel a heavy pounding in my head and my neck hurt a bit, too. With extreme effort, I raised my hand to the back of my head and felt a warm stickiness that could only mean one thing. I had been hit, but how badly I did not yet know, I was blind and that was plenty for me! Fortunately, I still had a dry handkerchief in my pants pocket and the soldier kindly tied it about my head to keep out the dirt. Throughout the remainder of the bombardment, which lasted about an hour, I prayed silently and fervently that God would spare my eyes, man's most precious gift.

At approximately 2000 the barrage lifted and the roads to Le Moulin and Vierville were opened to traffic at long last. I was piled into a truck with some twelve or fifteen other wounded men and taken inland. We were laid in a row in a small sheltered area on the seaward side of a ridge which began its rise some three hundred yards behind the beach. Army men gave each one of us a blanket to protect us from the chill and intermittent rain.

While we were being settled as comfortably as possible on the rocky ground, I heard a sharp command to move an anti-aircraft battery being set up nearby to a safer position, inasmuch as it was exposed to enemy snipers still active in this area. As the soldiers disassembled the unit, I asked softly, "Are you leaving a guard with us?"

"Sorry we need every man we have here," came the reply, "but you'll be okay buddy, until the medical men get to you in the morning."

Quietly, they slipped away and I resigned myself to sweating out a long and eventful night, turning my immediate attention to wrapping my single blanket closer around my weary body to ward off the damp cold. Sometime during the night, some enemy bombers came over and bombed the ships in the harbor. The still of the night was often broken by the sporadic burst of a machine gun, or the "clank, clank" of a tank's treads as it changed its position to cover some new sector with its guns. Not being able to see, I could only surmise and imagine what was happening.

The boy on the left of me was very restless and his body kept jerking spasmodically. I did not know what his injury was. The lad on my right moaned softly that he could not stand the pain in his right arm much longer. The cold ground and sharp stones we lay on caused us to shift our bodies often during the night. It was weird lying there blind, listening to the jerky movements of the chap on my left and the heavy breathing of the soldier on my right. I dozed off to sleep many times for short intervals; it seemed that the night would never pass. Guns began firing more regularly again, so I turned to the soldier on my left and whispered, "Hey, Joe, is it daybreak yet?" After receiving no answer or movement from him I rolled over and nudged the boy on my right. He, too, was unresponsive. Thinking out loud I mumbled, "What's wrong with these guys anyway?"

"They are dead buddy—lost too much blood," came the unexpected answer from farther down the row.

"Oh, sorry," I said, wondering just how many more of our small group would follow their example before medical help arrived.

Just before noon on June 7, an Army medic managed to get to us and gave us each some sulfanilamide pills and a sip of water from his canteen. He explained to us that the stretcher bearers could not come to remove us until all of the remaining snipers holed up in the side of the hill were rooted out. He said that probably some time in the afternoon they would get to us and move us to an evacuation center.

Four of our group died during the day from loss of blood. Finally, just before dusk, we were carried down the ridge to the beach. We were examined and then carried to an evacuation center. Those of us considered critical were placed on a jeep and taken to an LCM around midnight. About twenty of us were loaded on this small craft and then we bounced our way out to an LST. A crane was rigged to swing us aboard on our stretchers. As I was about one-third of the way up, one side of the sling slipped off and I was raised the rest of the way with my head hanging down. We had no sooner been loaded aboard than we experienced another brief but distasteful air raid, from which we emerged unscathed.

We had our damp, heavy clothing cut away from our dirty bodies and were given sulfa pills periodically. The pills stayed down but the water didn't; I couldn't hold a meal in my stomach until about June 13. We lay overnight in the Normandy harbor to await the formation of a convoy, and late on the night of June 8 we pulled out and headed for Portland, England. We arrived at the port on the afternoon of June 9. Those of us requiring immediate operations were taken by ambulance to the 228th Station Hospital at Mansfield, England. On June 10, X-rays were taken and pieces of shrapnel were removed from my skull. One piece, which I still have, measured three-quarters of an inch long by three-eighths of an inch wide and weighed approximately half an ounce. It was taped to my wrist after the operation.

Although limited vision had returned, I was permanently left with "gun barrel" vision and back problems. I also continued to have severe headaches. On June 30, after some misadventures, I was sent to an Army neurological hospital in Chester. There, Dr. William R. Lipscomb, a distinguished neurosurgeon, determined that further surgery was required. Dr. Lipscomb operated, removing bone and shell fragments and inserted a large tantalum plate. During the operation, Dr. Lipscomb reprimanded one of the assistants for humming "Blues in the Night." He found out, however, that it was I, trying to keep myself in a happy frame of mind.

Quartermaster (Signalman) Second Class William DeFrates, U.S. Naval Reserve.

"LET'S GET ON WITH IT!"

By Quartermaster (Signalman) Second Class William DeFrates, U.S. Naval Reserve. Adapted from unpublished manuscript.

I was a member of the 7th Beach Battalion. Like all the beach battalions, our mission was "to facilitate the ship to shore operation." Our five hundred men, who had trained together for months in Virginia and, more recently, England, were divided equally into signalmen, radiomen, pharmacist's mates, boat salvage and repair men, and underwater demolition teams.

On June 4 we boarded USS *LST-372* with full gear, including generators and fuel for our signal lights. We were pretty sure the invasion was about to begin, although we had heard that rough weather in the Channel was causing some delay. The entire craft resembled a giant poker game with everyone playing in hushed tones. On the evening of June 5, the P.A. system came to life with the voice of General Eisenhower and his "Great Crusade" speech. There was no yelling and cheering, but I could feel a general consensus around me: "All right, then. Let's get on with it."

At daybreak on June 6th, I looked about me to see what can only be described as a scene from a Buck Rogers comic book. As far as the eye could see, there were ships: cruisers, destroyers, transports, tankers, freighters, and hundreds upon hundreds of landing craft— LSTs, LCIs, LCTs, LSMs, LCVPs. Some two thousand in all.

The combat ships were hurling tons of shells against the beach. From overhead, U.S. and British planes were raining bombs upon the concrete pillboxes, and rockets from the LSM(R)s were flashing like a thousand sabres at the hilly terrain behind the beach. All this time, men were clambering down cargo nets hanging from the sides of LSTs into smaller landing craft.

On my LST we were given a plan for disembarking. We would go in five waves of one hundred men. Each wave would consist of twenty men from each of the five components of our battalion. The first wave would leave at H-Hour, the second at H+1, the third at H+2, and so on. Muster was called, and my designation was given: H+4. I was to land in the 5th hour of attack on D-Day, at about 1100 hours.

There was barely time to say goodbye to our buddies. Things were moving fast. There was equipment to check and adjust. We each carried a full field pack plus cartridge belt. We each wore a Mae West life belt and carried a carbine, a gas mask, and a pair of semaphore flags tucked in our belts. Over our fatigues, we wore a blue suit of "impregnated" (gas-proof) clothing and a cloth arm-band supposed to detect the presence of poison gas. Some men were also assigned generator parts or binoculars to carry.

As H+4 approached, I found myself wondering about my fate. I had turned eighteen in January, was five foot three inches tall, and weighed one hundred and thirty pounds. I was in good physical condition and knew what my assignment was. I had not been trained to fight, but rather to communicate. I knew that my safety depended on how well the guys before me had done their jobs.

At the signal of our commander, Captain Caplin, Wave 5 started down the cargo net. The Channel was still very choppy, and the waves repeatedly banged us against the hull of the LST. Before we could settle down in the LCVP, Captain Caplin called down, "You men down there, hang onto the net and steady it for these other guys."

As a result, we were subjected to several minutes of further banging, as the elements lifted us up, thrashed us, and then dropped us into the LCVP. Meanwhile, other seamen were clambering over our bodies, dragging their gear with them. By the time the craft was loaded and ready to head for the beach, my stomach had rebelled. I sank to the bottom of the LCVP, my skin a pallid green.

"DeFrates, stand up and get some air. You'll feel better," said Ensign Bean, our morale officer. But at that moment, standing was out of the question.

After about twelve minutes of pure misery, the coxswain cut the engine, the ramp was lowered, and somebody yelled, "Everybody out." I struggled to the front of the boat and stepped off the ramp. My hand reached for my life belt and squeezed. Only one air capsule released its charge and so only half my belt inflated. I was half submerged and half afloat. Whenever I could, I managed to wave my hand and say, "Hey!" to no one in particular. Fortunately, one of our pharmacist's mates—named Snowden and called "Ears" for obvious reasons—noticed my plight and dragged me ashore.

It took no more than twenty minutes for me to fully recover. After all, my head had ceased to spin and my stomach to agitate. I was on solid ground, and my body was intact. I felt a sort of elation.

As my head cleared further, I noticed the shambles around me: twisted iron obstacles had been torn from their moorings and flung everywhere; wooden and metal debris from boats and vehicles were strewn about; a human hand with a ring on one finger and bleached white by the water lay on shore; *LCI(L)-91* [Scheer's craft; see next story] and *LCI(L)-92* [Bacon's craft; see previous story] lay side by side, their twin ramps swaying to and fro in the water, huge gaping holes blown in their sides by German 88-millimeter guns. Devastation was everywhere.

I turned away, and there on a sand dune perched Friekin, a signalman and demolition expert with our battalion. He had opened a gallon can of fruit cocktail and was quietly eating it with a large spoon. I remember asking myself, "Is this guy for real?"

We were soon united with the rest of our group and shown where our signal station was located. It was atop a German pillbox and commanded a view of the entire beach as well as of the Channel facing it. Behind it, a narrow road led to the French village of Vierville. To our right lay the beach of Utah, and to our left lay Juno. Also at our left stood the huge portable dock called a mulberry. It had been towed across the Channel to speed up the unloading of men and supplies.

Our business, however, was the open water. We divided our men into watches and set to work. Visual contact was made with approaching landing craft by blinker light or semaphore. We ascertained which beach was their destination, which outfits or cargoes they were carrying, and whether or not they wished to unload. We also had an important bit of information to relay which we got each day from the beachmaster: a table of high and low tides for the area.

Sometimes, we received a message which read, "Request permission to unload immediately." If the vehicles involved were waterproofed, no great harm could be done, but usually they were not. So we would reply: "Send in one truck for trial run. CAT will stand by." If the truck made it, we would give the OK to beach. If it bogged down and got stuck, we would signal up the beach to the Army engineers, who would then dispatch a caterpillar with a winch and long cable. Our underwater men would attach the cable, and the caterpillar would pull the truck onto the beach.

As the hours and days passed, unforeseen problems arose due to the huge numbers of men and materials being brought to shore. As soon as troops were safely ashore, they discarded their life belts. By D+3 thousands of life belts littered the beach, making rapid passage impossible. In addition, and much to the consternation of their officers, many hundreds also ditched their gas masks. A solution was found by acquiring from the engineers fifty foot rolls of snow fence, which we formed into large circular bins. When we were not actively engaged in signaling, we spent our time picking up life belts and gas masks and pitching them into the bins. We built some mighty tall haystacks in this manner, but walking became easier.

On the midnight to 0400 watch on D+6 a British landing craft, without signaling or giving an explanation, discharged sixty troops in about six feet of water. A few who straggled to the beach told us their mates were having a rough time of it, and needed help. We reported to our commander, who managed to provide two DUKWs. We fished the troops out, hauled them aboard, and brought them ashore. As we attempted to remove their packs and loosen their collars, they fought our every move like demons. Only later did we learn that British soldiers were responsible for their gear, and any loss was replaced and the cost deducted from their pay.

The next morning found them waterlogged and snoring on the beach like so many beached whales. Their destination was Juno beach, located east of Omaha. They dried out and shoved off on foot.

We slept on cots inside the pillbox, the same area the German soldiers who manned the big gun had used. On the morning of D+9, we were awakened by a lively exchange of conversation. We found representatives of the Army, Navy, and Air Force, who told us they were gathering information for an official account of how the pillboxes were taken out. We knew from listening to our first wave of arrivals that the guns were still firing when they came ashore, so direct hits from the Navy and Air Force were ruled out. We told them that Army tanks, charging up the beach after being unloaded from LSTs, had blown the Germans to bits by firing directly into the bunkers. Some of our crew had themselves carried the bodies out to make room for our signal equipment. Our visitors made notes and left.

On D+10, we heard that a small café was opening in Vierville, a short walk from our signal tower. I joined other members of my signal watch and paid it a visit. They had bread, cheese, and wine, but we could not converse. When I mentioned that I had taken a high school French course, they insisted I act as interpreter. I agreed to try.

"Combien du franc pour un verre de vin?" I said to the owner, hoping first that I would be understood, and secondly that his response would make sense to me.

"Quinze," he replied.

"Fifteen francs for a glass of wine," I told them, not knowing whether my memory was accurate.

They eagerly put down the money. He set up glasses, poured the wine, and collected his fee, which he stuffed into an earthen jar behind him.

Once the ice was broken, a brisk business ensued. When the first lull occurred, he motioned me over, and set a small glass before me.

"Pour vous, mon ami," he said.

"What is it?" I asked.

"Cognac."

It burned all the way down, but it tasted very good.

Back on the beach, mines were a constant menace to our presence on Omaha. The Germans had planted them everywhere—in the sandy beach, on the roadways, and in the fields and hillsides throughout Normandy. The Army, using detectors, had cleared paths for the new arrivals to use to reach their destinations. These pathways were clearly marked and separated from the uncleared areas by strips of white tape. In addition, signs reading "Keep out mines," "Achtung minen," and "Attention aux mines" were posted throughout these areas. Nonetheless, either through stupidity or illiteracy, a man would sometimes dash under the tape to retrieve a German helmet or some other relic as a souvenir. The results were dire. On D+15, for example, we received a message to send a pharmacist's mate to treat a shattered leg. Once we were asked to summon the Grave Registration Service for a fatality.

On another occasion, a DUKW coming ashore directly below us with a cargo of rations struck something which blew off the right front wheel. The driver was jammed against the steering wheel and rendered unconscious. A soldier who was occupying the seat across from him jumped out and ran down the beach as fast as his legs could carry him. We suspected the driver had struck a mine, but investigation revealed that his DUKW had detonated a dropped hand grenade.

We had come to expect some sort of surprise almost every day, so we were not too astonished about sundown on D+17 to see two hundred German prisoners, guarded by a score of U.S. soldiers, pull up to our signal station and stop. We heard our Lieutenant Billings say into a walkie-talkie, "I see you sent me some boys. What in hell am I supposed to do with them?"

That is how four Navy signalmen armed with carbines came to stand guard over two hundred German POWs until 0700 the following morning. At that time, they were loaded into the holds of LSTs, carried to England, and from there shipped to prison camps in the U.S.

The captured men were as meek as lambs. Nothing equals the blank stare in the eyes of a defeated soldier. It is a wretched sight to see grown men so cowed with no semblance of hope. They neither knew nor cared what befell them. One of them showed us his field rations. It looked like a combination of sawdust and what I imagined Chinese bird's nest soup would resemble.

Meals improved quickly as our stay lengthened on Omaha Beach. For the first few days, we ate K rations, first from our backpacks and later from supplies our officers gave us. These rations contained small cans of cheese or ham and eggs, biscuits that tasted like dog food, a compressed bar of raisins, figs, and prunes, sometimes a bitter chocolate bar, and small packets of instant coffee, tea, or chocolate.

This grew old in a hurry.

We soon discovered Army C rations. These cans were the size used for canned soup, and they contained such delicacies as corned beef hash, beef stew, and beans and franks. When heated in our mess kits, they were a big improvement over K rations.

Often, a carton of C rations would fall off a truck. Other times, we would mooch a carton from a soldier riding on top of a supply truck; he would kick one off pretending all the while that he was unaware of what his foot was doing. And more than once, we hopped aboard a slow-moving convoy and liberated a carton, as Mark Twain used to liberate watermelons in Hannibal, Missouri.

Ten-in-one rations were our next bonanza. They were designed to feed one man for ten days or ten men for one day. With them, we graduated to canned fruit, pineapples and peaches, tinned ham and beef, rice pudding, and loaf cake. I began to do a little experimental cooking with Bisquick mix in the ten-in-one. My crowning achievement was a pineapple pie.

This Robinson Crusoe existence ended about D+20. Captain Caplin reported that he had arranged for us to be quartered in an apple orchard behind the beach. Henceforth we would sleep in pup tents and eat with an Army outfit stationed nearby. He decided on this, he said, because he thought we would get a better diet at the Army mess hall.

"No offense to your pineapple pie," he said. "That was good."

From the orchard to our signal tower was a fifteen minute walk. There was a shortcut we could take which led through an area surrounded by a high stone wall with entrances through iron gates. In the center of the grounds was a chateau, now being used as headquarters for the military police. I had noticed lanky guards at the gates and knew they were southerners, because they had once intercepted our signal team when we were trying to go sightseeing in Cherbourg. They had orders restricting us to the beach area, they said.

One night, I had a rather long message. The other signalmen had been relieved by the time I finished with it, so I started for the orchard alone. I decided to take the shortcut to catch up with my buddies.

Omaha Beach had been secure for some time, but every day we were given a password in case some emergency arose. There were always two parts to it, the "challenge" and the "response." Phrases only Americans might recognize were chosen. For example, the challenge might be: "Halt . . . hot dog," and the response, "mustard." We had never had need of using such passwords, so we paid little attention to them.

This night, I had just entered the gate of the chateau grounds when someone shouted, "Howt! ['halt' with a southern accent]"

I howted.

"Hamon!" said the voice.

My brain went dead. For what seemed to me an eternity, I kept repeating to myself, "Hamon, hamon, hamon . . . ham and . . ."

"Eggs!" I yelled, "eggs!"

"Paison ['pass on']," said the voice.

Nighttime was not the proper time to use the shortcut, I decided.

One bright morning, I left my tent in the orchard bound for the signal station. I was walking parallel with the beach when I was over-taken by a group of German POWs closely guarded by American soldiers. They were doing double-time, hands held over their heads. There had been several days without rain. Quite a bit of dust was being kicked up by their movement. As they passed me, one prisoner jumped out of formation and ran along behind, choking, and coughing as though allergic to the cloud of dust he had been engulfed in.

One of the guards, noticing him, ran back to him and slammed his gun butt against the prisoner's temple. He fell heavily onto the sweltering sand. The guard left him and ran back to join the group. I walked over and looked at his silent form. The hot sun had already begun to bake a thin trickle of blood that flowed downward in a wavy line from the prisoner's ear. At my station, I told the incident to my superiors. I heard nothing more of the German's fate.

On July 19, I was informed by V-mail of the death of my first cousin, Private Bob Whitlock, on July 11, somewhere in France. We were the same age and had grown up together. But I had gone into the Navy, and he into the Army. I thought of the many weekends we had spent on the farm and in the timber at Grandpa Whitlock's home near Nortonville. War, I thought, has no heroes—only victims.

One night, we received a message by blinker light that said: "Send MPs at once." It came from a freighter far out to our left, which we knew had been unloading ammo into smaller craft for transport to the beach and then to the front. We informed the detachment of MPs in the nearby chateau, and they dispatched two patrol boats to the scene.

When they returned, they had in custody several very drunk soldiers, who had been assigned the job of unloading the ammo. They had somehow obtained a quantity of medical alcohol from the ship's pharmacy, laced it with fruit juice, and had a party. The ship's captain had called for help when the men began to toss the large shells into the Channel.

You must realize that all I am reporting happened on a few hundred yards of Omaha Beach. There were other signal-stations manned by the 7th Beach Battalion all along Omaha, whose men were experiencing similar incidents. And I assume there were other beach battalions handling the landing of troops and supplies on Utah and Juno as well [Ed.: there were].

Our days in Omaha drew to a close. In the latter part of August, we boarded an LST and returned to England. Although we were not permitted to have cameras nor to keep diaries during the invasion, certain things you remember—even fifty years later.

Pharmacist's Mate Third Class Leo H. Scheer, U.S. Naval Reserve.

SALVE AND SALVOES

By Pharmacist's Mate Third Class Leo H. Scheer, U.S. Naval Reserve. Adapted from unpublished manuscript.

I was in Platoon B-5 of the 7th U.S. Naval Beach Battalion. Beach battalions had three companies and there were three platoons to each company. Each platoon had eight medics, a doctor, eight motor mechanics, eighteen seamen, some signalmen, the beachmaster, and the assistant beachmaster. The job of the beach battalions was to go ashore with invading troops and work between ship and shore.

After a few months of training and maneuvers in southern England, we went to Southampton. There, on June 4, 1944, we were put aboard the Coast Guard–manned USS *LCI(L)-91*. The invasion was supposed to happen the next day, but a sudden Channel storm came up and canceled the plans for that day.

There were Army engineers from the 6th Special Brigade as well as beach battalion members on the craft. For some reason, on the delayed day, the Army men were moved to the forward hold and the Navy men were moved to the aft hold. This move probably saved my life and eight of my buddies' lives the next day.

On the evening of June 5, we left the port, formed into a convoy and started across the Channel The water was rough, but not many men got seasick; they were probably too excited. None of us slept much. During the night, the cook of the LCI passed out canned goods which he had in the ship's pantry. He said the craft would never leave France, but that we would probably enjoy the canned food later on.

We were kept below decks all night. We knew our time to land was H+30 minutes. This was supposed to be after the Navy Demolition Team, Army Rangers, and parts of the Army's 1st and 29th Divisions landed, if I remember correctly.

Shortly after H-Hour, we felt the LCI hit Dog White Beach. The winches began operating to pull out the gangplanks. After I disembarked, wearing an oily set of coveralls that were supposed to protect us from mustard gas, the ship began to back off the beach, but hit a mine. I soon found that swimming in the heavy surf with all the clothing and boots that I was wearing was not easy. The Germans were hitting us with everything that they had—mortars, machine guns, rifle fire, and artillery. When I realized that the possibility of getting killed was very real, a feeling of sadness and worry came over me. How would my mother and father react when they got the news? This feeling of worry over causing my folks grief stayed with me all day.

While swimming toward the beach, I helped a man who was thrashing frantically in the water grab hold of a log tank and landing craft barrier. He was so fearful of drowning that he had put on two life belts. The barriers that he was grasping had several mines on them, and as he thrashed about he almost hit one of them. I left him unwillingly, fearing that he would hit a mine and kill us both.

A little farther towards shore, I came upon an Army engineer who was trying to swim while carrying large radio packs. He was so exhausted that he was about to sink. I wanted to take the packs off of him, but he would not allow me to do so. He said he was supposed to get this gear to the beach and would drown before he took it off. I swam and dragged and struggled with him until we realized that we were in water which was shallow enough to stand on the bottom. Artillery, mortars, and bullets were splashing in the water and moving towards us. The Army engineer indicated that I should go on in, so I left him there and started crawling onto dry land.

I finally got out of the water and onto sand. When I got in a little closer to the breakwater, I heard some of my buddies yelling encouragement to me to make it on in. I got up and tried to run, but finally ended crawling on all fours; not only from exhaustion, but because it was safer. The breakwater was made of logs and was four to six feet high in the area that I reached. After a while, I realized that everyone was using it for protection. It was the front line, at least in that area of the beach.

As I look back on that day, I guess everyone who was on the beach was the assault force. As far as I know, no other troops landed that day, so it was we who were expected to clear the beach. After a while, an Army officer started walking along the beach—I think he was a one-star general [Ed., this may have been Brigadier General Norman Cota of the 29th Infantry]—and started organizing things. He ordered anyone who had a gun to stick it up over the edge of the seawall and fire away. Anyone who did not obey his orders soon got a thorough cussing-out. I remember one machine gun crew that claimed they couldn't see what they were shooting at. He ordered them to shoot up the hill anyway and cussed at them while he was doing it. After some time spent firing, I heard whistles being blown and the infantry began to go over the seawall. It was not my job to go with them, so I put my back against the wall, made a step with my two hands, and helped a lot of the guys over the wall. I was damn glad that I did not have to go with them. They were really brave men.

I joined Mullen, one of my fellow medics, and we started treating the wounded. We were trained to stop excessive bleeding, to sprinkle sulfa on wounds, and to bandage wounds properly. We were also to give morphine as needed. Since we had left our medical pack and everything else on the landing craft, we used the bandages that each man carried. We soon learned not to pass by a dead man without taking his bandages and water to bolster our supplies. We had no trouble getting lots of extra bandages that way.

We were supposed to move to our right (the west end of the beach), to our beachmaster's area. As we moved, we treated the wounded. Moving consisted mostly of crawling behind the seawall. One of our big adventures moving down the beach came when we approached one of the few tanks that made it to the beach. The tank was sitting on the road that went along the beach, and German artillery was trying to hit it, but the artillery shells were landing just a little long in front of us. After waiting a while, Mullen got up and said, "Let's run past the tank!"

For some reason, I grabbed him and pulled him down. Seconds later, an artillery shell landed where we would have been. After our hearts calmed down, we smartened up and started to time the shells coming in. There must have been only one gun firing at the tank and it took the Germans time to unload, reload, and fire. As soon as a shell landed, we dashed by the tank. We made it past.

When we finally reached our area of the beach, we found our beachmaster, Lieutenant Fox. He was wounded, as was our assistant beachmaster and our company commander, who had been badly burned from fire. Our doctor was missing. These were all tough, brave officers who tried to do their jobs as well as possible given the circumstances. They told us that we were on our own and to do our jobs to the best of our abilities without a doctor. There was no way to evacuate the wounded because no landing craft were coming in and more men would be killed in the attempt to evacuate.

I asked if anyone had seen my best buddy, J.B. Shuman, a medic, or Cletus Shoptaw, a seaman buddy, but no one had seen either of them. As they day wore on, we treated the wounded when we found them. Other soldiers would see our Red Cross arm bands and they would yell: "Hey, doc, there is a wounded guy over here or over there." We would go to treat them.

The conditions under which we treated the wounded were brutal. We had no stretchers, so those who could not be moved lay where they were hit. We had no blankets either, so it was a good thing that the weather was not too cold. We kept hoping that things would calm down and some landing craft would come in so that we could evacuate the wounded. When I finally looked at my watch, it read 1600. Although the day had passed in a flash, in other ways it seemed to have lasted forever.

I suppose that everyone prays when he is in combat. I first prayed that I would not get killed; after a while, I prayed that it would be quick when it happened. On the shore, along the high water mark, there was a row of poor guys who did not make it to the beach. The sky was dark with bomber contrails. We were told the beach would be saturated with bombardment before we went in, but the bombs didn't hit where they were supposed to.

About this time, I ran into my buddy J.B. Shuman. We were really glad to see each other. I asked him about Shoptaw, and Shuman said that he had been wounded. They had treated his wounds, but he was hit again, this time mortally.

As evening approached, we checked on the wounded occasionally. We still hoped to evacuate them, but had begun to realize that it would not happen. It was a sad and bitter feeling when we realized that they were going to have to spend the night on the beach. At this time, we saw a row of eight or ten destroyers coming in towards the beach. They were going very fast and the rooster tails behind them were very high. They went past the beach and then made a big sweeping curve until they opened fire and began shelling our area of the beach. At the same time the Germans increased their shelling. All we could do was lie on the ground and try to be small as the shells whizzed back and forth over our heads. This went on until the destroyers moved back out to sea. One of our signalmen, a fellow by the name of Thomas, got the Navy Cross later for trying to let them know that they were hitting the wrong places on the beach. There was a large pillbox at the extreme west end of the beach which I think they were trying to hit.

After this was over and things calmed down, we stopped to think about food for the first time all day. We got some K rations from somewhere. I'll always remember that when I opened the food and started to eat, I noticed that my hands, fingernails, and cuffs were caked with dried blood.

Just before dark we checked on the wounded around our area and told them as best we could that they would have to spend the night on the beach. One guy in particular gave me and the other medics hell. I soon had enough of that and told him that there were a hell of a lot of men who would never leave the beach. Before dark, my buddy and I dug out trenches for sleeping in the front yard of a house. Naturally, I got completely soaked with sea water coming in the trench.

I was awakened the next morning when a shell landed nearby. The explosion shook the sand edge off of my trench and buried my face. The battle inland was going hot and heavy and artillery was still reaching the beach. There were still no landing craft coming in, so we took care of what we had. We found some men that were missed the first day and some other wounded men began to come to the beach from up on the hill. I remember getting wire cutters and cutting barbed wire along the road so we could place the wounded along the wall for more protection. As I was cutting wire next to a post, I saw a small wire going down into the ground. I pulled the grass aside and found that I was looking at a mine about one foot in diameter. I don't know whether it had a pull or release wire, but that incident was a close shave. I marked the mine and warned everyone around about it.

Sometime the second morning, a soldier came by and told me that there were three wounded men lying just inside a hole in the wall. They were just a little way down the road. I went to the place and carefully crawled in. Two of the men were dead, but the third was alive. He had been hit in the hip and lower leg. It looked as if all three had been hit with machine gun fire when they went through the hole. I treated his wounds and made him as comfortable as I could. He told me that they were hit D-Day morning in the first assault, so he had been lying there without help for more than twenty-four hours. I told him that he would have to remain there as we had no stretchers and I was afraid to move him without one. I hated to leave him there isolated and alone, but it was the best that I could do.

Another incident I remember on the second morning was when an Army Ranger came limping down the road. He stopped and sat down on the ground beside me, and asked if I could help him. I asked him what was wrong and he pointed to his foot. He had a bullet hole in one side and out the other just between the toes and the ankle. I said, "Sure, let's get your shoes off and I'll bandage it."

He said, "No, to hell with that. If you took my shoe off, I wouldn't be able to walk." He got up and limped away down the road. Another soldier came to me and asked for something for a headache. I asked why, and he took off his helmet and showed me where a bullet had pierced it. The slug had spun around inside the helmet and dropped out. He didn't have a scratch that I could see, but he sure had a sore head and neck.

Later that morning, a British LCM came up to the beach and unloaded some vehicles. I went aboard and asked them to stay a while so that we could get some wounded aboard. A few shells landed nearby, however, and the LCM skipper pulled up his ramp and backed off the beach. I ran after it, cussing the skipper out. I picked up some rocks and threw them at the LCM and hoped a German shell would hit it.

Meanwhile, the Navy was still interested in the pillbox on the west end of the beach. In the afternoon a battleship [USS *Texas*] moved in close to where we could see it pretty good and started shelling the pillbox. We were only about two or three city blocks from where the pillbox was and it was something to see the three 14-inch guns fire, see the clouds of brown smoke, hear the rounds coming in, and witness the explosions. The concussion was terrific and the ground shook when the shells hit. Their aim was pretty good because when we looked over the pillbox later, they had made some direct hits.

Another incident that I recall from the second day was when another medic, named Tony Campanelli, and I were kneeling down side by side treating the wounded beside our now beloved garden wall. Suddenly, a shell exploded about two or three hundred yards down the road. Although we hunched down, we were stung by flying debris. We thought everything was allright, but then Tony said that his butt felt funny. He reached back to feel and came away with blood on his hand. He had been nicked in the fanny. The shrapnel did not penetrate; it just took out a little chunk. He got a Purple Heart, but took a lot of razzing about having the biggest butt on the beach and about now having a much-needed air hole in his pants.

Judging by the sounds that reached us, the battle inland heated up on the second day. The rumor went around that the Germans were making a push back at us and that we might have to evacuate. Some joke; we could not even evacuate our wounded. Some of us began to practice reciting our name, rank, and serial number.

By the evening of the second day, I had become accustomed to warfare. I and many others felt that if we had survived this far, fate was with us, so we walked around freely, only kneeling or ducking when we heard a round coming in. The mortar and small arms fire was over by this time, and we could predict fairly accurately a shell's landing spot by its approaching whine.

I was very unhappy about having to go around to the wounded and tell them that they would have to spend another night on the beach. The guy who gave me hell on the first night really gave it to me on the second night. I didn't say anything this time. Chewing me out made him feel better. The guy who was isolated and alone with his two dead buddies took the news all right. He was a brave man.

On the third day, our hold on the beach must have appeared secure, because landing craft began to come in with troops and vehicles. We were finally able to get our wounded off into landing craft, although this was at times a harrowing process. I remember one incident in particular when a mortar or artillery round hit the hood of a truck twenty feet away from us. None of us—the truck driver, his passenger, or us medics—got a scratch. Even the windshield did not break. The truck driver just sat on the ground for a long time, shaking his head. We theorized later that the hood caved in in such a way that all of the shrapnel went straight up.

As the third day wore on, more and more troops came in, and those of us on the beach began to feel more secure. We observed the looks of fear and terror on some of the new men's faces when they landed and saw for the first time what they were getting into.

When an explosion went off, hundreds of them would drop to the ground. It was sad to think what they would yet experience.

The first German prisoners were brought down to the beach during the afternoon and it turned out that they were from somewhere in Russia [East Battalions]. I was shocked when I saw the prisoners and realized that they were kids just like most of us. I remember one incident when a German officer complained that he and his men would get wet wading out to a landing craft. One of our officers told him, in no uncertain terms, that if we got our asses wet getting into France, we did not care how wet they got leaving!

On the fourth day, the ships began unloading in earnest. All day long there was a steady stream of troops, vehicles, and weapons across the beach. They continued right off the beach and inland into the action. The beach had not been cleared of mines, and several trucks were blown up when they ran over mines. This happened more often to the DUKWs, because they went directly from water to land. As the wrecks piled up, the beach began to look more like a junkyard every day. Floating docks were brought onto the beach and a line of old ships were sunk out a ways to make a breakwater. The Army began to take the wounded directly into the landing craft now, so we were finally left without much to do.

The next day we noticed that the fire was out on our landing craft, so when the tide was out, we went out and went aboard. I found my backpack, gas mask, and medical packs where I had dropped them on the deck. We went into the front hold of the craft and found that the first explosion had resulted from a mine. It opened a six to eight foot hole in the craft's bottom. An artillery shell caused the second explosion. It tore a three to four foot hole in the side and flipped over one of the gangplanks. The cook, who I never saw again, had been right about this landing craft never leaving France.

After about a week or so on the beach, another storm came in the Channel and the water got really rough. Small boats began to wash ashore and even a coastal freighter was pushed up on the beach. All we could do was to try to keep dry from the rain and watch the show. The beach was really a pile of junk when the storm was over.

About ten days or so after D-Day, a group of men arrived at the beach. They were the grave registration detail. These men gathered up the bodies, registered them, took their personal items, and buried them. I knew where some of the bodies were that they might miss, so I took them around and showed them. They asked me to help, but I didn't have what it takes. They gave the German dead the same care.

The days wore into weeks. Then, we heard that the port of Cherbourg was taken. We now had a regular port and were not needed on the beach, so we would be going back to England. When I realized that I was going to survive this thing, I had a feeling that was new to me. I was depressed and sad. I wondered how men could do these things to other men. I wondered why I was alive and not buried with all those other men on the beach. I crawled into some thick bushes in front of a house and stayed there all day. My buddy wondered what had happened to me that day. I told him that I just went for a long walk.

Boatswain's Mate Third Class Julius Shoulars, U.S. Naval Reserve.

ON THE 7TH DAY . . .

By Boatswain's Mate Third Class Julius Shoulars, U.S. Naval Reserve. Adapted from unpublished manuscript.

The greeting from Uncle Sam came in early June 1943. I was inducted into the Navy and left for boot camp on July 5, 1943. After boot camp in Sampson, New York, I thought I would go aboard a ship as all Navy men do. But to my surprise, I was shipped to Camp Bradford, Virginia, to join an outfit known as the 7th Beach Battalion.

There were twelve beach battalions in all during World War II. Each battalion had approximately 450 officers and men. Each of a battalion's nine platoons was assigned to one of six functional sections. These sections included command, medical, hydrographic, communications, demolition, and boat repair. The command section was responsible for the direction of all other sections. The un-armed corpsmen of the medical section tended the wounded of both sides during an invasion and also helped wounded civilians. They had their hands full during any invasion. The hydrographic section was responsible for finding channels that the small landing craft could utilize. The communications section took the place of the Army shore party communication section because the Army was not trained in ship to shore communications. The boat repair section performed repairs on small boats that had been disabled so that the craft could return to the large troop ships to bring in more troops and supplies.

We were supposed to land on June 6, but the beach was so littered with bodies, vehicles, and other debris that our A-1 platoon could not land until the second day. On that day, June 7, we left our LST and climbed down cargo nets into the small landing craft that was to take us to the beach. The channel was still rough, and getting into the landing craft was a delicate balancing act. We had to coordinate the roll of the ship to the rise of the landing craft. Some did not do this and fell ten or fifteen feet into the landing craft. There were many broken limbs.

When I landed on Normandy, I was nineteen years old. During the landings, I couldn't help but wonder if I would ever get out of this alive or in one piece. I could hear some of the fellows around me praying; one friend of mine was furiously repeating prayers on his rosary.

The first four days on the beach were the roughest. There was utter confusion. There was no water for a bath or tooth brushing or shaving. We had only a limited supply of drinking water and K rations for food. There were body parts everywhere. The equipment coming ashore had to run over bodies which removal teams had not yet had the time to move. Speed was necessary because of the extreme tidal variation at Normandy; delays could result in the loss of valuable equipment.

My job on the beach was to wade out into the water and locate channels for the small boats to use. Once I located a channel, I would place a flag on the beach to mark it, so that the coxswains could bring their cargo ashore safely. On the beach, I was constantly in danger of being hit by sniper fire. In the water, I was constantly being bumped by body parts that were floating just under the surface. I tried to condition my mind to block out this horrible experience. I could not.

In addition to locating and marking channels, we also helped the medics bear litters of wounded down the shoreline to be loaded aboard available craft for evacuation to England. Other jobs included helping the boat repair crew and assisting the communications section. We were so busy that I did not sleep for three days and three nights.

On the third day, I walked toward Pointe du Hoc where the Rangers had scaled the cliffs on June 6. There was still a Ranger kneeling by his jeep with his hand on the steering wheel—and a bullet through his head. He was dead but still kneeling.

Some men cracked under the pressure, including our A-1 platoon leader. He had drilled us diligently prior to the invasion and was very gung-ho. Formerly in the Marines, he had transferred to the Navy aboard a destroyer. Hearing about the beach battalions, he asked for a transfer to that rugged group. He bragged to us about the number of German pillboxes that we were going to take upon landing. However, as soon as the first shot was fired at us, he flaked out. He commanded us to dig a foxhole six feet deep and cover it with logs. We had to stand guard over him so he would not be captured by the

Germans. He did not come out of his foxhole for about ten days until another officer replaced him and he was shipped back to England. We never heard what happened to him. His replacement, Sam Byrd, had been an actor on Broadway and later became an author.

Other men performed admirably. The youngest man in the 7th Beach Battalion, Paul Hernandez, was only sixteen years old when we were on the beach. He had lied about his age in order to join the Navy [Ed.: as had Jack Hoffler, in the first story of this chapter]. Despite his age, he performed heroically. One day, without permission, he put two stretchers on a jeep that he commandeered and went over the dunes picking up wounded and bringing them back to the beach for evacuation.

The nights were not easy, as we did not know if or when we would be strafed by the Germans. Then, a few days after the invasion, we heard a shout come down the beach: "Gas attack! Gas attack!" Well, by that time, we thought we were pretty safe and had stopped wearing our gas masks. Needless to say, we were terrified because now none of us could find them. Fortunately, it turned out to be a false alarm.

The word came to us, after three weeks on the beach, that we were going to return to England. I cannot express the joy that I felt. I said to myself, "Well, old boy, you made it through Hell!" How lucky I felt. No more days of working eighteen to twenty hours. No more days without a shower. No more days of constant fear. My prayers were answered.

Fifty years later, I returned to Omaha Beach with a group of my 7th Beach Battalion shipmates to commemorate the fiftieth anniversary of the Normandy landings. Only then could I and many of my buddies begin to talk about our experiences at Normandy. My shipmate, Leo Scheer, expressed our thoughts well when he said: "I never felt lucky, blessed, or fortunate to have been at Omaha Beach fifty years ago, but I feel all those things now." Echoing Scheer, I have often said that I would not give ten cents to invade Normandy again, but I would not take a million dollars for the experience.

Coast Guard landing craft prepare to hit the beach. *(U.S. Coast Guard; National Archives)*

Omaha Beach looms dead ahead as U.S. Army soldiers prepare to disembark from their landing craft. *(U.S. Coast Guard; National Archives)*

"Into the Jaws of Death." *(U.S. Coast Guard; National Archives)*

Wounded soldiers are evacuated by Navy Corpsmen. *(U.S. Navy; National Archives)*

Wounded are evacuated on a U.S. Navy LCVP. *(U.S. Navy; National Archives)*

Ensign Joseph P. Vaghi, beachmaster, explains the value of invasion money to villagers of St. Laurent Sur Mer on June 19, 1944. Fifty years later, Vaghi returned to France to reunite with two of the people pictured here. *(U.S. Army Signal Corps; Joseph P. Vaghi collection)*

Beachmaster headquarters at Normandy. *(U.S. Navy; National Archives)*

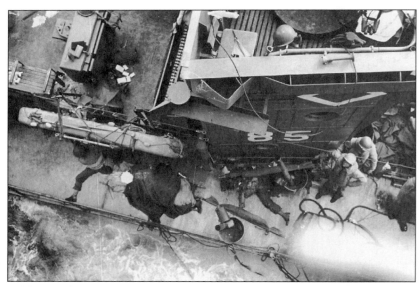

USS *LCI-85* lists after hitting a mine off of Omaha Beach. Wounded and dead are visible in the foreground although their faces have been obscured by censors. *(U.S. Coast Guard; National Archives)*

The damaged USS LCI(L)-85 with casualties lying on deck. *(U.S. Coast Guard; National Archives)*

Pre-invasion Roman Catholic mass on the afterdeck of an unidentified cargo attack ship. *(U.S. Navy; Robert Killie collection)*

USS *LCI(L)-85* prepares to evacuate troops and wounded shortly before capsizing. *(U.S. Coast Guard; National Archives)*

Garwood Bacon (front, holding raft) and shipmates drag their supply raft ashore after returning to their LCI to pick up wounded. *(U.S. Army Signal Corps; National Archives)*

Naval Beach Battalion members dive for cover during a German strafing attack. *(U.S. Navy; National Archives)*

U.S. Naval Beach Battalion command post. *(U.S. Navy; National Archives)*

During low tide, J.B. Shuman and Leo Scheer inspect the hole in *LCI(L)-91's* bow two weeks after D-Day. *(Leo Scheer photograph)*

Living with these men day in
and day out is a conditioning in
tolerance and selflessness that is
a paradoxical product of such an
insanity as war. Such a thing as
intolerance or prejudice simply
does not exist here, for it's not
real but artificial. I shall never
accept graciously any prejudice
that I encounter when I
get home.

VII
OF MINES, MEN, AND MULBERRIES

The Allies logistical supply line, stretching from North America to Great Britain to the Normandy coast, was vital to the success of Operation Overlord. This supply line kept the front well-stocked with men and machinery, and helped turn the tide of battle in favor of the Allied invaders.

The Normandy coast was chosen primarily for its harbors of Cherbourg and Le Havre, which the Allies hoped to capture quickly and establish as major supply depots as fighting moved inland. To bridge the interval between the invasion and the capture of those ports (Cherbourg was not captured until June 26), two artificial harbors known as mulberries were built in England and towed in several hundred sections across the English Channel. They were placed off Omaha Beach and Port-en-Bessin as soon as these areas were secured. The harbors were protected from the waves of the stormy Channel by gooseberries, or breakwaters composed of sunken, surplus ships. The Omaha Beach mulberry, however, was destroyed in the fierce gale of June 19, making the capture of Cherbourg even more essential to the maintenance of uninterrupted supply lines. U.S. Navy Armed Guard and merchant seamen manned these artificial harbors. The following stories demonstrate that although these men were in support roles, they were also in harm's way.

Many others in support roles also faced dangers similar to those at the front lines of the invasion. Troop transports, minesweepers, and repair ships were some of the many ships and craft that daily confronted the rigors and dangers of battle in their efforts to keep the invasion force armed and supplied with men, food, and matériel.

Signalman Second Class
Fred Harris, U.S. Navy.

MULBERRIES, GOOSEBERRIES, PHOENIXES, AND WHALES

By Signalman Second Class Fred Harris, U.S. Navy. Adapted from unpublished manuscript.

In January 1944, I had just completed signal school at the U.S. Naval Training Station (Newport, Rhode Island), and was assigned to a naval amphibious unit called Drew Unit One. After sailing on the *Queen Mary* with several thousand GIs, our group was stationed at the U.S. Naval Advanced Base in Roseneath, Scotland.

Toward the end of May our group was sent down to the south of England where I was assigned as a Navy signalman on an Army tug with a Merchant Marine crew. This was just one small example of the teamwork, coordination, and integration of services that went into Overlord. It was here that I saw some of the massive buildup of men, ships, landing craft, supplies, and equipment that had been cramming the southern seaports for weeks in preparation for the coming invasion.

The initial landings had already begun when we received our orders to sail. Leaving the Isle of Wight we joined a large convoy of auxiliary and supply craft crossing the Channel. We arrived off Omaha Beach just after dark on D-Day. I could hear the sound of gunfire close by and see the flashes from artillery fire in the sky.

Omaha was the most strongly defended and bloodiest of the five Allied landing beaches and by midnight the beachhead was barely a mile deep. Our job was to help position sections of one of the two artificial harbors known as mulberries which were vital to assure a quick and steady flow of men and supplies to the front until a major port could be captured.

Early the next morning (D+1), the larger, ocean-going tugs started bringing in the sections of the mulberry harbor. These consisted of huge, floating, concrete blocks which were partially sunk to form an outer breakwater along with twenty or so old block ships (merchant ships and freighters) that had outlived their seagoing days. They were given the name gooseberries.

There were also concrete and steel caissons called phoenixes. They were units with steel columns on each corner which were driven down into the seabed just offshore to anchor them in place and were designed to rise and fall with the tide. They served as a dock and unloading platform and were connected to the beach by pontoon bridges called "whales." Each of the phoenixes mounted two anti-aircraft batteries with crews' quarters. Many of the block ships were also armed with anti-aircraft guns.

During the first few weeks, the Luftwaffe bombed the beachhead regularly each night. We could see the colorful red and orange tracers arching up into the night sky like a huge fireworks display down at the British beach, and we knew they would soon be over us. The darkness gave us some sense of security until the Germans dropped those flares that hung in the night sky like a chandelier. They lit up the whole harbor like daylight and gave you a feeling of suddenly being exposed and vulnerable. When all those anti-aircraft batteries were firing at once the noise was terrific and nerve-racking.

Although the air raids did some damage, the worst destruction occurred when a channel storm—the worst in many years—struck the French coast about two weeks after D-Day. With gale force winds it virtually destroyed the mulberry harbor at Omaha Beach. Everything was breaking loose from the moorings. Small craft and larger ones too were washed up on the beach and smashed. Men were washed overboard and some drowned. Our tug and others were desperately fighting the wind and waves to assist the ships and supply barges in distress.

The storm lasted three days. When it finally subsided, the beach was a shambles and debris was scattered everywhere. We didn't realize until later what a serious setback it gave the Allied timetable at the front, and it was some time before unloading operations returned to normal. Finally, on June 26, the port of Cherbourg was captured and several days later I was assigned to a signal station there.

Looking back I can understand and appreciate the tremendous importance of those artificial harbors which kept the men and supplies coming ashore in those first few weeks and in no small way contributed to the success of the Normandy invasion and ultimately to victory in Europe.

With today's awesome nuclear capabilities, it is highly unlikely that any military operation of this size and scope will ever be seen again.

Seaman First Class Orval
Richard Allen, U.S. Naval
Reserve.

INNER VOICES

By Zora Schrieber. Adapted from unpublished manuscript.

This is a story of an experience my brother, Seaman First Class Orval Richard Allen, had in the D-Day invasion.

It was D+2 and his Liberty ship had been sunk just off the coast and run aground to form a breakwater. They were under sporadic but heavy fire. My brother manned one of the heavy guns, but all the men were exhausted, so they were doing this in shifts.

My brother had gone below to get a bit of rest. After this rest period, he donned all his gear to go back up top. He had to slush through a lot of water that they had taken on and then started up the steps to topside to man his gun. He got to the door and had one foot and leg outside, when he heard a voice which was very loud and very clear—even above all the battle sounds—telling him, "Stop!" He was so shocked and dazed that he jumped back in and pressed himself against the wall. The very next second, the entire area where he would have been was heavily shelled.

So if my brother Richard had not listened to the voice, he would have been killed or wounded. I know this is a true story because my brother was a very honest man and did not lie. He used to tell this story and he swore the voice was that of his guardian angel.

Signalman First Class Herbert Kearns, U.S. Naval Reserve.

LIFE ABOARD A GOOSEBERRY

By Signalman First Class Herbert Kearns, U.S. Naval Reserve. Adapted from unpublished manuscript.

I am a proud USNR veteran who served for three years in the U.S. Navy Armed Guard as a signalman, on board various flagged ships during World War II. In my role as a signalman second class aboard the *SS Audacious* (555), a Panamanian-flagged ship, I had the dubious honor of being on board her when we blew the ship up to serve as part of a twenty-five ship breakwater at Omaha Beach on D-Day, June 6, 1944. We had been selected for this honor when we came out second best in a collision at the entrance to Liverpool harbor.

Our English skipper had been in a rush to get home, and after the collision, we were deemed expendable.

We remained onboard her (with four feet of freeboard at high tide) for one week and experienced many harrowing and funny moments. Life was harrowing when we were attacked by German bombers and fighters at night. Times were funny when the old girl refused to sink properly when asked to and showed her underbelly to the world before finally doing as required and going bottom-side down (with the assistance of two British tugs).

Now, fifty-two years later, together with an aging shipmate from the *Audacious*, I play golf and reminisce about our youth—gone, but not forgotten.

"To our absent brothers."

Boatswain's Mate Richard A. Freed, U.S. Merchant Marine.

MOVING THE MEN ASHORE

By Boatswain's Mate Richard A. Freed, U.S. Merchant Marine. Adapted from unpublished manuscript.

I was aboard the merchant ship SS *Oliver Wolcott* on June 6, 1944. We had come over to England in the winter of 1944 and off-loaded our cargo in Plymouth. We were then sent up to Glasgow on the west coast of Scotland, where we were outfitted as a troop ship. Once this was accomplished, we knew that there was going to be an invasion, but we did not know where it was going to be. This was the early part of May.

They sent us up to the Orkney Islands, north of Scotland, where the sun did not go down until one o'clock in the morning and came up one hour later, at two o'clock. We thought that we were going to invade Norway at that time. But as it turned out, we stayed at anchor until almost the last week in May at which time we were sent down to Cornwall. [Ed.: The 29th Infantry Division was based in Cornwall.]

Around June 3 we started loading all the field artillery and artillery shells. Also on the third, 450 men of the 29th Field Artillery came aboard. We left from Cardiff, Wales on June 4 with the invasion planned for June 5. We were in the Bristol Channel, which is some distance away from Southampton and the Isle of Wight, where we were to rendezvous with the main invasion fleet. We left Bristol Bay about five o'clock in the afternoon on June 4, and rendezvoused sometime around three o'clock or four o'clock in the morning, off the coast of southern England, south of Southampton and the Isle of Wight.

However, nobody had told us young sailors that the invasion had been called off. We did not know we were supposed to meet the main body of the invasion group, and had absolutely no idea as to what was going on other than we were about to invade the continent of Europe. We sailed in circles all night and early on the morning of June 6 we sailed for the coast of France. This was about two o'clock [in the morning].

We arrived off the coast of Normandy about nine o'clock in the morning of June 6. We were about three thousand yards off shore. Evidently they had planned to drop the troops off quite a distance from the shore, and supposedly give them time to form up, but the British had argued against this. In retrospect I think the British were right, because we were much too far off and it was much too rough to put small boats out. On top of that it took them three hours to get in, and a lot of the boats were sinking, equipment was falling overboard, and all the men were seasick. Our group was supposed to be ashore about three hours after the first initial invasion. The artillery was the second wave to go ashore because the troops had run into a German SS division that was on maneuvers in Normandy and they met great opposition. The poor fellows on the beach took a severe beating.

We had a derelict ship alongside that we were towing. This ship had been torpedoed early in the war. It was a Greek registered ship that had a strange name. We brought this ship in early in the morning of June 6 and lined it up as one of the gooseberries. Explosive charges had been placed in the bottom of it to sink it in a line with others to form a breakwater.

We had to go back out later that same day because we couldn't get the men ashore, and we came back in the next morning, June 7, and at that time we went within two hundred yards of the beach and started to unload and get the troops ashore.

The beach was a terrible mess by this time. There were bodies all over, bodies floating in and out, and there was absolutely nothing we could do for them. You knew that those in the water were dead, and we just had to keep working to get our artillery and men ashore. While this was going on, the Germans were lobbing shells at us and they put a shell into the *Charles Morgan*, another troop ship, and quite a few were killed. There was also another ship off to our right that was sunk at the same time. The landing craft were running into mines and were being fired upon from shore. The noise was absolutely incredible. It's hard to even describe it, because we had cruisers firing and destroyers darting in and out, in back and in front of us. They were firing machine guns onto the shore at German gun emplacements.

It took us about another whole day to get everything off because we had to off-load it by booms and put it on barges. With the help of the Army men, we were out of there within two or three days, and we sailed back to England to pick up another load. We made ten trips like this to Normandy. We left Normandy early in September, after the break-out of the troops which was, in effect, the end of the Normandy campaign. From then on, it was a land campaign.

From there I was sent back to the United States and went on to the Pacific and to the Mediterranean on two different ships, but this ends my June 6 story.

Radioman First Class
James F. Meyer,
U.S. Navy.

THE DEATH OF THE "SUSIE BEE," PART I

By Radioman First Class James F. Meyer, U.S. Navy. Adapted from unpublished manuscript.

I was a radioman aboard the transport USS *Susan B. Anthony* (APA-72) when the Normandy invasion began. We had twenty-three hundred troops aboard plus six hundred Navy personnel.

On the morning of June 7, I was on the ship-to-shore frequency and heard a signal of four S's. I didn't know what that meant, but the communications book was right close to me, so I looked it up. The signal meant that enemy submarines were laying mines ahead of us.

I called the communications officer, and he said that there couldn't be mines ahead of us, because we had a minesweeper ahead of us. But about twenty-five minutes later, I was blown head over heels, with my feet hitting the deck above me. The explosion busted my shoe laces like they had been sliced with a razor, and stunned me for a while.

When I got my head cleared up, I looked around, and everyone was gone. A Navy tug was along our port side and I just stepped aboard her bow. They transferred me onto *LST-395* and then back to Portsmouth, England. I rode the *Queen Elizabeth* back to the States. I wound up with shore duty at the Norfolk Navy Yard at the fleet administration office, Building 48.

I have always said that the sinking of the *Susan B. Anthony* should have gone down in naval history. We had so many men aboard, but did not lose a single soul when she sank.

Quartermaster Second Class David R. Minard, U.S. Navy.

THE DEATH OF THE "SUSIE BEE," PART II

By Quartermaster Second Class David R. Minard, U.S. Navy. Adapted from unpublished manuscript.

During World War II, I was a quartermaster third class aboard the USS *Susan B. Anthony* (APA-72). The *Susan B. Anthony* was an attack transport and carried about eight LCVPs. She was formerly a fifteen-thousand-ton Grace liner that had plied its trade as a "banana boat" between South and Central America and New York. She had accommodations for about twelve paying passengers and, coincidentally, my grandparents had sailed on her in the thirties. Prior to Normandy, the *Susan B. Anthony* had participated in the invasions of North Africa and Sicily, and spent the rest of her time shuttling troops across the Atlantic.

We had sailed into Wales and picked up fifteen hundred members of the 101st Airborne Division (Screaming Eagle Division) and then sailed around the south of England. This was around June 5, and the shipboard chatter was alive with rumors of a large, impending invasion. We made one last stop in Portland, England, before heading across the Channel, and I remember how upset the harbor pilot was when our captain refused to let him off the ship.

At around seven o'clock on the morning of June 7, 1944, I was in the mess hall having a cup of coffee, when suddenly there was a huge explosion and my coffee went all over me. All of the lights went out and I thought that we were on the way down. The mess hall, which was full, emptied in seconds. As soon as I reached the deck above I knew that we weren't sinking fast, so I continued on up to the bridge, which was my General Quarters station. My position was emergency helmsman, but all power, including that to the steering engine, was out.

It seemed as if everyone except me knew what had happened. We had collided with two floating mines that had exploded just aft of amidships on the starboard side. The Channel had been swept of mines on June 5, but apparently the Germans had dropped parachute mines with dissolving shrouds the day or night before. I heard that two soldiers, whose bunks were near the point of impact, were injured. I asked the navigator (my boss), if there was anything that I could do and he said to just look out for myself. He pinpointed our location in the Bay of the Seine, and placed us about seven miles offshore.

The area was black with vessels for as far as I could see, and as soon as they saw that we were in trouble, the closest ones came alongside to assist. The first were two Canadian corvettes, and the ship was immediately surrounded. The troops had formed bucket brigade-type lines from the holds, where their packs and gear were stored, to the rescuing vessels. Nevertheless, many landed on the beach with nothing but the clothes on their backs.

Since I had no assigned duties, I hurried below to the crew's quarters to find my journal. The normally orderly area was in complete disarray, with personal lockers scattered around on the deck. The engine room, which was located aft of the crew's quarters, was ablaze and the passageway was filling with smoke. I finally found my locker and pulled out my journal and a government publication entitled *Survival on Land and Sea.*

When I made it topside, the boat deck was awash. The closest vessel to which I could evacuate was a seagoing tug (I believe its name was the USS *Robin*) and a number of my fellow crew members were waving and shouting for me to hurry. The tug stayed in the vicinity until the last signs of the *Susan B. Anthony* disappeared below the oily water.

Shortly thereafter, we were transferred onto an LCT and headed into a portion of the beach that had been secured. Our battleships were still shelling the coast to the south. When we were close enough, we pulled alongside another LCT and our ramp was dropped. There were four or five men on stretchers made from bunk bottoms on the ramp of the other LCT, and someone yelled for some help in moving them to our craft. I though it kind of odd that no one volunteered, so I did. The fact that the men on the stretchers were covered with Army blankets should have tipped me off, but I didn't realize that they were all dead until I noticed jagged bone fragments protruding through the flesh of one of their arms. And then I smelled them. They must have been killed early on June 6 and laid out in the sun all day. That smell stayed in my mind for days afterward.

Finally, we were loaded on an LST which, at that point, seemed luxurious. The quarters were clean, the bunks were comfortable, and the food was good. A number of the other crew members were also on the LST and we had an opportunity to swap stories and compare notes. I have never understood how anyone was able to round up all of the ship's crew in such short order, when everyone had evacuated earlier by the quickest and most readily-available route. Some of the crew had to get on the invasion craft with the troops and ended up landing on the invasion beaches with them.

One of the signalmen, a fellow named Ryan, was one of the crew that reached the beach with the troops, and was forced to take cover behind a disabled tank. He was a very compassionate and caring person, and aboard ship was referred to by some of the crew as Father Ryan. On the beach, he immediately started giving first aid to the wounded. I heard later that he was decorated for this.

None of our crew was lost in the entire operation. The LST on which we were aboard remained in the area for a few days, and then sailed back to Portsmouth, England. A number of us were sent to Scotland, where we awaited reassignment.

Chief Electrician's Mate John U. Smith, U.S. Naval Reserve.

TROUBLED WATERS

By Chief Electrician's Mate John U. Smith, U.S. Naval Reserve. Adapted from unpublished manuscript.

In April 1944, I was a chief electrician's mate aboard the fleet minesweeper USS *Nuthatch* (AM-60). Our ship had just picked up a cement ship from Charleston for towing across the Atlantic. We traveled at five to six knots across the ocean with three other sister ships, *Raven*, *Chickadee* and *Auk*. It took us twenty-nine days to reach Cardiff, Wales. After visiting a few other harbors including Plymouth, we ended up in Torquay.

After midnight on June 6, we left for the Normandy beaches. We were out in front and ships were lined up behind us as far as the eye could see. The sky was lit up by tracer bullets and even though it was the middle of the night, it looked like daylight. I could see the planes heading to France in droves to bomb the Germans.

As daylight approached, the battlewagons and cruisers opened up on the beach. Meanwhile, the Germans were shooting at the battlewagons and planes. It was a sight to behold.

Nuthatch and one of her sister ships began sweeping mines around Omaha and Utah beaches. Minesweeping went on for days, although the Germans were firing at us from Cherbourg.

On June 15, during one of our sweeping runs, we were three-quarters of the way into a U-turn off of Omaha Beach when one of our sister ships, which was close by, set off a mine with her magnetic cable. The resultant explosion rattled our entire ship and shut down our operations, for it had stopped our engines and made our electrical gear inoperative.

We couldn't move until our ship's degaussing was restored [until the ship was magnetically neutral]. In the meantime, the crew of a small minesweeper that had been hit brought all of their wounded to our ship. The decks and mess hall were filled with wounded men.

Our degaussing came back quickly, so we made it out of the range of the shore batteries and headed for Southampton. When we arrived, ambulances met us to take the wounded to the hospital. Afterwards, we washed down the ship to get rid of the blood on the decks and mess hall. We then headed to the shipyard for repairs.

When repairs were completed, we accompanied a couple of battlewagons and cruisers to Cherbourg to sweep mines on June 25. We were to sweep the mines so that the larger ships could get in close enough to shoot at the large German guns that were still operating. All hell broke loose because somebody miscalculated the distance between our ships and the shore batteries. All of our minesweepers were straddled, as were the battlewagons. The admiral in charge said: "Every ship for itself—let's get out of here!"

Our captain made a turn to get out. As we turned, one of the German shells landed about one hundred feet in front of us. Thank the Lord, it missed us!

The ships that were hit had to go back to the shipyard for repairs. The minesweepers in my division, MinDiv 21, headed for the invasion of Southern France.

Motor Machinist's Mate
Roy G. Settle, U.S. Navy.

SWEPT UP

By Motor Machinist's Mate Roy G. Settle, U.S. Navy. Adapted from oral history transcript.

I was assigned to *YMS-350,* a minesweeper, in World War II. We left the States in December of 1943 to go to the European area. For some reason, the sweep gear was removed from our ship and sent over on a freighter. A YMS is a rather small ship; one of the smallest or the smallest type that went overseas under its own power. It was only 136 feet long.

I spent my twenty-first birthday just outside the Azores. After staying there for a week or so, we went to England. Our first stop was Falmouth. As we were going into the harbor in late afternoon, the sirens started wailing and barrage balloons went up. We knew we were in a combat area. We were in almost every port along the southern coast of England.

One use for our ship, other than as a minesweeper, was moving mulberry portable harbors. We soon learned that the ship was not strong enough or big enough to pull those. Several of the minesweepers had their screws fouled-up by backing or by being pulled into the mulberries. It was then decided that we would be a minesweeper again. So we went to Scotland to have the sweep gear put back on. And from there we went to Londonderry, Ireland, where we stayed about a week.

Coming back into England, we practiced minesweeping in May 1944 as D-Day approached. A lot of the German E-boats came along and buzz bombs came over. In early June, D-Day arrived. And you know, it was supposed to be one day sooner. But when we got out into the Channel, it was too choppy for the LCIs, LSTs, YMSs, etc., so the invasion was delayed by one day. The weather was not bad on June 6, 1944.

H-Hour at the Normandy beach was 0600 [Ed.: 0630]. We were there, the minesweepers, at 0300 to clear or attempt to clear the area of any mines that might be in the way. We actually did not detect any mines during our sweeping operations before the troops hit the beach. And at that 0600 [0630] hour all hell did break loose.

A lot of German mines were brought out during the night by aircraft and would be dropped with some type of soluble attachments. They would float the parachutes away and then the mines were undetectable by sight. On one occasion, I happened to be looking toward the beach and saw a ship hit two mines. One on the bow and one on the stern simultaneously and that ship actually was picked out of the water. It came back down and went straight to the bottom.

We did a lot of minesweeping there for a couple of weeks or so. And then we were sent back to England for a few days of rest. I did a lot of praying on the way over for the invasion. I think that anybody who said they were not scared was not telling the truth because I don't see how anybody can be going into a situation like that without being frightened. I know that I repeated the 23rd Psalm many, many times on the way over there, before and after.

We went back over to Omaha Beach where our assignment was, and by that time the Army and other troops had taken Cherbourg. It was necessary for the mines to be cleared out of the Cherbourg harbor because that was the closest point across the Channel. Cherbourg juts out into the Channel and the harbor needed to be free of mines so they could use it.

On Sunday morning, July 2, a group of eight minesweepers was sent to the area to clear those harbors. We got there about noon and started sweeping. We started in the outer harbor first, moving on in closer to land.

Late in the afternoon, we started encountering mines that we hadn't seen before. They were going off sporadically, one after another. And it wasn't very long until all the ships had their sweep gear mangled and put out of order except ours. So the leader of the group decided that it was time to secure the operation and go back to Omaha Beach. And he gave that order.

Since our sweep gear had not been damaged, our skipper requested permission to make one run alone. This was granted. We started very close to the Cherbourg harbor. It wasn't very long until a mine exploded some seventy-five or one hundred yards behind the ship. It wasn't many seconds until another one exploded about half that distance. And it was not very many more seconds, about twenty-five to thirty, that one finally hit the stern of our ship. I happened to be standing near the stern when the concussion of the explosion pitched me into the air about fifty feet. The mast of the ship was thirty-nine feet high, and I was knocked out for a few seconds. When I came to and realized what had happened, I was above the mast and on the way down. The ship moved out and I hit the water, feet-first with a Mae West life jacket and thought that I would never get back to the surface.

There were some English ships in the area and they picked us up, took us back to Omaha Beach, and put us on a hospital ship. My YMS carried a crew of approximately thirty-two people. Ten of our crew members were killed outright and eleven were sent to the hospital for one type of injury or another. The other eleven escaped injury, although they got a tremendous jolt. Most of the eleven who were unhurt were up forward away from where the mine hit.

I spent the night on the hospital ship at Omaha Beach and then took off for England the following day. We went to Southampton. We went to a naval hospital at Nettley, England, across the river from Southampton. And it was determined after a day or so that I had a severe knee injury; posterior cruciate [ligament], whatever that means. My leg was put in a cast from my hip all the way down to my toes. And I also learned that I had a broken rib through that life jacket. I'll never know how that happened.

The Germans were using quite a lot of buzz bombs at that time and we could hear them coming over us. A buzz bomb sounded like an outboard motor. When it quit, you knew it was coming down.

After a week, I was transferred to a hospital ship bound for the United States. Following further hospitalization, I was eventually placed on limited duty. Near the end of the war, I was discharged.

Lieutenant Commander
Joseph H. Roening, U.S.
Naval Reserve (Retired).

Fixing 'Em Up on Utah

By Lieutenant Commander Joseph H. Roening, U.S. Naval Reserve (Retired).
Adapted from "USS Atlas," *unpublished manuscript.*

In 1943, the *LST-231* was commissioned, but shortly afterwards, was
decommissioned and redesignated as an amphibious repair ship, the
USS *Atlas* (ARL-7). This was a new concept, a repair ship that could
run up on the beach, stay there, do its repairs, and conduct diving
operations, all the while shooting down enemy aircraft.

I had been training about four hundred Seabees and civilian experts at Solomons Island, Maryland in repair work. Taking about 280
of the best for the crew, I headed to Baltimore, Maryland. We were
now ready to repair LSTs, LCMs, LCTs, and anything else that
needed help. *Atlas* was to be our home for quite a while.

The men needed training aboard the ship, so we proceeded to
Norfolk, Virginia and the Chesapeake Bay. Our captain, Lieutenant
Buell Nesbett, USNR, ordered pay clerk George Melbostad and me

to stay at Norfolk Navy Yard and assemble necessary stores and equipment for the ship. I felt that a repair ship needed more material than what I saw coming into our warehouse. Here was a good chance for me to go around the shipyard and do a bit of begging, called "cumshawing" in Navy language. Everyone was very helpful. We were getting loads of iron plate and everything else that a repair ship might need. It was like Santa Claus was here with us.

Melbostad, becoming frantic, said that I was going to sink our ship and that the captain would have a stroke. I told him to tell the captain that all the material had come in, and that I would take care of getting all the goodies aboard the ship.

The ship came in the yard and tied up to a pier. When the captain was asleep, my men helped load, and we put all the extra material onboard, filling up all sorts of empty spaces. Some were worried, however, that we might sink in mid-ocean, but I was watching closely the draft of the ship. All was well.

We headed up to Nova Scotia to pick up a large convoy and then headed to England. Upon arrival, we dropped anchor in the River Fal and started work immediately. We had very good, hard-working men, and were ready when the invasion of Normandy came.

We dropped our anchor on sandy Utah Beach on June 8, and stayed there almost until November. Our men did a wonderful job, and we were called the "miracle ship." We were able to take care of everyone, and did lots of diving, repairing, and chasing mines (that got away from minesweeps).

One day General Patton came to our ship, saying that he wanted the "miracle ship" and a "red-headed guy" with lots of Seabees and laborers. The "red-headed guy" was me, Chief Warrant Officer Joe Roening. I jumped off the ship and met him at the ship's bow. He said that he was having a problem with all his tanks; they could not break through the hedgerows. An Army sergeant had devised a solution by mounting a piece of angle iron on the front of his jeep at a sixty-degree angle, which served to cut down the hedgerows. However, the Army needed lots of angle iron and welding to get sufficient numbers of tanks through the hedgerows. I told him that I had all of the angle iron that he needed and six diesel welding machines. I said, "Bring in the jeeps, and we will take care of it."

I don't really know how many jeeps came, but it looked like there were two miles of jeeps lined up at water's edge. As soon as one was finished, off to the front lines it went. Patton sent word back to us that all was okay. The big tanks were on the move to the war lines to chase Germans. Patton was as happy as a lark.

Not long after, General Patton came back again. He had a big problem now. A British merchant ship named the *President,* which contained ammunition that Patton needed badly, could not off-load anything because the channel waters were too rough. Patton told the ship's captain to run his ship onto the beach. Captain Arnold did not want to do it, but Patton told him that it was urgent, and if he [the captain] did not come, Patton would blow the ship out of the ocean. I believe that a British admiral called General Eisenhower, who was extremely angry. He told Patton, "Don't you dare blow it up!"

Things were not well between the two generals. Finally, however, the ship ran into the beach, but the captain lost control of his rudders and smashed into an LCT that had been sunk by a mine. The collision knocked a hole in the merchant ship's plating, and it sank quickly in very shallow water. The British ship was now there for good.

It was rather funny, watching all the Army men climbing aboard the ship, like red fire ants, picking up their ammunition and heading towards the front lines. All was quiet for a short time, but the beachmaster wanted the sunken ship out of the way because it was taking up too much space for LSTs that needed to land on the beach. I heard that Eisenhower called Patton and said, "You got what you wanted, now how are you going to get that ship off the beach?"

Patton responded that it was an old ship, and that he wanted to blow it up. More arguments followed, so Patton again came to the USS *Atlas* and asked me if I could lift that ship off the beach. I told him that I would like to try it. The ship was down in the sand because of the tidal movement, and there was strong suction holding the ship in place. I told Patton that I would have to get all the sand out of the engine room and then weld plates over the hole in the engine room. I told him that I would need plows to make a dike from bow to stern so that the welders could weld the plates and not get electrocuted.

We had no heavy beams to work with, so what I had in mind was to rock the ship at high tide, with about two dozen LCMs tied to the ship's starboard side. I stood on top of the freighter, and when I waved a red "Baker" flag, the LCMs moved in order to rock the ship and, hopefully, break the suction. The LCMs moved, but it did not look like the ship was going to loosen. I was about to come down, when suddenly I felt a slight tremor. We tried again, and up she came; the suction was broken! The captain, crying, hugged me and gave me some Scotch. Captain Arnold had been a young boy on the ship many years ago and had moved up eventually to be the captain. This ship was his only home.

A British tug boat came over and took the ship in tow back to England. General Patton came to see me. He told the beachmaster to write up commendations for the men. Captain Nesbett was given a Bronze Star for the work that the "miracle ship" did.

"Can do."

Chief Commissaryman Harlin Kermicle, U.S. Navy (Retired).

CREAMED TURKEY AND OTHER TALES FROM USS *ATLAS*

By Chief Commissaryman Harlin Kermicle, U.S. Navy (Retired). Adapted from unpublished correspondence. Harlin Kermicle, the cook aboard USS Atlas (ARL-7), wrote this letter to Lieutenant Commander Joe Roening three years ago.

I was a crew member of the repair landing ship USS *Atlas* (ARL-7). I hope a time comes in the future when I will have the privilege of asking some bright engineer just how he visualized feeding a crew for six months (our fuel capacity), when at the very most the entire space for provisions would not allow more than thirty days with a crew of eighty men. When there were more attached to the *Atlas*, like its wartime contingent of Seabees, our complement was approximately 350. Thus, some of my problems.

As we cleared Plymouth Harbor, there was some excitement when a Charley Noble [a ventilation pipe] caught fire in the galley. Nothing of further notice occurred, however, until we came onto the scene at Normandy. Of course we went to GQ and then it became apparent that there were those in the crew who should have been somewhere else. Example: one of our supply officers—here was a man who didn't belong on a man-of-war and certainly not under GQ conditions. His battle station was the main deck aft, where the Seabee department had a .50-caliber machine gun on each side and our "main battery," an old 3-inch gun from World War I. This gun was mounted where the stern anchor had been on an LST. The supply officer drew and cocked his .45-caliber sidearm and walked from one side of the ship to the other threatening to shoot any man who even looked like he wanted to leave his battle station. A very interesting man to work with.

I believe we had GQ every night just about midnight, and on one occasion, the order came to fire the quad 40s (our other offensive weapon) on the fo'csle as a German plane was in sight. No shot was ever fired; the crew had forgotten to unlock the gun. Then there was the night when the Seabees got the old 3-inch loaded and decided the easiest way to unload was to fire it. My battle station was in the galley and that night there was nothing going on, so I went back to bed. But when that main battery fired, I just knew we had been hit. I came topside demanding to know where the hit was, only to find out we had fired our main battery. It was never fired again.

The greatest threat to our safety during our stay at Utah Beach was a German 88-millimeter gun stationed on the Cotentin Peninsula. The gun came out almost every night just at sunset and expended three rounds with little or no time to aim; it just shot down across Normandy beach. One night he cut our radio antenna—not a great bit of damage. If I read about today's Navy correctly, we should have been under a great deal of stress, but we didn't know that so we just carried out our orders. Captain Nesbett tried to get a [Presidential] Unit Citation for our action. Admiral "Betty" Stark in London didn't think we had earned one, and we didn't get the citation.

There was one other small incident that added to what was going on. I got provisions from an LST that had been hit and I was able to get some stores that had not been destroyed in the wreck. One of the items I found which we had never had on the *Atlas* was two cases of boned turkey. So to have something different, I put "Creamed Turkey on Toast" on the menu. The only problem was that, when it came time to break the turkey out, it could not be found. I tried again, but still had no luck. As I was searching, however, I noticed that the officers were being served turkey on toast. I found out that the stewards had seen the load of stores as we returned from the sunken ship, and they stole the turkey and had it hidden in lockers in the wardroom. From then on, the crew, not the officers, had turkey.

Soon after we moored at the position we were to occupy for the next several months, a survivor came onboard, a chief, who had managed to get off the beach, although just how, he was not sure. As we chatted in the chief's quarters, he took off his helmet, laid it on the table, and said, "You can never tell just what you will do under certain conditions. As I tried to avoid being hit, I just knew there was nothing that could hit me as long as I wore that helmet." It wasn't funny at the time, but he said it was real.

During the storm that hit on June 20 [Ed.: June 19], an LST hit a mine just outside our gooseberry and we tried to rescue survivors.

Not too many came to our ship. I recall one soldier who had a perfect cross on his face; his nose was split and across his forehead was a cut. His wounds were not life threatening.

The bow of the LST remained afloat for several days with a jeep secured right on the bow. All the time, our crew tried to find a way to get it off, but we were not successful.

I guess the greatest fun we had for pleasure was trying to sink an LCM that had capsized. We couldn't get it away from the stern of the *Atlas*, so we took turns shooting at it with a .30-06-caliber rifle. Occasionally, it would sink, then a day or two later, it would surface again. Finally, it went down never to rise again. Again, concerning the storm of June 20 [Ed.: June 19], we had a complete hospital unit from some Army outfit that came alongside until the storm broke. What a different way of life, between the Army and the Navy.

Very likely much more could be written about our stay at Utah. I do remember two pieces of German artillery that I thought were very interesting. Fortunately, I didn't have to worry about them as those in the field did. They were self-propelled explosive, radio-controlled, tank-destroying units. What made them so interesting was that when the explosive charge was removed, there was sufficient room for an operator to ride on top and steer with the control panel. The gun moved with a caterpillar track on each side; the whole unit was about three feet long and maybe two feet high.

Now it was time to leave our "Beloved Utah Beach" and return to England. I believe it was during the week of Thanksgiving.

Electrician's Mate First Class, Robert F. Yorke, U.S. Navy.

FIXING 'EM UP ON OMAHA

By Electrician's Mate First Class Robert F. Yorke, U.S. Navy. Adapted from "The Swivel," *unpublished manuscript.*

This is the story of a naval vessel that was not featured in any newspapers or television documentaries. She was known as the USS *Swivel* (ARS-36), an auxiliary repair and salvage ship.

Swivel was built in Wilmington, Delaware, launched on May 6, 1943, and commissioned on October 6, 1943. She was a wooden-hulled ship approximately 183 feet long and 65 feet wide. After a shakedown cruise in the Chesapeake Bay, she sailed in a convoy for Falmouth, England. She had a crew of about sixty-five men, including salvage divers.

On June 25, 1944, *Swivel* crossed the Channel to the Omaha Beach assault area with a mulberry unit in tow. There we found landing craft of all shapes and sizes strewn all over the beaches. *Swivel* immediately began the work of clearing the beaches of these craft to expedite the landing of troops and supplies. She also towed several ships back to England including the *LST-512*, which had been thrust up on the beach and across the pontoon landing, breaking her back [keel] in the process. Railroad tracks were welded to the deck and after several attempts, *LST-512* was floated and towed back to England.

There were many months of this type of work at Omaha and Utah beaches. *Swivel* also went to the southern coast of France to rescue a patrol craft hit by enemy fire and returned the craft to England.

In November she proceeded to Le Havre, France, and assisted in clearing the harbor. She then moved to Cherbourg on Christmas Day, 1944, where she received a battle star, and assisted in clearing that harbor. She remained there until June 27, 1945. She then returned to Le Havre and engaged in clearing screws, inspecting underwater bottoms and making temporary repairs. On January 10, 1946, she received a commendation from the war shipping administration.

Swivel was always on call and ready for any assignment. An LST hit a mine on the Seine River near Rouen, France. We were dispatched to the site and determined that the ship had to be beached. We then proceeded to remove everything that could be salvaged and returned the equipment to England. The LST was abandoned at that point and left for the locals.

Swivel returned to the United States in October 1945. She was judged to be beyond economical repair, declared surplus, and disposed of in June 1946. Here's a little poem a fellow shipmate wrote about her:

Swivel

Here on the battle-scarred Atlantic,
There steams a battle tug gigantic.
Short-handed and three-fourths reserve,
She doesn't get the credit that she deserves.

We have our radio and bridge gang too,
The engineers and deck force make up the crew.
We also carry divers, seven told,
And they bunk down in the salvage hold.

United and faithful we all stand together,
And manage to ride the worst kind of weather.
Not very scared though mostly alone,
We'll move with our tows through any war zone.

At times we wonder what it's like to fight,
As we dodge the subs during the night.
At times we are not so lucky of course,
As we maneuver around an enemy task force.

Millimeters fly and depth charges fall,
Yes, even a tug can be on the ball.
Now mates on the wagons and flat tops too,
We have our work but still envy you.

And like all others we know that it's true,
The heavy fighting is left to you.
But when the battle is over and the clean-up begins,
Fighters stand out and the tugs steam in.

Swivel's the name, just a tug,
But the beaches to her are just like a rug.
She'll clear them and clear them and even do more,
Believe me, without her, you couldn't win the war.

A mulberry caisson rests in an English harbor following its construction at Portsmouth Dockyard in March 1944. *(U.S. Navy; National Archives)*

A phoenix caisson is towed across the English Channel by the tug *Dexterous* for use in a mulberry harbor. *(U.S. Navy; National Archives)*

The June 19 storm batters the Omaha Beach mulberry. *(U.S. Coast Guard; National Archives)*

Remains of Omaha's mulberry fifty-two years after the invasion. *(Photograph by editor)*

A line of sunken merchant ships forms Utah Beach's gooseberry. *(U.S. Navy; National Archives)*

YMS-350 was not the only minesweeper fatality. On D+1, USS *Tide* (AM-125) sank off Omaha Beach after hitting a mine. USS *PT-509* and USS *Pheasant* (AM-61) stand by the stricken ship. *(U.S. Navy; National Archives)*

Members of the 2d Beach Battalion experiment with German radio-controlled tanks. *(U.S. Navy; National Archives)*

USS *Swivel* (ARS-36) en route to Cherbourg Harbor to assist in salvage operations. *(U.S. Navy; National Archives)*

For ten months I've been awed by the tremendous enormity of war material—the thousands upon thousands of planes and tanks and tons upon tons of explosives and death we were amassing on every road, field, and harbor in England. And since D-Day it's all been pouring through these beaches in a fantastic flood that staggers the imagination. But it's only the surgery. Whether the patient lives is what's really important.

VIII
MOPPING UP

The successful capture of the Normandy beaches was only the beginning of a year-long quest to free Europe from the suffocating embrace of the Third Reich. Operation Neptune was far from over after D-Day, and during the course of the next few weeks, more than 700,000 men and 100,000 vehicles would disembark from naval ships and craft. Neptune officially ended on June 24; on June 26, Cherbourg was captured and the Allies finally had a port to serve as a supply depot.

The following stories describe the roles that special naval task units played in the aftermath of the immediate invasion. Although they were not there at D-Day, the authors of these accounts were an integral part of Operation Neptune. More valuable than bullets, the intelligence that these men provided assisted Allied planners in plotting their advance off the invasion beaches and into Europe. The efforts of these task unit officers contributed to the success of what British Prime Minister Winston Churchill claimed was "undoubtedly the most complicated and difficult [invasion] that has ever taken place."

Lieutenant Angus
MacLean Thuermer,
U.S. Naval Reserve.

INTERROGATING THE GERMANS

By Lieutenant Angus MacLean Thuermer, U.S. Naval Reserve. Adapted
from "D-Day: You Went East, I Went West," unpublished manuscript; and
oral history transcript.

On D-Day, my shipmates forged eastward to dash ashore on the
Normandy beaches with the Big Red One and the Ivy Leaf, divisions. There, crouched down in the beach sand and under
whizzing bullets, these intelligence specialists interrogated German sailors.

On D-Day, I forged westward from London to dash into the barracks of the Wiltshire Regiment. Crouched down in a bouncing jeep,
I arrived in the town of Devises. From the Normandy beaches, my

shipmates and U.S. Army intelligence sent Kriegsmarine prisoners to us.

Although I'd been cleared as a "BIGOT"—had a complete top secret briefing all about the date and place of the Overlord operation—my chances of getting to Normandy seemed to be getting slimmer. [Ed.: The word "BIGOT" was the reversal of the words "To Gib," which was stamped on orders for those headed for Gibraltar and the invasion of North Africa in late 1942. This designation was later applied to those who were briefed on the Normandy invasion plans.] Among my intelligence shipmates, Lieutenant John Guise Lyons went ashore on Utah with the Ivy Leaf, the 4th Division, and Lieutenant Philo Tolman Dibble landed on Omaha with the Big Red One, the 1st Division. They helped pick knowledgeable POWs to send back to us for further interrogation.

With all the concentration and publicity on D-Day, it is hard to remember that at about the same time the Kriegsmarine's U-boat packs were playing hob with our convoys. We wanted to know why. We tried to learn from the POWs whether they had attended Torpedoschule, and if they had learned, at this school, anything about torpedo trigger number 7. This was in deadly earnest. We wanted to know how that trigger ignited a U-boat torpedo.

On Omaha, Dibble was called back off the beach to the flagship of Admiral Alan Kirk. He turned up looking mighty scruffy in Army khakis and a Navy helmet and was taken to the bridge. There, Admiral Kirk asked him what the prisoners were saying. He replied, "Sir, prisoners have said that the naval bombardment is so accurate that some have asked me whether we have a magic eye.'"

The admiral smiled and said, "Thank you lieutenant," and my comrade was sent back ashore.

The only bridge I was on was the one over a stream leading to the city previously known to me from a limerick. It can only be repeated in its Bowdlerized form:

There once was a man from Devises
Who had ears of two different sizes.
One was so small
It was no good at all;
The other had won several prizes.

268

I had no interest in Devises, or in squatting in the barracks of its gallant regiment which was fighting overseas. The town seemed to be devoted solely to making gunny sacking from jute. But what about the girls who worked in the mills and strolled down the street after work? Hanging heavily upon them was the scent of jute, the ultimate stink.

This was an added incentive to get over to Normandy, "the far shore" as the "in" phrase of day had it. For me, a less serious aspect of getting over to France had to do with my earlier days as a student. I was to have studied in Paris. This never happened. So, my first look at those world-renowned, chic French mademoiselles was going to have to wait until the landings in Normandy.

Finally, at an embarrassingly delayed "D-plus-something," I landed in Normandy. Two of our returning D-Day "veteran" shipmates from the 12th Fleet's Forward Intelligence Unit—the "FIU"—as our outfit was called, were with me as we went ashore from a U.S. Coast Guard cutter—which brought twenty-six Red Cross girls to Normandy.

But we made the best of it (and didn't mention the Red Cross girls in any "I have landed on the Far Shore" letters home). It was a medium-delightful, dry-footed disembarkation at the artificial harbor at Omaha Beach. Then, there followed a scenic jeep ride through coastal Normandy. We drove along the liberated strip of coastline to right behind Utah Beach into La real, genuine, belle France, the French countryside. We proceeded to the French village of Ste. Marie du Mont, and to our unit headquarters at the sturdy, great, French farmhouse of M. Hebert, sturdy French citizen, sturdy French farmer.

And it was there that I finally saw my first French mademoiselle. She was the hired girl; she was standing at the side of the Hebert house in a shapeless cotton dress, a pitchfork in her hands, up to her calves in real French cow manure.

Upon my recovery from this shock, we got on with the practice of naval intelligence in Normandy. All intelligence did not begin with the CIA, and most certainly not with the OSS, despite all their genteel hints. Aside from the Moses business in the land of Canaan, in more recent times, Great Britain has been a preeminent intelligence power.

That is especially true of naval intelligence. The oldest established part of the Royal Navy is the Naval Intelligence Division. That should surprise no one who has been awake. Our FIU (officially it was Task Unit 125.8) was closely associated with British naval intelligence. The Royal Navy also had a Forward Intelligence Unit. We worked with them. Encased in their FIU was a Royal Marine outfit known as the 30 Assault Unit. In the Admiralty, Commander Ian Fleming, RNVR, the creator of James Bond, was its chief. The assault unit's number, "30," did not mean there were at least twenty-nine other assault units. The "30" was the number on Commander Fleming's door in the Admiralty basement. We worked along with 30 AU in Normandy until the time came for them—with their orders signed by the Supreme Commander—to shoot up through American lines to Cherbourg to hit an intelligence target. They tried to get to enemy intelligence gold mines, headquarters and the like, before they were destroyed by the surrendering Germans or blown to bits by the U.S. Army.

In Normandy, our FIU had a colorful mix of men in navy blue. They tried hard, but there wasn't a real sailor in the whole outfit. For instance, I had been a language student and then an Associated Press correspondent in Berlin. I did my business in German. At one time in a headquarters slot, my yeoman—he emptied my "out" tray and put stuff in my "in" tray—was a Ph.D. from the University of Chicago. Hardly taxing on his talents.

This same high class arrangement persisted generally in the FIU: my shipmates included two distinguished Harvard University professors, a university ornithologist, a missionary of the gospel, a nationally known artist, and a professor of Greek at Vassar.

Whatever other funny occupation they had, they all spoke foreign languages. There was not a drop of tar in or on one of them, but they made a good effort to be "Navy."

Yes, and all of us came face-to-face with the enemy; those whom I encountered I met in sanitary conditions while interrogating them as prisoners of war.

One of the techniques we used in interrogating German prisoners was to pose as knowing more than we did. The German U-boat service had a practice aimed at maintaining the health of the U-boat crews. When the U-boat crews went ashore in the French ports they had occupied and visited German Navy bordellos, they were given a little card that said, "Wehrmacht bordello number such and such," and the name of the partner of the sailor. Her name was inscribed on a little card that they were instructed to keep. So they went to sea with a packet of these cards in their back pocket.

When their U-boat was sunk and they were fished out of the water, they forgot about their cards. By the time they were brought to interrogation, the packet of cards had been taken from them. So the interrogation officer sat there with the sailor in front of him and these cards spread out discreetly in the officer's lap. Then the interrogator would ask, "Well, is good old Isabella still functioning down at bordello number such and such? Ha, ha, ha." And then we would ask the sailor, "Well, how are things down at the Café Sechs Titten?" The Café Sechs Titten (Café Six Tits) was the name given to a French café named the Café Trois Soeurs (Three Sisters' Café). German sailors thought that we were really "in" when we knew this slang and this joke—"three sisters" translated into "six tits" in German Navy parlance. Thus, they would be more inclined to talk.

At about this point, we would bring around the conversation to the question: "So, do you have any relatives in the United States?" Well, everybody had some relative who lived in Milwaukee at one time or another, and it often turned out that they [the interrogees] had too.

We'd reply, "Oh my goodness, that's ole Fritz. Why, we know him well, yes, a good chap." As the sailor opened up, we could then slip in the questions, "Did you ever attend torpedo school and when?" and "Did you study the ignition device of trigger number 7?" In this way, we were able to obtain information from our prisoners.

One other tactic we used in interrogation was to pose as more senior than we actually were. I remember one officer declined to be interrogated by a junior officer such as myself. So, I asked our assistant chief of staff in London to lend me his captain's shoulder boards. Later I, the youngest-looking captain in the United States Navy, interrogated this man of equal rank.

Exceptionally, Lieutenant Joseph Kaitz's FIU career in Normandy was different from the rest of ours; he spoke no foreign language except New York City American. Nor did Chris Chattaway, the other half of a two-man team somehow extracted from New York's crime-fighting governor, Tom Dewey. What they did most of their Navy time I never did find out, which was perfectly proper. It was none of my business. One thing became clear when they joined the FIU in Normandy, however. They were direct action fellows.

But there were occasions when what was needed was pretty straightforward: entry into a safe in some recently evacuated German Navy headquarters. In it, for dead certain, were some GEHEIM documents. The FIU linguist/POW interrogators/enemy-document mavens and the like were pained to hear a London based Naval Reserve lieutenant commander speak of the need to get "those GEHEIM documents the Nazis have." Everyone else in the unit knew enemy secret papers were marked GEHEIM, and except for the London fellow, they all knew how to pronounce the word correctly, too. Inspecting the locked safe, the FIU academics, linguists, junior U.S. archivists, biologists, Harvard art professors, and similar gentle folk in Navy uniform were wondering how to get at the documents. What to do?

"Blow the damn safe open!" That was Kaitz's immediate solution. And so it happened enough times that Kaitz and Chattaway not only got the GEHEIM stuff but also became known and admired in the Forward Intelligence Unit as "The Blow Boys."

Deservedly, the two of them were at the ceremony in a Navy headquarters in a French chateau. For our work in Normandy, all of the complement of the FIU had been awarded the Secretary of the Navy's Commendation Ribbon. The ribbon pinning was held by the chief of staff to Admiral Kirk.

After the ceremony, all of the FIU, dressed up smartly in Navy blue and gold uniforms, stood drinking Navy coffee. That is a feat said by some to deserve a medal, even when sipped out of the admiral's four-star coffee service.

The chief of staff, looking down into his cup of java, shook his head resignedly and commented, "There's no coffee like the coffee served on your own bridge." All these FIU landlubbers agreed heartily.

"You're right, there, captain!"

"Aye, captain! Being on your own bridge puts quite a different taste to it."

The only bridges those fellows knew about were the ones put in their mouths by dentists.

But they carried it off well.

Recovery from fibbing to a four-striper was helped along by the FIU assignment to interrogations at the mouth of the Gironde outside the still-occupied "Fortress Bordeaux," as the German Navy called it. We made our headquarters in a chateau, too; in a chateau in Cognac. Monsieur and Madame Martell had us over for a drink . . . but Cognac's not in Normandy, is it?

That's another story.

Captain Quentin R. Walsh, U.S. Coast Guard (Retired).

CHERBOURG: CROWN JEWEL OF THE INVASION

By Captain Quentin R. Walsh, U.S. Coast Guard (Retired). Excerpted from: Little-Known Facts of a Well-Known War. (*Privately printed; reprint, 1995*). *Walsh's story also appears in Paul Stillwell's* Assault on Normandy: First-Person Accounts from the Sea Services *(Annapolis: Naval Institute Press, 1994).*

I was one of twenty-three thousand who sailed aboard the *Queen Mary* from New York on June 23, 1943. The troops aboard her slept "hot bunks"—three men to a bunk on a rotational basis. I was one of twelve officers assigned to a small compartment that had twelve metal-framed, canvas-bottomed bunks with a pillow and blanket. There were no portholes. Two overhead ceiling lights provided illumination. We had no chairs or toilet facilities and had two meals per day, at 0700 and 1700. We arrived at Gourock, Scotland on June 28. There I was assigned to one of the Coast Guard units tasked to deal with problems encountered by American ships and personnel at British ports.

In September, I was reassigned to the planning and logistic section on the staff of Commander, U.S. Naval Forces, Europe, Grosvenor Square, London, England. This transfer was at the request of Admiral Stark who wanted a Coast Guard officer assigned to his staff to deal with matters related to the future ports to be captured on the continent during the invasion. These were known as "advance bases."

Here I was cleared and briefed as a BIGOT by British and American intelligence. I was assigned to the planning for Operation Overlord, Phase Neptune, involving mulberries, gooseberries, PLUTO, the Quiberon Bay Project, Rankin Case "C," and establishing the logistic requirements for Cherbourg and Le Havre. [Ed.: Rankin Case "C," named after Jeanette Rankin (1880–1973), the first woman to serve in the U.S. Congress, was the Allied landing plan if the Germans surrendered prior to D-Day.]

Commander A.L. Stanford, Lieutenant Colonel Scott, and I were among a group of U.S. Navy and U.S. Army officers assigned to determine the cargo capacity required for Mulberry A. It was essential that at least eight thousand tons of cargo per day be landed in Normandy. Because of our participation on Mulberry A planning, none of us could leave Scotland or England until after the invasion.

It took months for thousands of men to build the two artificial ports at Selsey Bill at a cost of millions of dollars. About 150 tugs were needed to tow and erect them at the Normandy beaches. They were about the size of the port of Gibraltar, capable of handling twelve thousand tons of equipment per day. We planned to use them until Cherbourg was captured, cleared, and operating.

Another one of my assignments was laying out the anchorages and berths in Cherbourg harbor. The purpose of invading the Calvados area of the Cotentin Peninsula, Normandy, was to isolate and capture Cherbourg. We had to have a deep water port for men, equipment, and supplies to sustain the invasion forces after the initial landings over the beaches. There was never any doubt about getting ashore on D-Day. The problem was to throw back the German counter attacks, expected anywhere from a week to three weeks, while we were capturing and clearing Cherbourg and then preparing to break out of the Cotentin Peninsula.

The jewel of the game was Cherbourg. We had to capture the port, repair any damages inflicted by the Germans, and get the harbor into operational condition. It was determined that at least eight to twelve large cargo ships had to be accommodated simultaneously in Cherbourg to support our operations. I finished writing the plan for Cherbourg by January 1944, and it was approved by the chain of command.

Because the U.S. Navy was to be responsible for the clearing and operation of Cherbourg, it needed to obtain the earliest information on the condition of the harbor, the location of mine fields, sunken ships, etc. So that our Navy could get the necessary information as soon as possible on the condition of the port, I conceived the idea that the Navy should have its own reconnaissance party enter Cherbourg with the U.S. Army forces designated to capture it. The idea was approved, and I was ordered to organize, train, and command U.S. Navy Task Unit 127.2.8, whose purpose was to determine the condition of the captured ports in Normandy after the invasion. About three hundred men volunteered for the special mission; however, I was notified to keep my personnel and equipment to a minimum because of lift restrictions. Accordingly, only fifty-two men were selected. All could drive jeeps and trucks. All had basic training in the use of firearms. Some were divers, bomb disposal men, radio operators, and intelligence specialists. Many could speak French, and a few spoke German. All eventually proved capable of doing any duty to which they were assigned in addition to their specialties.

We trained intensively at Roseneath, Scotland, under Colonel Stribler and a contingent from the 28th Division. Our training schedule was set from 0500 to 2200 daily, six days per week. We ran a mile and had calisthenics before breakfast. After the evening meal we watched military movies dealing with bomb disposal, booby traps, reconnaissance duties, camouflage, and house-to-house fighting. My idea was to make the training so tough and arduous that combat would seem easy by comparison. Strict discipline prevailed and I ran a tight outfit.

Following training, we went south and bivouacked at what was known locally as "Camp Cadnam." While here I reported to General Lawton Collins at his headquarters at Breamore and to Admiral Moon at Plymouth. Collins ordered me not to carry any orders, keep a diary, or permit cameras. On June 4, we left Cadnam for the marshalling area near the waterfront. Messing facilities, movies, stage plays, and around-the-clock church services were provided in tents. It was my observation that there were no atheists going to Normandy.

While in the marshalling area, I briefed my command for the first time on their mission and objectives. We also shifted into outer garments which were wax impregnated for defense against possible gas attack. We were in these clothes until after the capture of Cherbourg (June 26, 1944). We got soaking wet going over the beach. As a result, it was like walking around in a steam bath all day when the weather was quite warm, but at night, it was like walking around with your clothes full of ice. As I recall, all personnel that landed before D+20 carried gas masks. During the planning sessions in London, they discussed the possibility of 70 percent casualties if the Germans used gas.

Shortly after 0200 on June 8, my task force was summoned for departure. We proceeded to the loading area, where we were marshalled alongside the Liberty ship *James A. Farrell.* I look back nostalgically on that roll call and muster. The morale and esprit de corps was excellent. The Red Cross ladies gave us tons of doughnuts and gallons of coffee. We joked and talked as if we were going on a picnic. It never occurred to any of us that some of us might not be coming back. Out of fifty-two men, three would not return. Ten men were wounded, four of them badly, and were returned to England.

We arrived off of Utah Beach on June 9 near La Madeleine and commenced off-loading of vehicles and men immediately. We were all ashore by June 10. We had trouble getting the vehicles ashore. The landing craft, which discharged earlier on the beaches, caused deep holes in the sand when they reversed their engines to back off. The landing craft that came in later would ground out on the rim of these holes. As a result, vehicles proceeding off the ramp were dumped in a hole. Several jeeps and trucks drowned out. About half the men stayed with me on the beach to get the submerged jeeps ashore at low water. The rest proceeded inland to Ste. Marie du Mont.

Those of us who remained on Utah Beach got orders that night to dig in and prepare for German shelling and counterattack, perhaps by paratroopers. My executive officer and I took turns sleeping in the same foxhole. It was very cold and we were soaking wet. The wax impregnated clothing only added to the misery because it kept our under garments from drying out. To the north, the sky was illuminated by a big conflagration which we learned later was the burning town of Mountebourg.

My men near Ste. Marie du Mont, along with 250 Royal Commandos, also dug in but were hit with an air attack in this area. Anti-personnel bombs were dropped. The commandos suffered heavy casualties and had to get replacements from England. Four of my men were badly wounded. The pellets from the anti-personnel bombs went right through jeep rims as if they were made of butter.

The unit finally reassembled near Ste. Marie du Mont. Equipment and supplies were checked. We had found and cannibalized some spare parts from jeeps from the wrecked Army gliders that had suffered heavy casualties in landing. After reporting to Colonel King, VII Corps Headquarters, we proceeded north towards Cherbourg via Mountebourg and Valognes.

On June 19, a big storm hit the Cotentin Peninsula. The dirt roads, turned into dust by hundreds of vehicles, turned to mud inches deep. The bocage country of Normandy, with its sunken roads and lanes, was one hell of a place to fight a war.

The rain and wind would have made a saint uncomfortable. We had four men to a jeep, each of which was combat loaded at all times. This required that we ride with the tops and windshields down. Wire cutting hooks were on the front of each vehicle which also carried four sand bags on the floor as protection against injury from land mines. Each man carried a knapsack with a blanket and a half of a pup tent, with K rations. He was equipped with a gas mask, trench shovel, dagger, hand grenades, helmet, bandoleers, and rifle. Most of the officers carried sub-machine guns and each had a .45-caliber automatic. Most of the men carried Garands; a few carried carbines. Each jeep carried a camouflage net, an axe, shovel, jerry can, and spare tire with tools.

Four men in a jeep with all their gear left little room. We slept on the ground, wrapped in our blankets, on the top of the tent half until it rained. Some men then pitched the pup tents, but they were useless in the heavy rain. Most of us just tried to sleep in the jeeps, but the jeeps filled with water because the sand bags on the floor prevented drainage. We had to bail them out with helmets. As my British friends remarked, "It was no bloody picnic." The two 2 1/2-ton trucks and communications truck were kept to the rear. The trucks carried a complete change of clothing and shoes for each man, but we never got to change clothes until we had been in Cherbourg for several days.

The storm showed the precarious situation we were in. We heard that Mulberry A [at Omaha Beach] was demolished and that the beaches were piled high with wreckage. The VII Corps and the three division headquarters emphasized that we had to capture Cherbourg quickly. The VII Corps was running short of ammunition. We were still around Mountebourg, about twenty miles from Cherbourg. DUKWs were used to ferry ammunition directly from the beaches to the front lines, but originally they were to have only about a five-mile complete turnaround from the beaches.

On June 22, I took a party of twenty-one men north of Mountebourg to a small hamlet called Delasse to await the outcome of a surrender ultimatum which General Collins had delivered to Cherbourg. The Germans were ordered to surrender at noon on June 22.
They refused. We bivouacked in a small fieldstone farmhouse a short
distance from the main road to Cherbourg. German shells were passing south over our heads; American shells were going north into
Cherbourg. While we were having breakfast, American planes attacked the area, which was full of German stragglers. We scattered.
I ran alongside the house and threw myself to the ground around
the corner but slammed into a dog house where I found a hen's nest
with about twelve eggs. We had not seen a fresh egg in months. After the planes left, we hard-boiled them in radiator water, and each
man got a small, but delicious-tasting portion. That afternoon, we
dropped back to Mountebourg, which had been destroyed by fire.
The statue of Joan of Arc in the town square appeared a dusty red
from the heat. I reported to the VII Corps that American planes had
strafed us well behind the American lines. They brushed it off with
the statement that they must have been German planes with American markings.

At 0600 on June 26, Perry, Boucher, and I approached Cherbourg
via Route 13, but found it blocked by shell holes and debris. We cut
east of the main road and proceeded via open fields to Fort du Roule.
The top of this heavily-fortified strong point had just been captured
by one company of American infantry. When we arrived, the company commander had just been killed by a stray bullet in the throat.
The officers and men were disconsolate. They insisted that I have a
drink with them in one of the strong points which had been set up
as a command post. It did not take much arm twisting. I enjoyed that
slug of whiskey.

While at this command post, I learned that Company G, 314th Infantry, 79th Division was departing shortly to carry rifle grenades to
a platoon which had been stopped by the Germans on Rue de Paris.
Perry, Boucher, and I moved out with Company G to the east of du
Roule to follow a country lane which brought us back to the bottom
of the hill on which the fort was located. German 88s were firing into

279

Cherbourg from caves made in the hill on which Fort du Roule stood even though satchel charges were being lowered from the top to blow off the muzzles. The country lane led into Rue de Paris which was the main road out of Cherbourg to the south.

While traversing the country lane, we witnessed German prisoners removing their dead. It was two men to a body, one on each foot. If the dead man fell on his back, he was dragged off on his back. If he fell face-down, he was dragged face-down. I wondered at the time what the Wehrmacht would have thought about this.

It was about 1100 when we turned right on Rue de Paris to proceed towards the waterfront. This is where the street fighting took place until about 2000 that night. The railroad yard to the left was an inferno of combat. The machine guns never stopped. American jeeps with Red Cross markings were going in both directions. Those headed to the south generally had a wounded man beside the driver and one stretcher across the hood and another running athwartships [across the jeep] behind the driver. German machine guns were zeroed-in on the intersections of Rue de Paris and the canal bridges which led to the west and main part of the city. The machine guns were placed at sidewalk level in the basements of the buildings fronting on the street. We would capture the upper part of the structure but the Germans had to be dug out of the basements. In the meantime, German guns in the caves under Fort du Roule, which had not been silenced by the satchel charges, fired into the rear of our American troops.

Perry, Boucher, and I were the first U.S. Navy personnel to enter Cherbourg. We reached the blazing and wrecked waterfront at Gare Maritime [the train station] in the eastern section of the port about 1700 on June 26.

Accurate casualty figures at Cherbourg are hard to come by, but as I recall we took thousands of prisoners in the last four days of an offensive that produced heavy casualties on both sides. There should be no doubt that Normandy was a blood bath and Cherbourg's house-to-house fighting produced a slaughterhouse. Dead and wounded from both sides littered the streets.

On the evening of June 26, I sent a message indicating that we held the eastern part of the port while the Germans held the western section. By June 27, our Army had silenced most of the remaining resistance in the western section of the city.

Many Germans, however, had retreated into the arsenal, a fortified area about a mile square on the western edge of the inner port. It contained E-boat pens, shops, and dry docks for repairing ships and wet basins for ships to discharge cargo. My idea at this time was to get the port open as soon as possible. However, we could not use the port until all resistance ceased and the harbor was cleared of mine fields.

On the morning of June 27, an American psychological warfare unit had persuaded some Germans to surrender in the vicinity of the arsenal entrance. But this did not include Fort du Homet nor the pockets of resistance throughout. The Army forgot about them. However, it had been decided in England before the invasion that the arsenal would be under our Navy's control after Cherbourg was captured.

This is why I took Ensign Daniel (Pop) Lauer and fifteen men to reconnoiter the arsenal and adjacent waterfront. We were heavily armed with Thompson submachine guns, Garands, bazookas, and hand grenades. We overcame snipers and resistance pockets by sheer firepower. By using hand grenades and bazookas, we blew open the steel doors of the underground bunkers. This method of persuasion to surrender produced hundreds of prisoners who had to be marched out of the area by armed escort.

The E-boat pens' four-foot reinforced steel walls had been blown outward by using torpedo heads as explosives. This allowed the eight-foot ceilings to drop down on the E-boats which had been set afire by the Germans.

Adjacent to the pens was a pile of rubble on top of which the Germans had left an E-boat flag flying defiantly on a short staff. I seized the flag, and it is now on display at the Coast Guard Museum in New London, Connecticut.

E-boats were about one hundred feet long, high-powered, with light armament and torpedoes. They were capable of making high speed attacks on enemy shipping and then retreating under their own smoke screen. It was E-boats from Cherbourg on the night of April 27, 1944, that attacked and sank two LSTs off Slapton Sands,

Lyme Bay on the south coast of England where the 4th Division was carrying a full scale rehearsal (Exercise Tiger) for D-Day. We lost seven hundred men and three LSTs (two sunk, one damaged).

It was near the pens that we captured a lone German who told Lauer and me in his broken English about the fifty-two American paratrooper prisoners in Fort du Homet under the command of a mad Nazi who threatened to kill any German that surrendered. That is why I decided to approach the fort under a flag of truce to negotiate its surrender and rescue the paratroopers. So long as our men were prisoners, their lives were in danger. After much negotiating, the Germans decided to surrender if I would separate the officers from their men. This was agreed, and an officer produced a bottle for a toast to Hitler. Lauer and I refused the toast.

We had gone only a short distance out of the fort with the captured officers when we met an American lieutenant colonel and about ten men. I briefed him on what had occurred and asked him to take over so I could complete my reconnaissance. The paratroopers appeared. First, they asked for cigarettes, then souvenirs. We told them that there was captured equipment throughout the area. That was the last we saw of the paratroopers. However, several days later a "Screaming Eagle" major came to my Place Napoleon headquarters and thanked me for getting the paratroopers released.

Once the arsenal had been captured, we embarked on a series of tasks designed to permit Cherbourg to regain its status as an active harbor. We obtained information on the mine fields from German prisoners, free French, and slave laborers, and sent it to minesweepers off the port. We established Navy headquarters, carried out a survey of the harbor, installed communications facilities, and reconnoitered and took over a number of buildings on the waterfront for port staff and U.S. Naval forces. We also provided transportation ashore for naval personnel, interrogated prisoners, determined the damage done to wharfs and piers, and established a first-aid station.

On June 29, Captain Norman Ives, USN, arrived at Cherbourg and relieved me as senior naval officer present. I was designated his chief staff officer in which position I served until July 15, 1944, until transferred to the staff of Admiral John Wilkes. In this capacity, I served as assistant port director until August 2, 1944, under Commodore Barton, USCG.

On August 1, Captain Ives departed with his reconnaissance party of approximately seventy-five officers and men to reconnoiter Granville and St. Malo. He requested that either Lieutenant LaVallee or I accompany him. However, Commodore Barton requested that I remain in Cherbourg, and Lieutenant LaVallee had been assigned to act as an interpreter and billeting officer for Captain Clyde Coryell, the officer in command of the Seabees. Neither of us, therefore, accompanied Ives.

On August 2, 1944, Ives's reconnaissance party was ambushed by a force of approximately six hundred Germans in the vicinity of Pontorson, Brittany. Captain Ives and about sixteen men were killed or wounded.

On that same day, Admiral Wilkes gave me verbal orders to stand by to carry out reconnaissance in Brittany. I departed Cherbourg on August 4, 1944 in command of a task force of about four hundred men.

Seaman First Class George
Hurley, U.S. Navy.

D-DAY

By Seaman First Class George Hurley, U.S. Navy. Unpublished poem. Written by Hurley, an Armed Guard veteran, while witnessing the invasion.

The thunder was the 88s,
Machine guns were the falling rain.
God waited at his golden gate,
To take away our pain.

Some were spared to live 'till noon,
On that fateful day.
All the world was warm in June,
We were there to pay.

Angels gathered up the souls,
All worldly troubles over.
Death had taken such a toll,
Where are the cliffs of Dover?

What was the terrible reason,
That we traveled to our doom?
I guess this is the season,
For cleaning out a room.

None of us ever asked why,
We had to reach that beach.
Sometimes at night I cry,
So far out of reach.

German POWs disembark from a British LCT in England following their capture at Normandy. *(U.S. Coast Guard; National Archives)*

A German sniper is searched after capture by an Army beach guard on June 9, 1944. *(U.S. Navy; National Archives)*

U.S. Army troops talk with French citizens at the village fountain of Ste. Marie du Mont, inland from Utah Beach, on June 12, 1944. The 12th Fleet had its Forward Intelligence Unit (TU 125.8) headquartered near here. (*U.S. Navy; National Archives*)

German prisoners transport their wounded to the beachhead for evacuation to England. (*U.S. Navy; National Archives*)

German POWs wait outside the pockmarked Fort du Homet. *(U.S. Navy; National Archives)*

Destroyed German E-boat pens at Cherbourg. *(U.S. Navy; National Archives)*

Naval beach battalion members demonstrate a radio to Cherbourg citizens, who express their happiness at the capture of the port. *(U.S. Navy; National Archives)*

It's hard to describe the pleasure I felt this afternoon when I saw whitewater bubbling behind in our wake. And the beach that had been our neighborhood for almost half a year flatten and fall into the sea. And with it went a whole part of my life. On that ridiculous bit of surf and sand dune I had seen men die. I had known danger and watched the machinery of war roll through and over us—leaving only lethargy and boredom. One more dead beach behind me. What lies before me now, I don't know.

All my love,
Tracy

THE U.S. NAVY MEMORIAL FOUNDATION

The U.S. Navy Memorial Foundation is a non-profit educational foundation responsible for the operation of the U.S. Navy Memorial and the Naval Heritage Center. Through ceremonies, concerts, seminars, displays, and written and oral histories, the Foundation is dedicated to honoring, preserving, and celebrating America's enduring naval heritage.

Active duty service members and veterans are eligible to become part of our perpetual Navy Log. To enroll yourself or a loved one in our Navy Log, or to learn more about the Foundation, please contact us at the address and numbers listed below.

Reproductions may be made of any of the photographs in this book. For information about ordering reproductions, please contact the Education Institute at the U.S. Navy Memorial Foundation.

U.S. Navy Memorial Foundation
701 Pennsylvania Avenue, NW
Suite 123
Washington, D.C. 20004-2608

Telephone: 202-737-2300
Web site: www.lonesailor.org

REFERENCES

Ambrose, Stephen E. *D-Day, June 6, 1944: The Climactic Battle of World War II.* New York: Simon and Schuster, 1994.

Astor, Gerald. *June 6, 1944: The Voices of D-Day.* New York: St. Martin's Press, 1994.

Barger, Melvin D. *Large Slow Target: A History of the LST.* 3 Vols. Dallas: Taylor Publishing Company, 1986–1994.

Belchem, David. *Victory in Normandy.* London: Chatto and Windus, 1981.

Bennet, Ralph F. *Ultra in the West: The Normandy Campaign, 1944–45.* New York: Scribner, 1980.

Chandler, David G and James L. Collins. *The D-Day Encyclopedia.* New York: Simon and Schuster, 1994.

D'Este, Carlo. *Decision in Normandy.* New York: Dutton, 1983.

Drez, Ronald J. *Voices of D-Day: The Story of the Allied Invasion Told by Those Who Were There.* Baton Rouge: Louisiana State University Press, 1994.

Gallant, Captain Jack. *D-Day, June 6, 1944; June 6, 1994.* Washington: Navy and Marine Corps WWII Commemorative Committee, [1994].

Garry, Johnson, and Christopher Dunphie. *Brightly Shone the Dawn: Some Experiences of the Invasion of Normandy.* London: Warne, 1980.

Gunther, John. *D-Day.* New York: Harper and Brothers, 1944.

Hagan, Kenneth J. *This People's Navy: The Making of American Sea Power.* New York: The Free Press, 1991.

Hastings, Max. *Overlord: D-Day and the Battle for Normandy.* New York: Simon and Schuster, 1984.

Hoswell, Jock. *D-Day: Intelligence and Deception.* New York: Times Books, 1979.

Hoyt, Edwin Palmer. *The Invasion Before Normandy: The Secret Battle of Slapton Sands.* New York: Stein and Day, 1985.

Karig, Commander Walter. *Battle Report: The Atlantic War.* New York: Farrar and Rinehart, 1946.

Kemp, Anthony. *D-Day and the Invasion of Normandy.* New York: Harry N. Abrams, 1994.

Man, John. *The Facts on File D-Day Atlas: The Definitive Account of the Allied Invasion of Normandy.* New York: Facts on File, 1994.

Marolda, Edward J. "Operation Neptune." In *D-Day: Operation Overlord; from Its Planning to the Liberation of Paris.* London: Salamander Books, 1993.

Miller, Nathan. *The U.S. Navy: An Illustrated History.* Annapolis: Naval Institute Press, 1977.

Morison, Samuel Eliot. *The Invasion of France and Germany, 1944–1945.* History of the United States Naval Operations in World War II, Vol. 11. Boston: Little, Brown, and Company, 1957.

Nigel, Lewis. *Exercise Tiger: The Dramatic True Story of a Hidden Tragedy of World War II.* New York: Prentice Hall Press, 1990.

Ruge, Frederick. *Rommel in Normandy: Reminiscences.* Translated by Ursula R. Moessner. San Rafael, Ca.: Presidio Press, 1979.

Ruppenthal, Roland G. *Utah Beach to Cherbourg (6 June–27 June 1944).* Washington, D.C.: Historical Division, Department of the Army, 1984.

Ryan, Cornelius. *The Longest Day: June 6, 1944.* New York: Simon and Schuster, 1959.

Stanford, Alfred. *Force Mulberry: The Planning and Installation of the Artificial Harbors off U.S. Normandy Beaches in World War II.* New York: Morrow, 1951.

Stillwell, Paul. *Assault on Normandy: First-Person Accounts from the Sea Services.* Annapolis: Naval Institute Press, 1994.

Sweetman, Jack. *American Naval History: An Illustrated Chronology of the U.S. Navy and Marine Corps, 1775–Present.* Annapolis: Naval Institute Press, 1984.

Symonds, Craig L. *Historical Atlas of the U.S. Navy.* Annapolis: Naval Institute Press, 1995.

U.S. Naval History Division. *Dictionary of American Naval Fighting Ships.* Edited by James L. Mooney and others. Washington: GPO, 1959–.

Wheal, Elizabeth-Anne, Stephen Pope, and James Taylor. *A Dictionary of the Second World War.* New York: Peter Bedrick Books, 1990.

Wilson, Theodore A. *D-Day, 1944.* Abilene, Kan.: University Press of Kansas, 1994.

Woods, Brian. *Footsteps of D-Day.* Kent Town, Australia: 1994.

Worth, Fred L., and Don McCombs. *World War II: 4,139 Strange and Interesting Facts.* New York: Wings Books, 1983.

Young, Peter. *D-Day.* New York: Gallery Books, 1990.

INDEX